NOT
TRAGICALLY
COLORED

ISMAEL HERNANDEZ

NOT TRAGICALLY COLORED

FREEDOM, PERSONHOOD, AND THE RENEWAL OF BLACK AMERICA

ACTONINSTITUTE

ACTONINSTITUTE

98 E. Fulton
Grand Rapids, Michigan 49503
Phone: 616.454.3080
Fax: 616.454.9454

Interior composition by Judy Schafer
Copyediting/Proofreading by Jan M. Ortiz and Patricia Murphy
Cover design by Peter Ho

Printed in the United States of America

But I am not tragically colored. There is no great sorrow dammed up in my soul, nor lurking behind my eyes.... Someone is always at my elbow reminding me that I am the granddaughter of slaves. It fails to register depression with me. Slavery is sixty years in the past.... Slavery is the price I paid for civilization, and the choice was not with me. It is a bully adventure and worth all that I have paid through my ancestors for it. No one on earth ever had a greater chance for glory. The world to be won and nothing to be lost.

—Zora Neale Hurston,
"How It Feels to Be Colored Me" (1928)

CONTENTS

FOREWORD

This is a brilliant, profound, and well-substantiated book. It is one of the best and most thorough books about race ever written. Ismael's accounts of personal experience enable him to get beyond the prevailing ideology of race and the clichés and impersonal talk we have become so habituated to for fifty years.

You will learn much from this book. For me, the learning began on the very first page: the passage from Zora Neale Hurston, whom I had not heard of until Ismael introduced her with the citation from "How It Feels to Be Colored Me." I have never read such words, and they throw a new light on the world around me.

There are many other such passages in this book—vivid, personal vignettes. Here is another one I love, in this case about Ismael's own father:

> Now and then, he would gather us to listen to Fidel Castro's never-ending harangues. My father's shouts of joy at the great Cuban leader's words were cause for both laughter and concern, as the loud noises often provoked marital discord in our own home and neighbors' complaints outside of it. My father was, nonetheless, unmoved. "Long live Fidel!," "Yankee go home!," and "Fatherland or death!" were his daily chants. I would also go with him to communist cell meetings lasting long into the night, where the dullness of discussion invariably put me to sleep.

On another day, Ismael was with his father all day defiantly waving a red communist flag, alone and outnumbered.

Still, there was something intoxicating in our efforts. Our hearts were neatly sewn with the thread of utopia. Being communists brought to us an aura of mystery and exclusivity. We were an embattled community, an enlightened vanguard who would eventually achieve victory. One day, we would cure the social pathologies of Puerto Rico and our flag would stand alone. At least, that is what my dad said.

Ismael Hernandez has diligently done massive research and reading on his subject. Yet he approaches his work with a novelist's eye for personal details and personalist narratives. Through twelve substantial chapters, he runs through the main themes of his own slow discovery of the meaning of liberty, and even of economic creativity. First, he tells some of his own life adventures and then turns in a more theoretical direction with chapters on anthropology and the philosophy of liberty. He takes on government and poverty, victimhood and dependency, the inner city and the family. He ends by describing his method and his point of view in "A Personalist Approach."

I promise the reader that he or she has never read a book like this before. It is both highly personal and brilliantly theoretical—the latter in order to clear away the thick underbrush that has been thrown out to prevent us from seeing the human realities behind our words. Reading through this book will require an effort to look at matters of race, poverty, separatism, and despair with shockingly new lenses. It puts one through a kind of cleansing and is well worth the effort.

My gratitude, Ismael, for what you have achieved.

Michael Novak
June 30, 2015

Acknowledgments

I have been fortunate to have the support, encouragement, advice, and friendship of the editor of this book, Dr. Kevin Schmiesing. Thank you, Kevin. I want also to thank Dr. Samuel Gregg for his insightful recommendations in the early stages of writing this book. I also thank him for his scholarship on many issues related to the questions addressed here, especially those related to the truth about the person. I also owe a great debt to Father Robert Sirico for, jointly with Kris Mauren, creating the Acton Institute, whose mission and work has been immensely important in my intellectual formation. It has been a joy for me to be associated with Acton during all these years.

Another important early encouragement came from a good friend, the late A. James Gallagher, Jr. His encouragement and insight made this book a better one. He was a great man and I was blessed in knowing him. How could I not mention the influence on my thought coming from the writings of Michael Novak? It is an honor that he wrote the preface for my book and his writings on liberation theology and markets were crucial in my ideological journey. Thank you.

My family has always been, after God, most important in my life. I want to thank my wife for her love and friendship, and my children for making my life so meaningful. Finally, I must acknowledge my deep gratitude to the many individuals whose stories and lives helped form my views through so many years. There were countless beautiful people in the poor barrios of Puerto Rico and the housing projects of Dunbar in Fort Myers; ministry coworkers at the African Caribbean American Catholic Center of the Catholic Diocese of Venice in Florida; and the simple people who helped me love the poor, love black people, and learn from them. Thank you.

1

Saved through the Waters of Liberty

The flag flew from my hands and landed in a ditch. I dropped to my knees to retrieve it from the filth. My father watched in pride. "Long live Socialism!" he yelled defiantly to passersby waving opposing political emblems. "Revolution or death!" I learned to yell with him. I would pump my tight left fist in the air with a grave look of intimidation, as if the strength of my grip and the frown on my face would magically bring elusive electoral victory.

Election time on the island was always electrifying. The rallies and long caravans were a sight to be seen. The motorcades' raging music and strident slogans led to verbal battles that often degenerated into physical violence. The oppressive heat might have been the culprit for the madness—but I think it was instead the release of a people longing, searching for a better life.

I never saw any car waving our red flag. It was always a sea of red and white "Jibaro" flags of the Popular Democratic Party or a flock of the New Progressives' white and blue coconut tree banners. Even the green and white of the "Independentistas" appeared occasionally amid the prism of pennants—yet, the scarlet flag of the socialists remained the rarest sight.

Still, there was something intoxicating in our efforts. Our hearts were neatly sewn with the thread of utopia. Being communists brought an aura of mystery and exclusivity. We were an embattled community, an enlightened vanguard who would eventually achieve victory. One day, we would cure the social pathologies of Puerto Rico, and our flag would stand *alone*. At least, that is what my dad said.

My flag safe and our duty fulfilled, we went back home to listen to the news of another devastating electoral defeat. I can see now that my devotion to the communist cause was an expression of my desire for approval. I was desperate for my father's love. He was everything to me.

Dad was short and stocky, with a Puerto Rican flag tattooed on his forearm, a silent witness to a life dedicated to the cause. Having found the truth of Marxism, he embraced it tightly and proclaimed it boldly. At home, books were everywhere and he was always reading aloud something interesting from Cuban newspapers. Articulate and sophisticated, my father was the neighborhood's intellectual who happened to be a vociferous radical. Everyone knew him as "Don Tito."

His late father, Emiliano, had been a storeowner and prominent Nationalist Party leader in their hometown of Isabela.[1] Albizu Campos, *el prócer de la patria* (the great man of the fatherland) stayed once at their home. The revolutionary spirit was ingrained early in Dad's psyche as he marched through town in military-style parades wearing the Nationalist uniform of a white shirt and black pants while carrying a fake wood rifle. Eventually, Dad moved to the United States where he spent many years inside "the guts of the monster."[2] His memory of America was sharpened by the grievances that he experienced. America was the enemy of humanity, and it was our sacred duty to destroy her.

While in diaspora he had financial struggles and quit his studies in engineering; something he always regretted. Staying alternately in New York and New Jersey, he settled into an underworld where excitement mixed with turmoil. Struggling to meet his needs, he engaged in black-market activity. He recalled the era with laughter: "There were basements in New Jersey that were like a mall, son. There, you could buy anything you wanted—and

---

[1] The Nationalist Party was founded on September 17, 1922, with the purpose of fighting for independence. In 1924, Pedro Albizu Campos joined the party, was named vice-president, and became its most prominent leader. By the mid-1930s, after several electoral defeats and police repression, the party opted for armed revolution to achieve its goals. After Albizu's death in 1965, the party split, and some factions joined socialist movements.

[2] The origins of the phrase can be traced to a political declaration of the First Congress of the United States Branch of the Puerto Rican Socialist Party, approved on April 1, 1973, and entitled *Desde Las Entrañas* (From the Guts). It was a seventy-seven-page document that examined the nature of Puerto Rican immigration in the context of capitalist exploitation of the working class.

the cops were in on it too!" Living desperately, he did not avoid brushes with the law, such as a court appearance for not paying child support. (That is all he ever revealed about a sibling I never met and about whom he refused to say more.) Attending boxing events at Madison Square Garden was his favorite pastime, but his commitment to radical causes, including an association with the Black Panthers, remained his devotion. Eventually, he met and married my mother, and they returned to Puerto Rico when he was offered a job with the Eli Lilly Company.

Through the years, we moved from house to house within the same small neighborhood in the city of Mayagüez, my mother's hometown. Our longest-lived dwelling was simple and small. Sergeant Vicente M. Torres and Detective Santos Toro Vargas, investigative intelligence agents, described it in a confidential police report. Working under the COINTELPRO program of the FBI,[3] they conducted routine surveillance of our home:

> Description of his residence: Wood house with "four waters" zinc roof, chalet style. It has a cement half-balcony and the house is painted yellow.... It has one front door and a Miami-style front window. On its East side, the house connects with Garnier Alley and on its West side with a patio.[4]

There I spent some of the most wonderful years of my life. Closing my eyes, I can still see the views and nearby homes. I can hear the old noisy cars and see the big mango trees that always had a treat to offer. I have been told that we were poor, but I had all I wanted: friends, family, and food on my plate.

---

[3] For decades, socialists and other individuals advocating independence for Puerto Rico had been the target of FBI COINTELPRO operations. COINTELPRO was a counterintelligence program instituted by the federal government between 1956 and 1971 to follow the activities of organizations and individuals who were considered a threat to national security. The goal was to "disrupt" the work of leftist groups and labor organizations. Files were kept on organizations and individuals who had at any time made any comments in support of independence for Puerto Rico.

[4] See Police Report 18 December 1967, case #15467 that was submitted to and reviewed by Abraham Diaz Gonzalez and Commissioner Angel Manuel Martin. Report on file in his secret Intelligence Division of Puerto Rico Police Department; record obtained through the Freedom of Information Act.

Take Me to the Waters!

What made the home comfortable was my mother. She was beautiful, tall, with yellow-black skin and wavy gray hair. For her, being a mother was everything. As my father worked nightshifts, Mom was the eternal presence and feared enforcer. A few times, I ventured to challenge her control only to learn my lesson and adopt the wiser policy of conformity. Yet her tender side was always dominant.

Although Mom was always busy with chores, she was usually happy and talkative. Still, there were melancholic moments when she recounted sad memories that weighed on her soul. She would talk of experiences of loss during times of economic hardship. Her sadness grew most intense when it came to her father, Gumercindo. Others in the barrio called him "Don Gume," but, at home, he was "Papú," an elderly yet tall and elegant man with Spanish features.

Divorced from our grandmother, he occupied a tiny dwelling off the patio of the home where she lived. His only worldly possessions were a small bed, a few clothes, and a portable gas stove. His painful death from stomach cancer was a heavy blow to my mother. In the midst of my increasing hatred of a political system that I blamed for his suffering, I questioned how it could be that he died without finding justice.

Mom's relationship with my grandmother was another story, complicated by years of animosity and notions of race and shame. Grandma Vicenta was a dark black woman with kinky white hair who loved to dance while performing African Bomba songs with her maracas.[5] Called "la negra," her color was a source of embarrassment for her and conflict with my mom. Mom's half-brother was light-skinned, and Grandma preferred him over Mom and Uncle Ismael, the darker siblings.[6] Every time Mom visited Ismael,

---

[5] "Bomba" is a music and dance genre unique to Puerto Rico but with deep roots in Northwest Africa. It became a source of strength to slave communities. During ceremonies with Bomba music, the slaves celebrated baptisms and weddings, and even planned revolts. Spanish authorities allowed it only on Sundays or saints' feast days.

[6] The "color line," to use W. E. B. Du Bois's phrase, divided the black community in Puerto Rico and elsewhere based on shades. Ostracized by the larger population, those of very dark skin were often rejected by their siblings and even parents, who favored the lighter-skinned children. Sometimes, ironically, lighter natives will marry darker partners so as to fit better within the black community.

they greeted by embracing while weeping, as if the commonality of suffering united them. The sight always left me sad and bewildered.

Due to the scarcity of white Spanish women during colonization, intermixture and intermarriage were common in Puerto Rico.[7] Even so, many Puerto Ricans today classify themselves as white and deny any black heritage. While she often tried to minimize its importance, Mom did tell us about her lineage.[8] My grandmother's surnames were Perocier and Gordils, both indicative of slaveowners' ethnic lines.

Through the efforts of Puerto Rican deputies to the Spanish courts, a partial abolition of slavery was achieved through the Moret Law of July 4, 1870. As a result, the Central Registry of Slaves was established.[9] There you

---

The common attempt to hide any traits of blackness was immortalized in a song by the great Puerto Rican Negro poet Fortunato Vizcarrondo (1895–1977) and popularized by Juan Boria (1905–1995):

> Eres blanquito enchapao, que dentra en sociedá, temiendo que se conozca la mamá de tu mamá... Muy bien que yo la conozco se ñama Siña Tatá tú la econde en la cocina porque es prieta de verdá.
>
> [You are made of a white veneer / and want to be in "society" / Fearing that anyone may find / The mother of your mother / But I know her very well / her name is Mrs. Tatá / You hide her in the kitchen / 'Cause she is black, very black.]

[7] By 1530, Spain began to import African slaves to work the mines after most Taino Indians disappeared due to cruel treatment, smallpox disease, suicide, or escape. Their work in the fields and mines was soon taken over by Africans bought from Danish, Portuguese, British, and American slavers. Most African slaves came from the Gold Coast, Nigeria, and Dahomey and belonged to the Yoruba, Igbo, and Bantu ethnic clans. See Fernando Picó, *History of Puerto Rico* (New Jersey: Marcus Weiner, 2006); Arturo Morales Carrion, *Puerto Rico: A Political and Cultural History* (New York: W.W. Norton, 1983); Irving Rouse, *The Tainos: Rise and Decline of the People Who Greeted Columbus* (New Haven: Yale University Press, 1992); Olga Jimenez de Wagenheim, *The Puerto Ricans: A Documentary History* (New Jersey: Marcus Weiner, 1994).

[8] In fact, my mother often got upset with me for my attraction to black women. She thought I should try to "improve the race" by marrying a white woman. At other times, she expressed contrary feelings of love toward her race and the culture of blacks in Puerto Rico.

[9] Among its provisions, we find that all babies born of slave women after the passing of the law were to be freed and those born from 17 September 1868 until the passing of the law were bought by the state from their owners for 125 *pesetas*.

find the surname that Antonio Gordils y Colón and Simón Gordils y Colón gave to their slaves. This explains why my mother often brushed off my questions saying, "That is not my last name. I don't use that slave name!"[10]

It is remarkable to see how politics and life intersect, changing history for ill or for good. The depletion of the gold mines on the island provoked the shifting of Spanish slave-trading routes to the north, causing the island to become a garrison for naval vessels. To provide the work force for the Puerto Rican garrison, African slaves from British and French possessions in the Caribbean could then enter Puerto Rico. It was likely at that point that some of my Perocier ancestors migrated to the island instead of staying in Hispaniola or some other French or British possession.

The family's oral history tells of an early African ancestor whose freedom was "bought in gold."[11] After the Spanish Crown Decree of 1789, African slaves were able to acquire their freedom by paying their weight in gold or by offering some other monetary payment. This possibility is consistent with the fact that some of my kin migrated between the Spanish decree of 1789 and the abolition of slavery in 1873. In any case, it was common for Puerto Rican abolitionists to purchase slaves' freedom. In 1856, a group of abolitionists founded the Secret Abolitionist Society with the objective

---

[10] Perocier is a French surname that seemed not to fit in an island conquered by Spain. My great-grandmother, Ynes Perocier, was born around 1880, only six or seven years after the abolition of slavery in Puerto Rico; she is registered as a mulatto in the 1910 U.S. Census (*Thirteenth Census of the United States, 1910* [NARA microfilm publication T624, 1,178 rolls], Records of the Bureau of the Census, Record Group 29, National Archives, Washington, DC). Mulattoes are the first generation offspring of a black person and a white person or simply the descendants of both black and white ancestors. According to the 2000 census, 80 percent of the four million inhabitants of Puerto Rico described themselves as "white"; 8 percent as "black"; 12 percent as "mulatto" and 0.4 percent as "American Indian" or "Alaskan Native." Anyone who visits the island, however, can easily observe that the percentage of mulattoes is much higher.

[11] During the eighteenth century, slavery was brought to the Caribbean islands by varied European nations, including France, England, and Spain. European markets demanded high quantities of sugar, which grew easily in the Caribbean's temperate weather. As demand for sugar increased so did the demand for plantation labor. With the speedy disappearance of the indigenous population of Taino Indians, African slavery under the plantation slavery model grew. In Puerto Rico, however, slavery was focused mostly on gold mining.

of freeing slave children by the sacrament of baptism.[12] The committee included some of the most illustrious men in Puerto Rican history such as Ramón Emeterio Betances, known as the father of the Puerto Rican nation (1827–1898),[13] and Segundo Ruiz Belvis (1829–1867). The tactic was known as *aguas de libertad* (waters of liberty) and was carried out in my family's hometown church, Nuestra Señora de la Candelaria, now the Catholic Cathedral of Mayagüez.

Because buying the freedom of slave children cost 50 *pesos* for a baptized child but only 25 *pesos* for the unbaptized, Betances and a few associates would wait next to the baptismal font on Sundays. As slave masters brought African women in to baptize their children, Betances would give money to the parents to pay for the child's freedom. Once freed, the child was immediately baptized. I am filled with pride when I imagine that glorious moment when my ancestor was immersed in the waters of salvation that broke the slavery of sin on the same blessed day as the ignominious chains of captivity were smashed forever.

LONG LIVE FIDEL!

My father was present on January 11, 1959, when the Pro Independence Movement (MPI), precursor of the Marxist-Leninist Puerto Rican Socialist Party, was formed. Now and then, he would gather us to listen to Fidel Castro's never-ending harangues. My father's shouts of joy at the great Cuban leader's words were a cause for both laughter and concern, as the loud noises often provoked marital discord within our home and neighbors' complaints outside of it. My father was unmoved. "Long live Fidel!," "Yankee go home!," "Fatherland or death!" were his daily chants. I would also go with him to communist cell meetings that lasted long into the night, where the dullness of discussion invariably put me to sleep. Our home became a gathering place for socialist meetings and rallies.

Even Mom readily helped in any way possible. In retrospect, I see that these activities gave her a rare opportunity for the cultivation of an elusive closeness with a man more enamored by an idea than by her. The only moment of tenderness between them that I can remember is both of them

---

[12] See James L. Dietz, *Economic History of Puerto Rico: Institutional Change and Capitalist Development* (New Jersey: Princeton University Press, 1986), 71.

[13] For a biography of Betances see Félix Ojeda Reyes, *El Desterrado de París: Biografía del Dr. Ramón Emeterio Betances (1827–1898)* (San Juan, PR: Ediciones Puerto, 2001).

laughing and dancing with joy after watching on TV as the Soviet Union's Alexander Belov sank a basket to send the US team to its first-ever Olympic basketball loss at the 1972 games. Their marriage would one day break down under the heavy weight of years of despondency and turmoil fostered under the great red flag of socialism. Socialism destroyed their marriage; I blamed America.

GOD IN THE MIDDLE

Although my father was a socialist and atheist, our family was never insulated from questions of faith. In fact, he was the barrio's official rosary prayer leader! Puerto Rican leftists were prone to preserve at least a semblance of religiosity—if not a fervent adherence to Catholic practices. How does one explain such a dichotomous stance toward religion? I remember a story told by one of my Jesuit seminary directors. As he arrived at the deathbed of a prominent radical lady, the priest saw the main leaders of the Puerto Rican Communist Party and other socialist movements gathering around her bed, encouraging her to make a good final confession. This was testimony to the depths of nationalist sentiment among Puerto Rican socialists: adherence to what made our culture distinct from Yankee culture—including the Catholic faith—trumped ideological orthodoxy.[14]

Occasionally, Mom sent me to Mass with neighbors. She was fervent in her religiosity yet also attached to the spiritualist practices common in the syncretism of Caribbean Catholicism. Seeing no contradiction between Catholic practices and *espiritismo*,[15] many participated in both. Each town had its resident medium, a woman believed to be able to communicate with the spirit world, and Mom often visited ours, Doña Ino. I remember the

---

[14] The Nationalist leader Pedro Albizu Campos, "The Teacher" to all who love him, including Marxists, was not a socialist. Albizu was a deeply religious man and a Catholic. He was not anti-American although he was in and out of prison due to his activities against American colonialism. He continues to be a hero and martyr for the cause of independence, and he is one of my heroes.

[15] The origins of espiritismo are to be found in the writings of the French Allan Kardec. It spread to Puerto Rico in the middle of the nineteenth century and became a framework for other traditions. The more popular form (*Espiritismo popular*) integrates Catholicism, African religious elements, and aspects of Spanish popular religion. See Bettina E. Schmidt, "The Power of the Spirits: The Formation of Identity Based on Puerto Rican Spiritism," *Revista de Estudos da Religião* no. 2, year 6 (2006).

day my mother took me to a session. The room contained numerous potion bottles, candles, statues, and other Catholic and not-so-Catholic-looking artifacts. She placed me on a circle drawn on the floor and sprinkled me with some nasty-smelling stuff while circling around me as she prayed. I was terrified and confused.

I grew seriously interested in the question of God only gradually. When I was about twelve, I joined a church youth group called Catholic Action Youth, mostly because of the girls and a desire for social interaction—but I soon found myself intrigued by what I heard there. The group was headed by two men, Chuíto and Maximino, who piqued my incipient religious interest. We went to visit the sick at hospitals, and every year we role-played the Passion of Christ on the streets of town before great crowds. I was attracted to the message conveyed by Chuíto and Maxi, but I would not yet permit any seed of faith to take root. Socialism remained my true religion.

A SON OF THE FATHERLAND

At the close of one hot Puerto Rican summer day, Mom started to cry. I saw a look of pain and desperation, and I became sick with worry when I saw her storm outside. I could hear the hum of inquisitorial voices and the pleading responses of my mother coming from her interaction with two men inside a vehicle. Later I learned that the men were investigators from the Intelligence Office of the Police Department who were always monitoring us. I hated them.

My father had long been under the Intelligence Division's watchful eye. As I leaf through the yellowed pages of his Intelligence Office file, obtained through the Freedom of Information Act, I find his first case file, dated July 7, 1963. I was less than one year old. It contains a detailed demographic record and an account of my father's alleged threats of violence against the police: "On 17th of July, 1963, [Mr. Hernandez] manifested that he was going to use violence against the police after the police interfered with him while pasting posters." Although the event is only alleged, I have no good reason to doubt that it happened. My father was not an idle observer; he was a front-line fighter.

In a confidential memo dated August 1969, for example, Lieutenant Cesar Soto, Chief of the West Coast Intelligence Unit of the Police Department, writes about my father's application for a job at a local factory. It also makes reference to a letter my father sent to the governor of Puerto Rico asking for a job. There, my father writes, "The sons of the fatherland cannot be left without sustenance and without food they cannot defend it."[16] In the memo, the factory's general manager said that my father would not be hired. The report also shows the authorities' efforts to find out from neighbors if my father was violent and if he possessed firearms. At the time of this report, he was an employee of a factory called I.B.E.C. in Mayagüez, a job he soon lost after accusations that he threatened to explode a bomb there.

I do not know whether every accusation was true, but I do know my father believed in violent revolution. After his initial firing for political reasons, his career was troubled, as investigation after investigation found him actively promoting revolution and distributing communist propaganda. Many times he recruited my brother and me to sell the communist newspaper *Claridad* in the neighborhood.

For those who thought as we did, being dangerous was a badge of honor, as violence against "empire" was love of humanity. My admiration for socialist leaders deepened. Fidel Castro was the master and Ché Guevara (we called him "El Ché") was the patron saint. Socialist Party leaders Juan Mari Bras and Carlos Gallizá were my heroes, and I met them many times at rallies. One of my favorite socialist leaders was Luis Lausel Hernandez, the president of a powerful trade union that fought a fierce battle with the government throughout a long and violent strike in the late 1970s.[17] I loved Lausel because he was a true communist who opposed the party's participation in the 1980 general election. His rhetoric was clear and powerful.

---

[16] Within the Intelligence Office's confidential file on my father I found a postcard signed *jinn* by an agent assigned to follow him. Hundreds of suspected socialist militants, leaders, and sympathizers were followed for decades and illegal files (*carpetas*) were kept on them. On the postcard I read, "Attended the commemoration of Grito de Lares, on the 23rd of September of 1977, as noted on the report A.A. 7-1-573, dated on the 26th of September, 1977." The Grito de Lares [The Cry of Lares] was an armed rebellion staged against Spanish rule in 1868. About a thousand men participated in the revolt, organized by Ramón Emeterio Betances and Segundo Ruíz Belvis.

[17] On January 19, 1978, six bombs were deactivated at an electric energy tower in the town of Aguas Buenas. Four days later, three more bombs destroyed a tower in the town of Trujillo Alto. Dozens of powerful bombs were found at various government facilities over the ensuing months. Lausel consistently denied any involvement in public; we in the party all knew he was behind the acts. Many years later, Lausel abandoned the Socialist nightmare and admitted the union's involvement in the bombings. Several years ago Lausel renounced Marxism and is now an evangelical pastor in the city of Yauco.

During the 1978 strike he declared, "We won't leave anything standing here. We are willing to allow for all we once built with our own hands to fall if necessary!" I thought he was uncompromising and pure. Only now can I see, through a prism of new understanding, that he preached death to our people.

Despite my eventual recognition of the harmful nature of communism, I still admire the thriving force of lives dedicated to a cause. "Do not be a fence-sitter," my father often said. He was right. Theories can be shrouded by a thick fog of irrelevance when those insistent on their truthfulness do nothing to advance them. Rationally articulated ideas must intersect with action if they are to become a driving force in the affairs of men.

Yet, the quest for practical results can lead men to enthrone mobilization and action as masters over reality. We can easily lose sight of the ultimate basis of activity and give free rein to the tyranny of the will. My socialism was deeply embedded in my personal history, and I purposefully studied it and learned to articulate it well. Only later would I examine its foundational vision and find it wanting.

A New Beginning

By the time I went to high school we had moved out of Mayagüez. My parents were building a modest home in a different town. It is never easy for young people to detach from normalcy, and the move for me was especially difficult: I was fond of our next-door neighbor's daughter, and I was leaving behind all I had ever known, including my best friend Stanley. The sadness was soon lifted, however, by the excitement of moving into our house. It was a simple, prefabricated wood-panel design, but it was new—and, best of all, each room had a door! A complete change of heart concerning the move came later, as I met new friends whom I have taken care to keep. There were "Peewee" and Lyn, Steven and "Bambi," and many others. Our home was directly across from a baseball park and a basketball court where we spent countless hours of carefree fun.

Isabela was a great place to live. Known as the "Garden of the North-west," it features mountainous peaks that descend to majestic coastlines. Countless times I took the short stroll toward the striking grandeur of the ocean shores. The walk took several turns through rich vegetation, a path probably journeyed before by the Igneri Indians.[18]

Soon after our move, my father joined the local Socialist Party. Often I accompanied him to meetings and continued to make socialism the center of my existence. One of my goals was to graduate from high school and go on to study political science in college so that I could be ready to defeat the Yankees. By the time I was seventeen years old I was fully engaged in political activity and steeped in socialist theory. It was about this time that I made my first trip to America.

My local amateur baseball team was traveling to New York to play against local teams, but I could not go. Perspiration oozed from every pore as I hacked at the tall grass on Mom's patio on the day of their departure. Not having the money to pay for my flight, I was upset but resigned. Suddenly, the team's manager appeared; he ordered me to pack my bags immediately. "Hey, you have five minutes, go!" Somehow he had found money for me. I packed a bag, kissed Mom goodbye, and headed for New York.

My brief encounter with what we thought of as the American Empire only solidified my hatred of it. I was scared, penniless, and could not understand a word. Each night I lay down on a cold motel bed only to be kept awake by the strange noises of a city that never slept. The only comfort came when I entered the Puerto Rican barrio, where my people lived and English was a foreign language. Surrounded by the collective reality of the American people, I was unable to detect any cogent cultural connection. These barbarians were strangers to me (although, as a socialist, I believed I knew their innermost thoughts). Homesickness accompanied me through each at-bat and each harrowing ride through the crazy New York streets. Do they care to slow down or rest? I wanted to go back home where things made sense.

---

[18] The Igneri were pre-Columbian natives originally sprung from the Arawak tribe. Probably originating from the Orinoco region in Venezuela, they moved to the Caribbean Sea to inhabit the Lesser Antilles and Puerto Rico. In Puerto Rico they were preceded by the *Arcaico* (Archaic) culture and later followed by the Taíno Indians, also from South America.

THE ADVENT OF CHANGE

I went off to the University of Puerto Rico at Mayagüez and lived in the familiar and friendly quarters of my uncle "Nono"[19] on Garnier Street, my beloved old neighborhood. He was a fiercely pro-American patriarch who controlled the household with an iron fist. At times, I would sit down and listen for hours to his tirades against communists and other political enemies. Before moving to Isabela, he often battled my father in long political conversations. They yelled, pounded, and pointed fingers in a manner that always left us expecting a physical confrontation. It never happened. They ended up laughing, only to go at it again another day.

While in college, I attended meetings of the University Federation for Independence (FUPI) and the Socialist Youth Union, and participated in several sit-ins during a socialist-led student strike. The Federation ("La FUPI") was a small and autonomous Marxist group founded in 1956, and the Socialist Youth Union was the result of a split within the Puerto Rican Independence Party. After the latter rejected Marxism, a youth contingent left to form the Union. These organizations were small youth movements aligned with the Cuban Revolution and in perennial ideological struggles with each other. I also had my first experience as a poll worker for the Socialist Party during the 1980 general election in which our party received a minuscule 0.3 percent of the vote. Political science became a passion of mine, and it provided the intellectual weaponry to attack America.

After graduation, I was admitted to the prestigious Pontifical Catholic University School of Law in Ponce, Puerto Rico. Regrettably, I was compelled to pass up the opportunity and went in search of a job, as the cost of studying there was prohibitive and my mother needed my financial support. I saw no means by which to escape my predicament at a time when my father was detached from the family's affairs and his money disappeared into not-accounted-for activities. I nearly despaired of finding a job until, by a stroke of luck (or Providence), I found myself employed at the local Catholic school. Father Pedro, the town's beloved pastor, interceded for

---

[19] His real name was Francisco Silva and he was the half-brother of my grandmother. Thus, he technically was my great-uncle. His relationship with us was somewhat strained for years due to family disputes and—again—the color line. He shared the same mother with my grandmother but had a different father, my grandma's father being the African-ancestry kin who brought to her the dark skin and with it, the great family divide.

me with the school principal and got me a job as a history teacher making five hundred dollars a month.

My dormant religious interests were finally awakened and so was the reality of my contradictions. Yet, during this time, I continued to be both an active and believing communist and a practicing Catholic. I had compartmentalized my religious and nonreligious commitments so neatly that some thought I had a vocation to the priesthood. The irksome tension of my dual inclinations soon eased thanks to changes brewing in Latin America. Liberation theology was on the move.

Although its roots are often attributed to Latin America, liberation theology was born in German schools of theology in the early twentieth century.[20] From this birthplace in the ivory towers of the Old World, priests and theologians brought it to the jungles and plains of the New. Troubled by the genuine needs of the natives, these populist theologians challenged the precapitalist system that perpetuated poverty in Latin lands. Energized by their vision of change and social justice and eager to make a mark of their own, they went to the *favelas* and *barrios* where desperate poverty cried out to God. They found no solid middle class and no traditions of democracy, only abject poverty on one side and heedless opulence on the other. In the Church, they found the piety of folk Catholicism with no social conscience and a structural alignment with elites. They offered as a solution a concoction of Marxist analysis and Christian praxis.[21]

All of this was music to my ears. For the first time, I perceived that Catholic faith and communist faith might be compatible. It now seemed

---

[20] Latin American liberation theologians also studied in other European centers such as Rome, Belgium, and France. There, they were exposed to the *nouvelle theologie*, a reaction against the traditional theology of Thomism and deeply dedicated to a renewal of the Church from biblical and patristic sources.

[21] See Michael Novak, *Will it Liberate? Questions About Liberation Theology* (New York: Paulist Press, 1986), 20.

Catholic and Protestant thinkers with the group Church and Society in Latin America (ISAL) took an early lead in the development of Liberation Theology. Catholic theologians such as Gustavo Gutiérrez, Segundo Galilea, Juan Luis Segundo, Lucio Gera, and Protestants such as Emilio Castro, Julio de Santa Ana, Ruben Alves and José Míguez Bonino began to share their analysis of the interaction between the gospel and social justice. In December 1971, Gustavo Gutiérrez published his seminal work, *Teología de la liberación*. Theology of liberation became more than an intellectual curiosity as its adherents increasingly became activists in trade union politics, community organization, and armed struggle.

possible for me to consider a religious vocation. Only one religious order could satisfy my quest: the Jesuits. What was a good Catholic and communist boy in the 1980s to do if not enter the Society of Jesus? I hesitated at first. The prospect of a Jesuit life among the Latin American poor thrilled me, and yet this was a move with steep consequences.

After flirting with the prospect for a while, I attended a Jesuit retreat. By the end of the weekend, I was asking to join. I rushed in on the impulse of a sheer lust for knowledge and a passionate commitment to a cause the Jesuits were offering me on a platter. Their academic prowess and social commitment captivated me. I discovered later that it was almost a requirement of admittance to be a Marxist.[22] I marveled at the existence of such a place, where my apparent dichotomies would finally merge in curious harmony.

Back home, Mom was not happy, while Dad seemed delighted. As I explained to him Jesuit life and beliefs, the stridently leftist personalities among them, and the prospects of going to Sandinista Nicaragua, he salivated with contented jealousy and pride. After saying my farewells to school colleagues, friends, and family, I departed for my ceremony of entrance. It was a beautiful and meaningful event attended by a man I much admired and whose presence I had requested—the revolutionary bishop Antulio Parrilla, SJ.[23]

The fierce light of the Jesuits' intellect and their commitment to socialist liberation obscured the shadows of any doubt I still had, and the goodness of the two superiors at the seminary made my life there a joyous experience. Father Orlando Torres, a biblical languages expert, and Father Fernando Picó, a prominent historian, lived in the residence, and I remember them with affection. Their talents and styles complemented each other, and they

---

[22] To be admitted, four Jesuit priests must interview a prospect. One of them seemed very interested in my politics, especially my willingness to disobey the Magisterium. He asked me, "Are you willing to disobey your bishop? In what ways are you willing to disobey him?" This was asked with a clear desire to hear an affirmative answer.

[23] Parrilla was the Titular Bishop of Ucres and a lifelong patriot who valiantly fought for Puerto Rico's independence. He was a fierce defender of human rights, opposed the American Navy base on the island of Vieques, and protested military conscription that forced Puerto Ricans to fight in "Yankee" wars. Active in the cooperative movement, he became program director at the Cooperative Institute at the University of Puerto Rico. The Marxist newspaper, *Claridad*, which I often sold in town, frequently printed his articles.

were exemplary priests. I abandoned myself to the life of a Jesuit seminarian: daily prayer, study, work, Mass, and more study. I seriously contemplated taking the final step of being ordained as a Jesuit priest.

Then came shocking news: the murders of six Jesuits in El Salvador.[24] Jesuits at the José Simeón Cañas Central American University had long opposed the government in El Salvador and the activities of the army. Throughout Central America, the Jesuits had been at the forefront of "liberation movements," supporting leftist insurrection and spreading liberation theology. Nearly a decade after the murder of Archbishop Oscar Romero, their deaths triggered outrage and pushed the government into negotiations to end the civil war. They also signaled the profound conflicts within the Latin American Catholic Church and the Jesuit order itself.

Indignation is too weak a word to convey what we felt. The tragedy only intensified our commitment against capitalism and American imperialism. We saw the unpublished bloody pictures and went to the vigils and ceremonies as anger raged, especially among Jesuits who personally knew the victims. An immediate effect was that we were not going to Sandinista Nicaragua for our studies in philosophy; it was too dangerous. Because I had longed to go, the news hit me hard.

Shortly after, I faced the most exhausting and frightening experience of my life, the hospital ministry. Father Orlando had made the decision to send us to the AIDS Hospice *Santo Cristo de la Salud* (Holy Christ of Good Health) in San Juan. I did not want to go and contemplated leaving seminary rather than working at such a place. Most Jesuit priests themselves would not visit; AIDS was sweeping the country and knowledge of the disease was sparse. The night I was notified of my assignment, Orlando's presence seemed like an apparition. Stupefied, I received the decree and barely assented as if condemned already to a horrendous fate.

Life at the hospice was an experience of constant pain enveloped in the stench of death. The chilling cries for help, the sorrowful words of regret, the curses to God even now reside in my memory. I can still feel the cold touch from a once-beautiful girl, confusing me with her beloved father

---

[24] It was November 16, 1989, when the news flashed out from El Salvador about the murders of six Jesuits and two women who worked with them at the Jesuit residence on the campus of the University of Central America (UCA). The murdered Jesuits were Fathers Ignacio Ellacuría, Martín-Baró, Amando López, Segundo Montes, Juan Ramón Moreno, and Joaquín López y López. The cook Julia Elba and her daughter Celina were also killed.

and beseeching me to come to her rescue; tightly grabbing me with the faint strength of a life almost lost. In recalling her, a human skeleton, full comprehension still escapes me.

Even more frightening was the day I rushed into a room to assist with a patient. Leaning heavily against a wall, and with a look of terrified apprehension, a volunteer refused to move. On the bed, an uncooperative and bloodied man struggled with a doctor. I found myself holding him while drips of blood fell all over my gloves and shirt. "What in the world am I doing here?" I thought.

It was with profound relief that I completed the assignment and went on to my spiritual exercises of St. Ignatius of Loyola—a thirty-day retreat in silence. The long hours of reflection helped me realize that there was no vocation to the priesthood in me. Desire to have a family had been buried deep under the sad experience of my parents' troubled union and my admiration for the Jesuit socialist haven. Although I had no true vocation to the priesthood, I did have a passion to merge God and Marx and go to Nicaragua to be in the midst of the revolution. Soon after finishing the spiritual exercises, I left seminary and grudgingly returned home. As I strolled near Isabela, a car stopped to give me a lift. It was my former employer, Sister Ida, principal of the town's Catholic school. She rehired me on the spot.

I found no relief from my struggles. I tried to lean on the belief that there were now opportunities before me but I knew that I did not belong there any longer. After less than a year, I decided to move on. The music teacher at St. Anthony College had just returned from studying at the University of Southern Mississippi and insisted that I consider going there. He argued that it was an enjoyable place and that the tuition was a bargain as well. Mississippi? I was incredulous at the thought of living in a place I knew little about and that seemed far removed from the main attractions of American culture. Resolved to pull myself out of my stagnant situation, I applied. I was admitted under a special program allowing me to study during the summer and return to my job in Isabela, so as to save money for the next summer.

I candidly admit my apprehension to cross the sea toward the hated behemoth, America. My heart was pierced as the plane took off over the deep river intent on returning me to Pharaoh. "Take me back home from the waters, Lord," I prayed. Still a communist, I landed in America where, though I was unaware of it at the time, my lungs filled with the air of true freedom.

Before I could realize the benefit of this freedom, however, I went through a trying time. The initial cultural shock was traumatic and I was apprehensive, isolated, and distrustful of all Americans, especially whites. Southern English was unintelligible. Driving up to Hattiesburg, Mississippi, from Louisiana, I pretended to understand those around me but mostly kept to myself. The voices were an incomprehensible buzz. To decipher an English word, translate it in my mind into Spanish, find English words to answer, and then pronounce them correctly was more difficult than cranking an old Russian car in Cuba! The initial weeks were tough, but I soon made friends who, for reasons I did not understand, found my thick accent appealing.

Getting used to American food was another challenge. Where is the rice with beans? Are you offering me a salad instead? Do you not know that I went straight from breast milk to yucca root and fried plantains? How do you expect me to drink that cup of black water you call coffee? It was not easy.

Embracing New Ideas and New Loves

In spite of these challenges, I began to enjoy myself. The voices of the multitude around me were still a buzz. Slowly, I began to better understand, as if someone from the high-tech country I now occupied were reprogramming my ears. Fully dedicated to my classes and making friends, I began to think that living at the university and in America was not that bad after all. Finally, I concluded that staying there and finishing my studies was my preference.

By the end of that first summer semester, I was not looking forward to leaving, but there was little hope of anything else. Then one day I was unexpectedly called to the dean's office. Some professors had recommended me for one of only three foreign-student assistantships, which would pay all my expenses. "Would I accept?" he wondered. Tears of joy gathered in my eyes as I left his office after giving my enthusiastic reply.

For the first time in my life, the thought formed in my mind—weakly at first—that possibly things were not as I had been told. There I was, still spewing words of hate against America, yet out of nowhere, and based only on my achievements, I had been offered a reward. Why? About a year before my arrival in the United States, I was leading an anti-American campaign in my hometown of Isabela, calling on young Puerto Ricans to refuse to fight in the first Persian Gulf War. Paying for anti-American propaganda posters myself—they read, "George Bush and Saddam Hussein are the same. Do not fight in the Iraq War"—I took pleasure in distributing hundreds of them.

Why offer me any benefit at all? Yet, America embraced me and gave me opportunities I had never dreamed of.

I soon found myself troubled by heretical thoughts, though I zealously resisted. How could I contemplate abandoning the familiar ideas that gave me life? I mourned over the possibility and refused to allow my thoughts to cross my lips. Beneath the silence, however, there was a movement of spirits. Reality was insistent.

The fall of the Berlin Wall threatened to strike another nail into the coffin of my self-confident ideology. It was not supposed to happen. Socialism, however, is not an ideology that can be defeated by facts or by reality. It is instead a sea of emotions, an infused essence without which a socialist thinks he shall perish. In short, socialism is a great lie.

Beginning to read what I previously considered meaningless Yankee propaganda and re-reading what was familiar without the easy assumptions of socialist orthodoxy to come to my rescue, a new world opened. I still fought the thoughts with appeals to the last of all socialist excuses: "Socialism has never been tried." For a communist, the embarrassment of reality must be opposed by a stubborn insistence on airbrushing history to preserve a semblance of respectability. Having been so wrong for so long about politics, life, and economics, it was exceedingly difficult to face the devastating truth.

I discovered that socialism survived in me as an idea to be pursued but never attained. If I were to find it, in reality I would have had to dig under a pile of corpses. Socialism is a utopian plan to build what cannot be built, to realize what is only illusory, and to destroy what works even if the result is chaos and death. Because its analysis of reality and its anthropology are faulty, socialism fails not because a given radical experiment fails. It fails because it is false in its essential premises. One day I would finally accept the error of my poorly crafted deception. I would then realize that socialism had been tried, and the result had been, and always would be, the gulag.

While still in the throes of my struggle, I met my wife, Crystal. A beautiful and intelligent African-American woman, she captivated me with her love of God and her assertive confidence. My encounter with her and other American blacks aroused in me a desire to know even more about issues of race in America. Not only did I attend classes on black issues and devour tome after tome about history, I also enjoyed being around my black brethren. My first attendance at a southern black Baptist church Sunday service remains one of the most inspiring events of my life. The memory of my first "soul food" meal at Crystal's family home in Hazlehurst still whets my appetite. Crystal and I were married and left Hattiesburg after graduation to move to Fort Myers, Florida. There we have raised our beloved children Lael Ann, Mateo Amiri, and Miriam Anne.[25]

No longer shielded from the fangs of a fiend called liberty, my past assumptions met another powerful opponent who made my views on race and ideology fall into utter silence: the remarkable scholarship of Thomas Sowell. As I began to read, especially his formidable *A Conflict of Visions*, I learned how my views on race were imbued with the same failed paradigm of victimhood proposed in the dialectics of history that were explored by Feuerbach, developed by Hegel, and popularized by Marx. They had made me think that out of the horror of revolution comes triumph; thus the travails inflicted by revolution pale in comparison to the evils of capitalism. Similarly, racism was the pernicious effect of a capitalist system forever in search of power, and race was nothing more than an epiphenomenon of class. Later, David Horowitz's autobiography *Radical Son* made me shudder. His account of second thoughts and political transformation punctured my soul to its core. The story of his estrangement from family and friends and his initial resistance and eventual surrender to the truth made me feel as if I were living the experience myself. It was as if the corrosive ideology that penetrated every cell of my body was now being decoded, and I saw that my experience was not unique.

The final blow came from the *The Content of Our Character* by Shelby Steele. I discovered the falsity of the victimhood narrative. American whites had not yet had the opportunity to oppress me, and I was already considered a victim, a wounded casualty of a race war that tied my future to an identity as victim. The moment I stepped off the plane, I was considered a victim, in spite of the freedom and opportunity I encountered at every corner. I was a protected specimen of an endangered group. My future achievements were not the deciding factor; in fact, the law dampened them, offering instead the appearance of benefit. The government had become my protector when in reality it was a hindrance binding my destiny to my status as victim.

I cannot identify exactly when I finally surrendered to the truth. Experience after experience and book after book shattered preconceived notions about America and capitalism that formed the basis of my worldview. I

---

[25] A fourth child and our firstborn, Jamil Ismael, was born in Mississippi while we were students there and died just two days after birth.

cannot offer a single blinding flash of conversion; my road to Damascus did not include any intellectual or experiential bolt of lightning. Like Paul, I may have been breathing murderous threats against empire when I fell from the horse of socialism, but my foot was stuck in the saddle and it dragged me for a while. One day I simply woke up realizing that I had become what I had always hated, a lover of freedom and a believer in "the American way."

Another discovery helped me considerably as I struggled to understand the full implications of my new situation. While watching TV one night, I heard a Catholic priest speak in ways that powerfully articulated my new thoughts. It was Fr. Robert Sirico, president of the Acton Institute for the Study of Religion and Liberty. Father Sirico spoke in a language I had never heard before from a priest: the language of faith, human freedom, limited government, and entrepreneurship. At the time, I could not yet merge my new ideas about freedom with my understanding of the Catholic faith. I had abandoned communism, but I could not reconcile my new politics with Catholic social justice. Father Sirico helped me cross the Tiber again, understanding that the things I appreciated about American freedom and capitalism were—the content of my Jesuit training notwithstanding—perfectly consistent with what the Church taught about human dignity and social justice.

BAPTISM BY FIRE

Renouncing socialism was not only a baptism of water but also of fire and blood. My situation brought to me great joy and new enemies. As socialism is a mood more than a cogent system, it uses shame as a weapon against those who dare to abandon the fellowship.[26] In this book, I will recount some of these experiences. Nonetheless, when you reach a transforming truth, you cannot hide it from others. "Don't be a fence-sitter," my dad said, and I have kept the family tradition of rebellious insistence.

---

[26] During Stalin's purges, those murdered were already dead before their deaths. They were erased from history books and their images erased from photographs as if they had never existed. If the sweeping force of the revolution turned against you, your humanity was denied and immunity from disappearance denied to you regardless of your labors for revolution. See David Horowitz, *Left Illusions: An Intellectual Odyssey* (Dallas: Spence Publishing, 2003), chap. 10.

A few years ago, I buried my father, his beloved Puerto Rican flag embracing his casket as he had embraced it with his life. He died a communist. At that time, I again silently sang the revolutionary songs to pay homage to the fallen warrior. While burying him, I remembered his laughter and joy when I, long before, had waved my retrieved red flag and pumped my tight left fist by his side. I mourned his death and I still honor his life.

His final days were met by a measure of God's love. Absolute coalescence between his politics and faith was never achieved, but I know that God likes fighters on his side. Although his revolutionary utopian plan remained unrealized, he fought the good fight. Where there is no passion for truth, there can be no yielding before his throne. Therefore, by the end, the communist rosary leader prayed it daily with devotion and received communion often. Looking back on his journey, I feel a sense of contented thankfulness for God's mercy in revealing through my father that life is finally meaningless if truth is not passionately pursued. It is true that the air of freedom now filling the lungs of my soul killed the fantasies of socialism within me, but Dad's committed life taught me how to retrieve and wave a new flag, the flag of freedom. Now, I am convinced, he still looks on in contented approval.

As I type these words, it has been only a few weeks since my mom joined my father in heaven. For the last few years, we saw her gradually slip away as her mind dissipated in advance of her death. The strength of her love, however, refused to surrender. At Mom's funeral, there were no flags over her coffin and no one to intone any revolutionary songs. There were only tears from those who loved her and for whom she offered her life. My brother Augusto tells me that she slowly and peacefully fell asleep while all my brothers gathered around and assured her that all her children were happy and safe.

Mom died on Thanksgiving Day, a holiday invented in the land I now call home. She died on a day that reminds us of the beauty of faith and freedom, the two gifts that long ago were poured over the head of a little child-slave at the Cathedral of Mayagüez. It makes perfect sense. As I flew home to bury my mother, I cried with sadness but even more with joy, thanking God for giving me a special mother. Thanking God for the waters of liberty; waters that broke the yoke of slavery and sin and realized my dreams of freedom. Returning to America, my new home, I again gazed through the plane's window upon the waters of liberty below. Waters I once crossed over in fear I now beheld in gladness.

2

WHAT IS MAN THAT YOU CARE ABOUT HIM? AN ANTHROPOLOGY

Whatever the man called every living creature, that was its name.

—**Gen. 2:19 (NRSVCE)**

One late afternoon in the early 1990s, I found myself in the midst of a colorful gathering at the home of a fellow Jamaican parishioner, Deborah.[1] It was a small, cozy home that made human closeness almost inevitable. A narrow family room with nice paintings and beautiful furnishings gave way to a kitchen full of pots and pans. The waning daylight made the atmosphere even more intimate, and the flavorful aromas coming from the kitchen invited all to venture close and peek at the variety of West Indian cuisine.

About ten of us, mostly black Caribbean and African-American, sat and chatted while awaiting the feast. New to the church and still somewhat insecure in my English, I mostly listened while enjoying my surroundings. As the night advanced and the magic of good Caribbean food began to work, everyone got more comfortable and talkative. Suddenly, and seemingly out of nowhere, an argumentative middle-aged African-American man—I will call him Lawrence—interrupted the amicable conversations with a provocative monologue on race. "We are all black—that is our identity, and nothing supersedes that reality. It does not matter whether you are from Jamaica or anywhere else, you are first and foremost black," he declared.

---

[1] In most cases, I have changed the names of the individuals in my stories.

The evening's peace and goodwill hung in the balance. Most blacks, and the couple of white women present, seemed to give at least faint assent to Lawrence's words, though they subtly sought to move away from him or turn the conversation in another direction. Lawrence, however, remained adamant, defiant, and loud.

It soon became obvious that Lawrence's harangue was a repeat of many others and was targeted especially at our host. (As the months went by, I would get used to Lawrence's "expert" proclamations on the race issue). Deborah was the only one who argued against him. "I am Jamaican, that is all we are in my country," she replied with conviction and offered no further explanation. Her strong posture and his accusatory insistence made the whole discussion a pointless battle of wills between two seasoned warriors. Nefarious triangulation was inevitable, I guess. You could see it in the penetrating eyes of the contestants and in the spectators' desperate attempt to avoid being drawn in to the conflict. Being the new kid on the block, I was even more vulnerable.

"You are wrong and this brother here knows it is true. He knows he is black," Lawrence answered, looking right at me. I felt the penetrating gaze of all eyes awaiting my reply, waiting to see whose casualty of war I would become. Taken off guard, I awkwardly blurted, "Yes, I am black." My poor response was a weak attempt at a Solomonic reply, accepting my blackness without denying my ethnic pride, all done with a sad-puppy look toward Deborah as if pleading, "Please do not take my plate away." Proud of his conquest, the African-American warrior decreed me a black brother and the discussion was over—at least for the moment.

Driving home, I felt upset. I thought about the incident and how it embodied a kind of received wisdom on black identity. Even more, I thought about how my intrinsic personhood faded behind a veneer of pretense about race in America. I marveled at how a nice gathering of good people was disfigured by a stance we all obviously wanted to avoid. Even those who obliquely assented to the proclamation of what it means to be black gave no clue as to what they *really* thought. They went with the flow, abiding by the authoritarian demarcation of authenticity they were expected never to cross. It was a perfect illustration of a phenomenon described by one of the foremost champions of black self-reliance, Shelby Steele: "The allure of race as a human delineation is the very shallowness of the delineation it makes."[2]

---

[2] Shelby Steele, *The Content of Our Character: A New Vision of Race in America* (New York: HarperCollins, 1990), 5.

Making race the principal source of identity empowered those who offered the crudest and most simplistic explanations of black experience—people such as Lawrence.

Race was presented to me as the great boundary, placing limits on my identity, rather than as one aspect of my deeper reality as a person. One camp offered me redemption by totalizing race and the other suggested an ethnic safe haven where I could deny it. Assessing the moment later, I was ashamed that I had given assent to a distortion. My affirmation of blackness was indeed meaningless and probably only a way to acquiesce to an intellectual bully. I had, as Steele says, "put on my race mask." Too often, we hold tight to race so as to ignore the reality of true self. If we were honest, however, we would admit that lurking beneath the skin-deep cover of race is insecurity. We either make race the totality of our existence, denying the more penetrating realities of our lives, or we reject our race in an attempt to forget what, deep inside, brings us shame.[3]

It is true that in our search for identity we must at times remember and at times forget our race. The forgetting is important as it allows an unimpeded search for the universality of existence while the remembering allows us to place racial specificity in the context of such universals. However, the back and forth of racial memory often becomes a simplistic tool of avoidance of that which is at the core of existence. In the give and take of racial labeling and racial strategizing that goes on in our society, the ultimate reality of our being is often dismissed. In that context, the hierarchy of the goods of human nature is ignored as we engage in grand proclamations about what it means to be black.[4]

Through the incident at Deborah's, I discovered that the real question before me was a deeper one, a question about what is prior and what is derivative in human reality. The choice seemed to be to succumb to the lure of racial pride as if the racial question is *the* question of my life or to shun it as if it is within my power to make it disappear. However, the racialists reject the deeper question by denying my individual right to challenge the boundary of race; there is no deeper reality than race, and I must embrace it or cease to be. For them, my ideas and individual understanding of the race issue are not dependent on a prior reality of existence; instead they are the central question of my reality.

---

[3] Steele, *Content of Our Character*, chap. 2.

[4] Steele, *Content of Our Character*, xi.

A few months later, I found myself again in the midst of the racial rumble. Once Lawrence found out what my real ideas about race in America were, ideas that strayed from the plantation of racialist ideology, he changed his mind. "He's not black; that guy is Puerto Rican or something," he commented. Although initially proclaimed a brother based on my skin color and ancestry, I was now orphaned and disowned. Now, it did not matter whether or not some of my ancestors came on the boat and were shackled with the chains of shameful oppression. What mattered were my views on race and politics. I learned then that the racialists see themselves as the gatekeepers of identity, and race is dependent on agreement with the liberal/radical consensus; race *consciousness* determines my belonging.

The racial identifier has become so overwhelming, so complete, that it places before us a new set of questions—not about the place of race and ethnicity in our lives as persons but about what it truly means to be human.

A CHRISTIAN VISION OF IDENTITY

The way out of this impasse is a true understanding of human identity. Evil surrounds us. Yet, in spite of the realities of a broken world, the certainty of a singular dignity in man is inescapable.[5] This reality denies the possibility of man's being merely putty in the hands of evolutionary forces or a token in an unfortunate game of fate. There is something in each of us that refuses to fade even in the very act of wickedness. At times, it escapes our gaze, but it is there. "Even in vice there may be a bond not untouched by grace," as Richard John Neuhaus put it.[6] The very capacity to make choices helps us to see that the space inside of us is not empty. Every attempt to deny this spark, every new and self-serving psychological theory designed to refute the possibility of moral freedom, reveals the opposite: that men choose, even if at times we choose the easy route of the denial of agency.

The reality of our personal freedom is of immense value in the study of the effects of racialism and other dualisms. The frontier of personal freedom is one that shall not be tampered with by a misdirected racial affirmation. It is in discovering the greatness of the human person *as person* that we will find answers to our questions about "the race problem." In such an account

---

[5] Throughout this book, the traditional designations of *man* and *men* refer to the human person, both male and female.

[6] Richard John Neuhaus, *Death on a Friday Afternoon: Meditations on the Last Words of Jesus from the Cross* (New York: Basic Books, 2000), 36.

of value, collective racial identity has no priority; race is but the shallow projection of a false depth in search of power.[7] In other words, racialism is an error of anthropology because race is not destiny and race is not who we are.

Among all comprehensive systems, the Christian worldview assigns the greatest dignity to the human person. As the late Charles Colson said, Christianity is the surest ground for defending human dignity because it holds that human beings "actually reflect the character of the ultimate source of the universe. How could anyone even theoretically conceive of any more secure basis for human dignity?"[8] Called into existence as members of the human species, we possess intrinsic worth as a gift from God. Christians believe that such dignity mirrors the Creator. Made in his image, we bear the marks of our origins as we resemble our uncreated maker as goods flowing from *the* Good.[9]

According to Christian anthropology, man is at once a task and a gift. There is in us a twofold dignity brokering for completion. Our personhood guarantees a certain status, yet we are called to self-determination at the level of action. Simply put, we make ourselves to be who we are by the way we live. We cannot be fulfilled by remaining what we are by natural endowment or by limiting our actions to reactions such as that of one chemical to another. Human action cannot be absolutely determined by training, circumstance, or racial identity.[10]

---

[7] Steele, *The Content of Our Character*, 5–6.

[8] Charles Colson and Nancy Pearcey, *How Now Shall We Live?* (Wheaton, IL: Tyndale House, 1999), 131.

[9] "Every human being," writes theologian William May, "is intrinsically valuable, surpassing in dignity the entire material universe, a being to be revered and respected from the very beginning of its existence." William E. May, *An Introduction to Moral Theology* (Huntington, IN: Our Sunday Visitor, 1991), 23. See also Richard L. Fern, *Nature, God and Humanity: Envisioning an Ethics of Nature* (New York: Cambridge University Press, 1992), 140.

[10] Karl Rahner writes:

> [Man] is that being who is responsible for himself. When he explains himself, analyzes himself, reduces himself back to the plurality of his origins, he is affirming himself as the subject who is doing this, and in so doing he experiences himself as something necessarily prior to and more original than this plurality.

From the beginning of life, we are created as subjects; as agents of choice. The human person is called not only to *change* but also to *choice*. We are not only capable of choosing but we also *know* that we choose. This self-awareness, or subjectivity, means that we are cognizant of our self-reflection and can recognize the particularity of our existence.[11] No amount of theorizing can eliminate that awareness deep in our hearts. Even if later on we point fingers and give excuses, we know better.

A deep dishonesty is inherent in the denial of our self-awareness, such as when some adduce ignorance of our capacity to choose or offer racial theories of oppression, thus excusing individuals when they refrain from choosing what is good. In pursuit of the safety that a parasitic life offers, some find comfort in the boredom of meaningless life with its unavoidable encroachment upon freedom where the denial of the capacity to choose is the ticket to a safe emptiness.[12] A racialist examination of social interaction is often tied to a denial of the human capacity for moral choice.

To examine social conditions while denying the human capacity for self-awareness and free choice is fruitless. Morality is empty without freedom. Our self-awareness creates a singular condition: We are unique and exceptional among known creatures, and exceptionalism is what we call dignity.

RACIALIST THEORIES VERSUS CHRISTIAN DIGNITY

Recent centuries, however, have seen the development of theories denying our radical capacity for freedom, denying that we can choose in the face of the binding power of psychological, biological, and social influences. Ironically, many of these theories attempt to create better conditions, in moralistic fashion, by denying freedom. They often focus on collective rather than

Karl Rahner, *Foundations of Christian Faith: An Introduction to the Idea of Christianity* (New York: Seabury Press, 1978), 31. See also Gregory Beabout et al., *Beyond Self Interest: A Personalist Approach to Human Action* (Lanham, MD: Lexington Books, 2002), 60.

[11] See John Paul II, *The Theology of the Body: Human Love in the Divine Plan* (Boston: Pauline Books & Media, 1997), 30; Rahner, *Foundations*, 12–14; Germain Grisez and Russell Shaw, *Beyond the New Morality: The Responsibilities of Freedom* (Notre Dame, IN: University of Notre Dame Press, 1974), 13; Anthony J. Santelli et al., *The Free Person and the Free Economy: A Personalist View of Market Economics* (Lanham, MD: Lexington Books, 2002), 7.

[12] Theodore Dalrymple, *Life at the Bottom, The Worldview That Makes the Underclass* (Chicago: Ivan R. Dee, 2001), chap. 1.

individual identity, grouping individuals in classes of people such as the workers, the poor, black people, and whites. The reality of our great value, however, refutes the idea of racial priority in establishing personhood or identity. What is truly determined is precisely a beautiful gift of humanity that facilitates choice instead of being a fixed identity that narrows it within the precincts of racial identity. Our calling into existence as members of the human family is a special one: We are called personally, by name, as beings affirmed for our own sake.[13]

In the first Genesis account, humans were made "male and female" (Gen. 1:27) not black or white. In this passage, man is shown as created for interpersonal communion by being provided with a specific *sexual* identity. As science has discovered, this sexual identity is established from the moment of conception depending on the presence or absence of the Y chromosome and its secreted antigens. The body is thus more than interwoven with the fabric of the human person; it is intrinsic to the understanding of what a person is.[14]

Interestingly, "original solitude" is our state in the second account of Genesis. This aloneness is a stark reality not only for the male but also for man as such (male and female), as revealed by the reference to the male only *after* the creation of the first woman (Gen. 2:7; 2:21–22). Placed among the beasts of the earth, the male journeys onward, looking among the different shapes and forms, only to find himself alone. His loneliness was real even as his body was similar to those of the other beasts; theirs were formed, like his, from the dust. From the beginning, he finds himself "as if in search of his own entity." We can say that he was searching for his identity.[15]

It is very important that, in this original quest, race does not show up. From the beginning, racial or ethnic identity, however defined, was not a part of the quest for meaning. It is in our sexual reality as individuals, not in our race, that we find the first quest for identity and togetherness. The essentialization of race often found in racialist theories of self betrays the deepest reality of the human person created as an individual called to communion. In a sense, the awareness of our loneliness and our conscious

---

[13] Vatican Council II, *Gaudium et Spes*, 24.

[14] Vatican Council II, *Gaudium et Spes*, nos. 12–14. For this, "man," as taught by the fathers of Vatican II, "is not allowed to despise his bodily life; rather he is obliged to regard his body as good and honorable since God has created it and will raise it up on the last day." *Gaudium et Spes*, 14.

[15] John Paul II, *Theology of the Body*, 35–36.

pondering about the meaning of our lives reveals our status as "partners of the Absolute."[16] We marvel at this unique feature that allows us to realize what is happening. As humans, we question our existence, are troubled about the meaning of our lives, and seek fulfillment and peace.

Genesis 2:25 stresses the point that man and woman were naked but not ashamed. They were able to participate in the vision of God as creator and saw themselves through that mystery. They were also capable of experiencing the pure value of their bodies and of sex as a gift. "They see and know each other," Pope John Paul II reflects, "with all the peace of the interior gaze, which creates precisely the fullness of the intimacy of persons."[17] This "reciprocal complementarity" allowed them to experience the gift they were to each other in the fullness of humanity expressed in their masculinity and femininity. Nakedness deprived of shame signals the mystery of man's creation in integrity and love. It points to a true communion of persons. In Genesis, we see humans as a unified community of male and female called to self-donation; not as a kaleidoscope of varied human subgroups. In that account, humanity is not divided in any essentialist way into tribes, races, or colors. The logic of Genesis is antithetical to that of Jim Crow, where persons were separated into the categories of "whites" and "Negroes and other races" by the obscene "one-drop rule."[18] The same logic also confounds the judgment coming from the other side of the same racialist coin—that which would divide us into neat segments determined by race and ethnicity. "Jim Crow is now dead," Professor Stephan Thernstrom tells us, "but its legacy lives on in current racial-classification practices. Ironically, though, it is now those on the left, who are pleased to call themselves liberals, who insist that we all belong in rigid, mutually exclusive, color-coded compartments."[19] By essentializing race, we have created another boundary of shame: the classification of race. Instead of the peace of the interior gaze, we get preoccupation with color and antagonism of race as a totalism—a comprehensive worldview.

[16] John Paul II, *Theology of the Body*, 38.

[17] John Paul II, *Theology of the Body*, 57–58.

[18] In the South, the one-drop rule established a black racial identity on the basis of any trace of African ancestry. Jim Crow laws disfranchised blacks and segregated them in public places and accommodations.

[19] Stephan Thernstrom, "One-Drop Still: A Racialist's Census," *National Review* (April 17, 2000).

In my work in "black" ministry, I try never to forget that I am not working with blacks or Hispanics but with persons, each of them of unsurpassable value and deserving from me a reverence due to persons made in God's image. We are not tokens in a massive collection from which we acquire meaning and value; the individual human person is the measure and starting point of social interaction and grouping. In other words, man is *an end* in himself. Hence, his dignity refers to the individual and intrinsic rather than to the collectivized and instrumental value of his life.[20]

Racialism has become a reactionary force by abandoning the civil rights movement ideal of erasing the importance of racial differences. "As instituted in movements such as multicultural education, diversity training, and cross-cultural counseling, [racial ideology], seen as the most radical, avant-garde thought on race by its proponents, emphasizes coming to grips with difference, not moving beyond differential thinking."[21] By contrast, in his original situation, mankind experiences harmony independent of tribal identity. By disobedience, he abandons this harmony and thus must rediscover his roots by means of contrasting his historical (or sinful) condition with his earlier condition. He must now try to reconstruct his original innocence through the agency of conscience. Tribalism and racial or ethnic essentialism are found only *after* sin enters into the affairs of humanity. What is interesting is that humanity was already a community *before* the fall, a male and female community in no need of racial or tribal classifications.

The law of that community was within their beings, not attached to the label of agglomerated identity. Before a written law was promulgated, they shared in divine governance by obeying a law written in their hearts. In a sense, God imprinted a hidden memory of a past without shame into our beings. In this sense, to remember—to remember in line with right reason—is our salvation. Radical consequences sprouted from breaking this law.[22] We

---

[20] Immanuel Kant understood this in affirming that the human person "can never be used merely as a means by any (not even by God) without being at the same time an end also himself, that therefore humanity in our person must be holy to ourselves." Immanuel Kant, *The Postulates of Practical Reason* (1788), chap. 2, n. 5.

[21] Elisabeth Lasch-Quinn, *Race Experts: How Racial Etiquette, Sensitivity Training, and New Age Therapy Hijacked the Civil Rights Revolution* (New York: W. W. Norton, 2001), 230.

[22] See Russell Hittinger, *The First Grace, Rediscovering the Natural Law in a Post-Christian World* (Wilmington, DE: ISI Books, 2003), 5–7.

will see later how important the idea of memory is in analyzing the black historical condition.

Genesis also relates the fall that produced the foundation for man's abuse of freedom. With disobedience Adam and Eve discovered their nakedness and lost "original fullness" (Gen. 3:7). We can see the fall as the expansion of human appetite beyond what is truly good. A totalism was established, the totalism of self-assertion and self-absorption, a refusal to deal with the reality of our dependent nature. Racialisms of all sorts are but a continuation down that path into the territory of sinful self-assertion and wrongheaded autonomy.

It is clear that human beings were created without absolute authority over the practical norms that will judge them. God did not grant us autonomy to create the moral law as we move on in history. The first dignity of man is a gift from a good God, not the result of human action. It is a gift inherent in the nature of persons from the first moment of their existence. Thus, as we try to understand human interaction and social processes, we must seek explanations that are realistic and personalistic. It is only when certain values are recognized as intrinsic goods of the human person that collective entities can act to craft policies that uphold such values. In our study of black reality, we will see how utopian and structuralist explanations have been preferred and how they consistently fail to connect with a correct vision of man. We will also see how modern liberal understandings of social processes misunderstand human autonomy.

Autonomy is a good not because persons are islands but because a self-directed life is a constitutive good of the human person. "Neutrality" with regard to the content of our choices betrays autonomy by failing to consider other aspects of human dignity and well-being. As philosopher Joseph Raz observes, autonomy has no real value apart from the content of the choice being made. "Since autonomy is valuable only if it is directed at the good," he writes, "it supplies no reason to provide, nor any reason to protect, worthless, let alone bad options. To be sure, autonomy itself is blind to the quality of options chosen.... Providing, preserving or protecting bad options does not enable one to enjoy valuable autonomy."[23]

In the case of modern liberalism and its influence in the lives of the underclass, we have seen the conflation of radical individualism in the moral sphere and asphyxiating collectivism in the economic and racial sphere.

[23]Joseph Raz, *The Morality of Freedom* (Oxford, UK: Clarendon Press, 1986), 411–12.

Both errors can be traced back to the threshold between original innocence and historical man. Both are a misunderstanding of what is essential about the human condition. Even in the moral sphere where modern liberalism seeks to assert individual autonomy, it sees choice as a byproduct of binding antecedent factors outside of individual control. Humanity is seen as destined *to be changed* but not *to make choices*.

AGAINST ESSENTIALISM

A radical separation of the human body from consciousness or personhood triggers self-alienation and disintegration. Not only might our physical body be seen as instrumental to our consciousness but also the volitional and existential aspects of the person become instrumental to biological aspects of self (be it race, gender, or even disability). My race becomes the determining factor in the way I see the world and analyze society.

A particular aspect of the person can then be seen, at least existentially if not metaphysically, as the total true self. In her autobiography, Zora Neal Hurston wrote of how the "race problem" was unavoidable among black writers and how she countered the temptation of forming a totalistic view of black folks based on race:

> Negroes were supposed to write about the Race Problem. I was and am thoroughly sick of the subject. My interest lies in what makes a man or a woman do such-and-so, regardless of his color. It seemed to me that the human beings I met reacted pretty much the same to the same stimuli. Different idioms, yes, inherent difference, no.[24]

I am also sick of the race problem discussed in essentialist mode. Against the assertions of the "Lawrences" in our community, we must not reduce the race problem to a battle of "us versus them." The disproportionate concentration of certain ills in the black community is real, but it serves no purpose to attribute such problems to essentialist assumptions. The history of the twentieth century is replete with examples of dangerous ideologies based on erroneous dualistic anthropology. Essentialism and totalism are concepts providing an illusion of understanding. The affirmation of human dignity is an important step in escaping this totalistic dualism and the social policies that derive from it.

[24] Quoted in Paul Witcover, *Zora Neale Hurston* (Los Angeles: Melrose Square Publishing, 1991), 144.

3

THE ARDUOUS APPRENTICESHIP OF LIBERTY

It cannot be repeated too often that nothing is more fertile in prodigies than the art of being free; but there is nothing more arduous than the apprenticeship of liberty.

—Alexis de Tocqueville[1]

My bicycle came to a screeching halt, and I crashed to the ground. There I was, trying to get up, and Maria was angry. Careening through the streets, I had almost hit her. "Oh boy, it's going to be one of those days," I thought. A torrent of angry words flowed from her mouth as I lay there with the burning rays of the Caribbean sun on my face.

"Why don't you watch where you're going?" she blurted.

"I'm sorry Maria, I didn't see you," I replied.

"Didn't see me?" she exclaimed; then, dismissively, "Well, you're just a nigger anyway."

Those words punctured my soul in a way my childhood friend could not have imagined. I wanted to crawl away and hide. I lay there in agony and silence. The whole incident could not have taken more than a few seconds, but it felt like an eternity.

---

[1] Alexis de Tocqueville, *Democracy in America* (1835; repr., New York: Bantam, 2000), 147.

Suddenly coming to my senses, I became angry in turn. My mind filled with confusing thoughts as my body tightened, prepared to launch a physical assault at Maria. But, thank God, at that moment, I happened upon the idea of a less violent form of retribution.

"Yes?" I said. "Well, remember that when you come back asking me to draw something for you!"

Maria retreated immediately as if in fear, or perhaps in shame. She frequently needed my assistance with schoolwork and other tasks, and I perceived that my words had gotten her attention.

In the midst of this confrontation, I had remembered the wisdom of my saintly mother. She always stressed the importance of accomplishment and the need to be studious. She had only a third-grade education, any aspiration to continued schooling unwillingly abandoned in the face of the pressing needs of a family mired in the Puerto Rican poverty of the 1930s. In spite of this—or because of it—she always understood how important books are. Loving, protective, and rigorous, her influence on me was considerable. Her wisdom led me to make a fateful choice that sunny day when I was confronted viscerally with the reality of racism for the first time. Instead of retreating into myself in shame or lashing out in anger, I had recourse to my inherent dignity and capacity for achievement.

Maria remained a good friend and readily came back for help, which I offered without complaint. Without knowing it at the time, I had found the antidote for racialism. The reality of my race took a backseat in my life. I recognized that my accomplishments and my skills had a power that transcended the accidents of my birth. I knew that, whatever my race, I had dignity.

THE REALITY OF FREE CHOICE

Men choose as individuals, not as races. Human dignity resides in our being intelligent and free beings capable of determining our lives by our choices. "Action *reveals* the person," writes Polish philosopher Karol Wojtyła (later Pope John Paul II).[2] We are not animals moved by instinct. Calculations or techniques to achieve specific goals would be sufficient if the problem were to *become* persons—as if personhood was some sort of static reality or attainable goal. Our challenge, however, is not limited to becoming persons,

---

[2] Quoted in Samuel Gregg, *Challenging the Modern World: Karol Wojtyła/John Paul II and the Development of Catholic Social Teaching* (Lanham, MD: Lexington Books, 2002), 55.

but, as Germain Grisez and Russell Shaw tell us, "We are instead coping constantly with the difficult but fascinating problem of how to *be persons*."[3]

Every action requiring technique involves some sort of manipulation of physical objects or mental elements. "Every technical manipulation, even the simplest," says personalist philosopher Gabriel Marcel, "implies the possession by the manipulator of certain minimal aptitudes, without which it is not practicable."[4] Our lives, however, are always a "project under development."[5] Conversely, our minds must transcend the boundaries of mere manipulation achievable through basic human intelligence and cross that transcendent threshold of what Marcel calls an "inner urgent need," a move from *aptitude* to *participation*.

The job is not transferable to entities, labels, or groups. The human person, not the racial group, has the task of participating in his own development and growth. Race consciousness is offered as an infallible sign of authenticity, luring us to abdicate responsibility and liberty. I know the temptation well, because I succumbed to it on that Saturday afternoon at Deborah's house. No matter how many times we are shamed by those telling us that the boundary of race must not be crossed, we must press forward. The call is to affirm our individuality and our capacity to choose our path in life in spite of social pressures. The task is to be free.

Free choice is, according to philosopher John Finnis, a decision "between open practical alternatives ... such that there is no factor but the choosing itself which settles which alternative is chosen."[6] These practical possibilities are *options for choice*, that is, options I can adopt among real alternatives. Racialism prevents the person from fully realizing this magnificent gift and wondrous responsibility, by channeling choice through the prism of race in

---

[3] Germain Grisez and Russell Shaw, *Beyond the New Morality: The Responsibilities of Freedom* (Notre Dame, IN: University of Notre Dame Press, 1974), 14.

[4] Gabriel Marcel, *Mystery of Being: Reflection & Mystery*, vol. 1 (South Bend, IN: Gateway Editions, 1950), 20–21.

[5] Anthony J. Santelli et al., *The Free Person and the Free Economy: A Personalist View of Market Economics* (Lanham, MD: Lexington Books, 2002), 51–52.

[6] John Finnis, *Fundamentals of Ethics* (Washington, DC: Georgetown University Press, 1983), 137. Finnis summarizes elsewhere, "Choice, then, is of proposals, and the proposals one shapes in one's deliberations include one's ends and one's means." Everything included in a proposal "has the character of end, of purpose, of objective." John Finnis, *Moral Absolutes: Tradition, Revision, and Truth* (Washington, DC: Catholic University of America Press, 1991), 69.

a search for power. Found at both ends of the spectrum of race consciousness, racial oppression denies our capacity to choose. Shame is the preferred instrument in the pursuit of control, and shame feeds on weaknesses in our self-esteem.[7]

Racialism insists that certain alternatives are not real; they are thus accessible to the acting person only at the expense of losing the self. In this view, the self is in meaningful ways predetermined by adherence to the group. To say, "this is the way blacks act," or "this is the way blacks think," is to lower the person to an element in a collection; to reduce free choice to group instinct. In fact, it is an insult to the dignity of persons. *Human action is not herd behavior.* I experienced this intensely in my encounter with Maria. Who can say how another person of color would have acted in the same situation? Any number of possibilities present themselves; the fact is that I acted in a certain way, and I did so by choosing. It was my own action, not that of a race or of a representative of a race.

We give ourselves existential dignity by formulating moral judgments and choosing rightly. My participation has an existential and transformative quality that is not merely a transient exertion or an agglomeration of events but is integral to being. "Choosing," says John Finnis, "is adopting a proposal, and what one thus adopts is, so to speak, synthesized with one's will, that is, with oneself as an acting subject. One becomes what, seeing reason to, one chooses."[8]

This capacity to choose establishes our difference in kind from other living beings. As philosopher Mortimer Adler notes, "Freedom of choice is involved [in the question of man's fundamental constitution] and with it a radical difference in kind between men and other animals that have no moral problems, no moral rights, and no moral responsibilities."[9] So much of modern racial theory denies such capacity for free choice and, in the process, diminishes the stature of those for whom the theories are supposedly created. Racialism impedes true autonomy and individuality by tying human behavior to preconceived modes of action. Racialism animalizes.

---

[7] Shelby Steele, *The Content of Our Character: A New Vision of Race in America* (New York: HarperCollins, 1990), 3–4.

[8] John Finnis, *Moral Absolutes*, 72.

[9] Mortimer J. Adler, *The Difference of Man and the Difference It Makes* (New York: Fordham University Press, 1993), 272.

Individualism properly understood does not fail to recognize biological connections or social ends, but it recognizes the limits of the collective in explaining the person and the need for individual agreement for the collective to execute its intentions. If the ability to choose is hampered by the collective, then the group dominates the vision of the person to the detriment of human dignity.[10]

Free Choice versus Hard Determinism

Is there such a thing as free choice? Common sense seems to answer the question in the affirmative. However, not all believe that we can freely choose. Materialist determinists consider choice to be the output of an efficient biological machine.[11] In the world of hard determinism, the intricate and perplexing labyrinth of hormonal fluctuations do not commingle with personal agency. In that universe, likewise, the features of systems and of genes determine the fate of our existence. Choices that seem to be free are instead said to be determined by unconscious motives or "gaps" in our brain functions controlled by chance or by the process of natural selection. This understanding of reason as possessing purely biological existence denies the possibility of transcendental or ontological value.

For biological determinists, both consistent patterns of behavior among certain groups and the evolutionary divergence of races enthrone heredity as the basis of identity. It is a position shared by racialists on the left and the right. From the right, there are those who insist on black genetic inferiority by pointing to achievement gaps or intelligence studies. From the left, we find the same insistence on genetic determinism joined with accusations that opponents are hiding the truth about black superiority. Both insist on a kind of *practical absolute*, one establishing that for all socially relevant purposes one race is superior, even if an absolute scientific proof cannot be provided.

Over a century ago, biological determinism became the engine of political agendas under the banners of Social Darwinism and eugenics. Genetics

---

[10] F. A. Hayek, *The Road to Serfdom* (1944; repr., Chicago: University of Chicago Press, 1994), 66–68.

[11] Philosopher Daniel Dennett writes, "Our brains are made of neurons, and nothing else. Nerve cells are very complicated mechanical systems. You take enough of those, and you put them together, and you get a soul." Daniel Dennett, "The Nonbeliever," *New York Times Magazine* (January 22, 2006). Quoted in Dinesh D'Souza, *What's So Great About Christianity* (Washington, DC: Regnery, 2007), 240.

justified discrimination; it was believed to consistently predict behavior and station in life. Such determinism was paternalistic for as long as the oppressed group went along with the program. It became savage and brutal once those sentenced to inferior status refused to accept their fate. Today, biological determinism does not attract many adherents. Only fringe elements on both racialist poles openly advance deterministic theories of race.[12] Determinism remains, however, in the recesses of political movements that are willing to weaponize the ideas that spring from evolutionary theory.

Many thinkers outside of the Judeo-Christian tradition have denied the existence of free will. Some have offered a "hard" deterministic account where both free choice and moral responsibility are absent. According to these theories, all of our actions genuflect before factors prior to choice. Similarly, modern psychology attempts to explain human behavior by appeals to unconscious forces and a naturalism that denies reality apart from the material body. Naturalism, in contrast with duality, holds that our mental states are identical to our bodies, with some naturalists claiming that, if the mind is nonphysical, then it is not scientifically meaningful. As a result, consciousness is nothing more than the effect of chemical reactions within the brain. When this mentality of a "tyranny of genes" spreads to the underclass, its destructive result is to reclassify irresponsible behavior as "normal" (e.g., biological imperatives make it impossible for black men to remain faithful to one woman in marriage), with negative effects to society as a whole, especially to the way we approach the problem of race.

The fallacy of deterministic sociological arguments lies in their equation of *inclination* with *compulsion*. It is true that antecedent factors, whether socially or biologically construed, strongly affect some aspects of human behavior. After all, human action does not take place in a vacuum but in the midst of life circumstances, which have a conditioning influence. A young person

---

[12] F. C. Welsing, Wade Nobles, and Leonard Jeffries, for example, have advanced the theory that levels of melanin affect the psyche of individuals belonging to racial groups. Welsing states that black men have the potential to destroy "melanin recessive" white men genetically and that is why whites must destroy them first. According to Jeffries, higher levels of melanin in black people allows them to "negotiate the vibrations of the universe and to deal with the ultraviolet rays of the sun." See Massimo Calabresi, "Dispatches Skin Deep 101," *Time Magazine* (February 14, 1994); F. C. Welsing, "Blacks, Hypertension, and the Active Skin Melanocyte," *Urban Health* 4, no. 3, (1975): 64–72.

growing up surrounded by dysfunctional families will find it more difficult to construct a functional family for himself.

It may even be true that certain biological differences exist among genetic groups. This reality, however, is irrelevant to the question of whether we possess the radical capacity for self-determination. I could have physically attacked Maria or retaliated with insults, as I was strongly tempted to do. These inclinations stemmed from the meaning her words had for me prior to the incident, as well as other familial and cultural factors. I chose otherwise. There were contradictory messages coming at me from antecedent sources, some urging me toward one set of choices and others pulling me toward another. In fact, those that seemed more forceful to me commanded me to attack. In the face of countervailing forces, I made a decision, one that was free.

Unconscious motives or other antecedent causes may make certain options more attractive than others, but this does not mean that such inclinations eliminate the human capacity to choose. The reality of our experience of deliberation prior to choice shows that not all our actions are predetermined. Those who assert that choice is an illusion stand on an internal contradiction: Presupposing the existence of norms of rationality to disprove the reality of free choice demonstrates that we can freely choose.[13]

Some try to accomplish this by doubting the efficacy of human reason. But if these skeptics are right, moral philosopher Samuel Gregg points out, "then it is impossible for people to know the proper ends of human choice through reason. Such ends do not therefore exist for man."[14] In presuming to know the truth of skepticism, the skeptic engages in a quest for truth on the foundational assumption that it is possible to know it. We must presume that he believes it is reasonable to distrust reason.[15] He fails to distinguish between *practical reasonableness*, which provides adequate certainty for most decision making and action, and *absolute certainty*, which excludes all possible grounds for doubt.

Critics of free choice attempt to refute the self-referential argument by saying that unless antecedent factors cause actions, actions are arbitrary;

---

[13] Robert P. George, *In Defense of Natural Law* (New York: Oxford University Press, 2001), 55.

[14] Samuel Gregg, *On Ordered Liberty* (Lanham, MD: Lexington Books, 2003), 35–36.

[15] *The Catholic Encyclopedia, Volume 13*, Robert Appleton Company, 1912, s.v. "skepticism."

hence, there is no freedom to choose. Reasons are said to be antecedent causes "by a different name." This retort fails to distinguish between *causes* and *reasons*. Reasons, as noted by Robert P. George, can exist without effects; one can have reasons to act but not act at all. One can also have reasons *not* to perform an act.[16] Either through action or inaction the possibility of free choice is demonstrated as nonarbitrary and thus intelligibly grounded.

The same confusion occurs among those who insist on safeguarding racial barriers. Culture and history may provide reasons for a given individual to identify with a racial group, or better, identify with a set of political and ideological propositions. Yet, these elements are not in themselves causes. They may incline the mind and move the will, but, then again, they may not. Thus, we are free to accept the political paradigm racialists abhor and still be free individuals, taking pride in but not being controlled by or reduced to a given ethnic identifier.

"POOR US" AND "DAMN THEM!" SOFT DETERMINISM

Determinism is often not so bold. It is more frequently so subtle that we do not notice its influence. "Soft" determinism accepts the premises of those who deny free will, albeit with crafty strokes, helping it maintain collective moral approval. This kind of determinism accepts limited personal responsibility for *some* of our actions. According to this view, those actions said to be determined by an intrinsic factor, namely our character, are seen as noncoerced and thus "free." This version becomes deterministic by stating that our character itself is determined, and we simply cannot help but choose the way we do.

At bottom, this kind of skepticism denies the possibility of free choice as genuine self-determination. The cleverness of this position is its adherence to egalitarian dreams and its appeal to racial sensibilities. While it stirs the emotions in favor of minorities, the poor, and the subjugated, it is grounded in oppressive external influences. It is a kind of "poor us" and "damn them!" version of determinism. The determinism of victimhood finds here an ally against enemies who must be destroyed because they cannot be redeemed.

Positing the management of human choice in the hands of reason does not deny the place of our emotions in the act of choosing. It does, however, establish reason as the guiding criterion of choice. Choosing is the decisive

---

[16] George, *In Defense of Natural Law*, 56–57.

act by which the person decides, after deliberation, which proposal is more attractive.[17] Emotions or feelings are always present in choosing, but these are not leading the process. Human beings can choose among intelligibly attractive proposals that move the will to action. These *reasons for action* constitute the basic motivations for choosing, helping us mold our character. Can we allow ourselves to be driven by emotion and appetite? Yes, as at times we may act irrationally by allowing our feelings to deflect our reason.[18] This, however, does not equate to an inability to choose.

Still, skepticism about human freedom is rampant in modern thought under the rubric of relativism. Morals and ethics are assumed to be relative to one's opinion or desires. As long as we are "honest" about our condition, many suggest, the content of our choices is secondary. Within the sphere of moral relativism, however, there is a secondary force that relegates reason to the periphery: the *will*.

That is why moral relativism can be so judgmental and moralistic while rejecting objective morality. Relativists have established a set of "practical absolutes" against which no one is allowed to resist. This phenomenon of intolerance in the name of tolerance has been widely recognized; Pope Benedict XVI memorably called it a "dictatorship of relativism."[19] The new culture of relativism indicts a preferred set of evils: homophobia, racism, sexism, and the like.

Contemporary culture's support of racialism comes mostly from the left but remains bound to earlier racialisms that occupy the other side of the same racialist coin. Soft determinism is the air that breathes life into the corpse of racialism. The destiny of the racial victim remains dependent on the racial oppressor, and the victim is blameless for his own condition. Because this relativism is moralistic and emotive, it encourages antagonism and fear of impending doom while squarely rejecting individual self-determination. The white supremacist side of the racialist coin, for example, upheld the

---

[17] See John Finnis, *Aquinas: Moral, Political, and Legal Theory* (Oxford, UK: Oxford University Press, 1998), 56–71.

[18] See John Finnis, "Natural Law and Legal Reasoning," in *Natural Law Theory: Contemporary Essays*, ed. Robert P. George (New York: Oxford University Press, 1994), 136–37.

[19] Pope Benedict used the expression on several occasions; the first public instance was during a homily shortly before he was elected pope. "Homily of Joseph Cardinal Ratzinger, Dean of the College of Cardinals, Mass for the Election of the Supreme Pontiff," St. Peter's Basilica, 18 April 2005; available at www.ewtn.com.

determinism of race by appealing to fears of mongrelization, communism, and the loss of the traditional American way of life.[20] Today, white racism continues to appeal to the fear of disintegration due to increased racial harmony and interracial marriage.

Although apparently opposed to white racism, the Black Power movement and later radical theories of race similarly suffer from determinism embedded in the anger of victimhood. As a political slogan used by Stokely Carmichael (later Kwame Ture) and Willie Ricks (later Mukasa Dada), Black Power became a cry for the release of base instincts against oppression.[21] Control of the will by the intellect and restraint of the appetites by reason, in the extreme racialist view, are tools of oppression. The racial mandate is to indict, to vent anger, to shame the oppressor, and even to riot.

THE NEXT PHASE OF CIVIL RIGHTS: MASTERS OF OUR OWN DESTINY

The more our society has opened to the possibility of integration, the more separatist movements and groups have sprung up. This trend was certainly justified in many instances as the growth in the number of black professionals triggered a healthy desire to create new organizations among a growing professional class.[22] Side by side with the growth of worthy associations, however, emerged a more radical movement that deliberately undermined

---

[20] In 1947, Mississippi Senator Theodore Bilbo wrote,

> The campaign for complete equality launched by the Negro leaders has now reached alarming proportions. The communists in this country have secretly and openly tried to indoctrinate the Negroes with the idea of social equality with the white race for their own purposes and as part of their plan to overthrow the American dual system of Constitutional government.

Theodore G. Bilbo, *Take Your Choice: Separation or Mongrelization* (Poplarville, MS: Dream House, 1947).

[21] *Black Power* is an ambiguous term that meant and means different things to different people. Its pan-African and nationalistic wing went beyond advocating black unity and cultural pride into separatism and black supremacy.

[22] Elisabeth Lasch-Quinn, *Race Experts: How Racial Etiquette, Sensitivity Training, and New Age Therapy Hijacked the Civil Rights Revolution* (2001; repr., Lanham, MD, 2002), chap. 4. The Association of Black Psychologists seceded from the American Psychological Association (APA) in 1968 to attend to what they perceived as special

integration for ideological reasons. If the very essence of American society is built on what we ought to reject, activists in this movement asked, why integrate at all?

Therapy and other social services fields provided ammunition for this assault by lending respectability to deterministic explanations of America as being racist to the core. In the field of social work, a rational, problem-solving method attempts to eliminate all "non-quantifiable values" because values are "helpless in understanding or developing social goods and fail to assist in overcoming social problems or social 'bads.'"[23] Rationality is here perceived as applying only to what is measurable. Under this utilitarian system, "decisions themselves are not judged according to their intrinsic worth, truth or goodness, but rather in terms of their *utility*." The content of choice is not deemed relevant. Values are individually determined by adopting a subjective hierarchy. Thus, instead of performing evil actions individuals are said to "make mistakes." As the late philosopher Henry B. Veatch states,

> One can still, perhaps, venture with impunity to admire examples of courage or integrity or decency, but one can hardly stand up and claim to know what is right and wrong without being laughed out of court, or at least out of a cocktail party.[24]

Based on this position, every dysfunctional behavior could be interpreted as the result of racial oppression. Highly politicized new therapies began to focus on empowerment and on helping individuals as members of groups deal with the scars of racial oppression. These therapeutic models have become morally hollow weapons in the race and class warfare inaugurated during the 1950s and 1960s. In effect, much of what passes as scientific theory on racial identity can be better described as pop psychology.

To reduce the extraordinary ascendancy of negative behavior in the inner city to irresistible effects of racial oppression is to avoid serious discussion. Likewise, to minimize pathology by either renaming it as resistance or by

---

needs of blacks neglected by the APA. A new field called "black psychology" developed, complete with its own journal.

[23] William G. Brueggemann, *The Practice of Macro Social Work*, 2nd ed. (Belmont, CA: Brooks/Cole, 2002), 63.

[24] Henry B. Veatch, *Rational Man: A Modern Interpretation of Aristotelian Ethics* (1962; repr., Indianapolis: Amagi Books, 2003), 13.

focusing only on white guilt and structural change seems more like throwing counterpunches in a political battle than honestly searching for answers. A balanced approach that values what we can discover about the effects of antecedent factors while acknowledging personal responsibility is essential for racial progress. Antecedent factors may have a powerful formative effect, but they do not have absolute binding power over the human person; if they do, morality is nonsense.

Balanced analyses take into consideration the distant West African past, the experiences of slavery and segregation, past and present socioeconomic factors, and the most pertinent present cultural challenges. This externalist analysis, necessary as it is, will be faulty and incomplete if it avoids focusing on the radical capacity of every living human being to transcend inclination and environment and reach toward personal self-affirmation. The isolation of American blacks can be curbed, and *has been curbed*, by individuals making courageous decisions to break from the chains of separatism and isolation imposed on them both by a past of oppression and by the siren songs of present "patrons."[25]

The emphasis on particular grievances and victimization has degenerated into the adoption of separatism as the best alternative for black survival. If endogamy,[26] spatial segregation, and other separatist practices are disconnecting elements, why are they now heralded by the black liberal and radical elite? In fact, the very isolation and exclusion imposed in the past by a racist society is now pursued by blacks themselves. It is true that in social contexts of dramatic change adherence to past strategies for success may become detrimental to the group if such strategies are simply reactive. Yet, to hold on to certain values and strategies proven effective in the past while at the same time adapting them to the variations of time can serve the

---

[25] Patterson tells us of the black internal and external isolation from the mainstream and from each other. Orland Patterson, *Rituals of Blood: Consequences of Slavery in Two American Centuries* (New York: Basic Civitas Books, 1999), 155–58.

[26] Endogamy is the practice of marrying within the same social or ethnic group. As Patterson observes, endogamy is stronger among blacks than among any other group.

purpose of effective and nonreactive change. If separatism then imposed and now adopted triumphs, what we can expect is increasing isolation.[27]

Referring to threats of collectivism during the French Revolution, Alexis de Tocqueville discussed the existence of two impulses in opposite directions: "the one was favorable to liberty, the other to despotism."[28] A similar dichotomy has brought about a fervent call for black "self-determination" against "white society," while insisting on a deterministic understanding of oppression where racism exhaustively explains black powerlessness. By identifying blackness within a narrow ideological universe and shunning those refusing to live on the ideological plantation, determinism and tyranny triumph under the guise of freedom and self-determination.

The French Revolution, writes de Tocqueville, declared itself "the enemy of royalty and of provincial institutions all at once." He explained well the harm of this merging of targets as "it confounded all that had preceded it—despotic power and the checks to its abuses—in indiscriminate hatred, and its tendency was at once to overthrow and to centralize."[29] We see the same error at work when leftist racialists declare themselves the enemies of both white supremacy and of black individuality. The new despotism of race attempts to centralize thought by channeling it toward leftist politics. In the process of dethroning the perceived tyranny, true self-determination is precluded by denying our responsibility for our condition. Calls for responsibility are answered with deterministic accusations of "blaming the victim." The accusation forgets, however, that self-determination

> means that, despite all external pressures and prior causes that can and do influence our choices, we retain at least some options of choosing or not choosing, of choosing one thing rather than another. In cases

---

[27] As Orlando Patterson states,

> To hold someone responsible for his behavior is not to exclude any recognition of the environmental factors that may have induced the problematic behavior in the first place. Many victims of child abuse end up behaving in self-destructive ways; to point out the link between their behavior and the destructive acts is in no way to deny the causal role of their earlier victimization and the need to address it.

Orlando Patterson, "A Poverty of the Mind," *The New York Times* (March 26, 2006).

[28] Tocqueville, *Democracy in America*, 107.

[29] Tocqueville, *Democracy in America*, 107.

where there is no such option there is no real choice and no real self-determination.[30]

A return to the human person and the recognition of his radical capacity to choose can move the debate forward. Made in the image of their maker, men and women possess the wonderful gift, if at once still a daunting task, of moral self-realization. Moral self-realization demands a transition to the next great phase of the civil rights movement: *an uncompromising personal responsibility movement.*

In fact, an attempt to convince the oppressed of his dignity and worth rather than to redress unjust social conditions would be a return to the values present at the heart of the civil rights movement. The first and most important stage of the movement was not a campaign to end bigotry and discrimination but an effort to awaken the spirit of those still under the bondage of self-doubt. "The non-violent approach," said Martin Luther King Jr.,

> does not immediately change the heart of the oppressor. It first does something to the hearts and souls of those committed to it. It gives them self-respect; it calls up resources of strength and courage that they did not know they had. Finally, it reaches the opponent and so stirs his conscience that reconciliation becomes a reality.[31]

"YOU SURELY WILL NOT DIE!"

Modern accounts of race relations and racial progress fail to do justice to the reality of the human person's capacity to choose evil and to the consequences of the abandonment of ethical and moral standards. Our discussion of human dignity cannot be complete without some treatment of the reality of *sin.*

Yes, that word still has meaning for contemporary persons. Our entire experience of choice becomes unintelligible without reference to sin and its effects. Understanding sin helps us bridge the gap of knowledge between ourselves and our Creator. Without such understanding, the mysteries of pain, suffering, and despair burden human experience intolerably, for vested

---

[30] Grisez and Shaw, *Beyond the New Morality*, 6.

[31] Cited in Juan Williams, *My Soul Looks Back in Wonder: Voices of the Civil Rights Experience* (New York: Sterling, 2004), 1.

in this recognition of sin is also the faculty to penetrate (if imperfectly) the mysteries of love, grace, and redemption.

Sin can be defined in many different ways. A common word used in the Jewish Scriptures is *chatta`ah*, which implies falling short of a certain mark.[32] Another Old Testament term is *pesha*, which points to a revolt against God—a defiant attitude toward his will.[33] Additionally, the Hebrew word `*avon* is often used to refer to the way sin distorts the being of the sinner.[34] Under this last term, sin is an existential condition embedded in the very heart of man. Sin is then not simply a historical datum but a free act of the will by which man misuses his freedom and transgresses the objective order created by God—in the process depriving the sinner and the entire cosmic order of interior equilibrium.

Thus, racial issues are not only issues of economics, ideology, and institutions, but they are also especially connected to moral transgressions that affect the very being of the sinner. The more racialism insists on structuralism, the more it departs from the core of the racial problem, which is found in the heart of every man. In confronting the sin of racial oppression, we often absolve the racial victim of responsibility for his own sin, and victims easily become victimizers.

Additionally, the sinner offends the holiness of God. The concept of God as holy is present throughout the Hebrew Scriptures. The God of the Israelites is *sadiq*, or morally righteous, partial only toward what is good.[35] God's concern with the observance of right order establishes human transgressions not as divine arbitrary assessments based on the whims of deity but as offenses against the truth. God's concern for the objective order is what we call holiness—and a transgression of that order is what we call evil. A transgression against right order affects the entire system, including the character of the sinner.

---

[32] Transliteration from the Hebrew *hattx*. From the primitive root word transliterated as *atx* meaning "miss the way, go wrong." *Strong*'s number 2402.

[33] From the primitive word transliterated as *pasa'* meaning "to step forward." *Pesha'* is *Strong*'s number 6588.

[34] `*avon* is the transliteration of the original word *aw* and means "perversity, depravity, iniquity." *Strong*'s number 5771.

[35] See William G. Most, *Our Father's Plan: God's Arrangements and Our Response* (Front Royal, VA: Christendom Press, 1988), 33.

In the deepest sense, sin explains racialism, and only God can lead us onto the path of reconciliation. Crucial to this formulation is a rejection of economics and class as the central axis to understanding the social reality of race. Sin cannot be subsumed under purely secular categories, and its personal character can never be reduced to discussions of social structures. Understanding race, then, does not mean seeing it as a complex of social meanings transformed by political struggle.[36] It means seeing it in relation to what it means to be human in the context of both the holiness of God and the individual nature of sin.

In the Greek translation of the Hebrew Scriptures, we find the verb *aphiemi* used to denote the *forgiveness* of sins.[37] A debt is owed and must be repaid by the one who infringes the moral order. However, as Father William Most observes, "Sin, under one aspect, has infinity about it: The person offended, God, is infinite. Hence, there was an infinite imbalance, which could only be rectified by an Infinite Person."[38] We can thus make sense of God's mercy and Christ's suffering and atoning for our sins. Only an infinite being, out of pure love, can come down to our level and repay the infinite debt, thus balancing the scales and restoring the order's integrity. Our union with this infinite sacrifice makes it possible for our transgressions to be truly forgiven and to have restorative power (Rom. 8:17; 2 Cor. 4:17). The recognition of this objective order with its prior reality in God is essential for understanding the human and social order and for understanding the journey of those who came here in bondage.

[36] See Michael Omi and Howard Winant, *Racial Formation in the United States: From the 1960s to the 1980s* (New York: Routledge, 1986), 66–69.

[37] From the original Greek word *afiðhmi* meaning "to send away to permit, allow, not to hinder, to give up a thing to a person." Strong's number 863.

[38] Most, *Our Father's Plan*, 36.

4

DETERMINISM SLIPPING THROUGH

---

*And does not anti-social behaviour increase
in proportion to the excuses that intellectuals
make for it?*

—**Theodore Dalrymple**[1]

The stench coming from the house was repugnant. Trying not to be insulting, I still hesitated to step inside. My purpose in being there was to support a young man whom I had taken under my wing. Antwan was a tall, heavyset black kid who regularly attended our mission church and was in dire need of attention and guidance. Recollecting the circumstances of his life is unpleasant, as they are fraught with pain and loss. Living through those circumstances with him, however, helped me learn about the human tragedy that the ideology of victimhood causes—but also about the victory that can be won by truth and love.

Antwan was about to graduate from high school even though, as a result of a learning disability, he could not read beyond a third-grade level. Political correctness, racial promotion, and a pitiful school system advanced the boy repeatedly as a way to get rid of him as soon as possible. I took an interest in Antwan because he was kind and respectful. Underneath the surface of a rough life and innate intellectual constraints, I detected in him a drive to

---

[1] Theodore Dalrymple, *Life at the Bottom: The Worldview that Makes the Underclass* (Chicago: Ivan R. Dee, 2001), 133.

make something of himself. He also needed a male role model in his life. His biological father had spent most of his adult life in prison, punishment for a series of crimes that made me wonder if incarceration was his goal—as if life in the outside world was intolerable. I resolved to do my best to be there for Antwan and to offer some of the closeness he was crying out for.

Nevertheless, as I stepped inside his home I had second thoughts. I should have known what to expect; I had been warned. Mission parishioners who volunteered to clean had long ago given up. It was a tiny, bleak house in a bad neighborhood. The walls were dark, suppressing the brightening effect of any ray of light willing to venture inside. The floor was more or less covered with a pale carpet whose original color was impossible to ascertain. Blocking my path were a couple of sofas that looked like they could be hiding creatures from an episode of *The Twilight Zone*. I feared being invited to sit down. Trying to hide my disgust, I engaged in conversation while standing immobile by the door. In a distant past that I forced myself to imagine, this was a different place, filled with peace and happiness. Maybe some cleaning was all that was needed to inject freshness and beauty into this precarious setting.

The only place where there was real activity was the kitchen. Something was frying there in thick and smoky oils. Bottles of alcohol covered many of the shelves, silent witnesses of a somnolent existence. Their presence made sense: efficient instruments to numb the senses and escape an existence of boredom and meaninglessness. My investigation had lasted long enough, and I sought the exit.

What shocked me most about my brief visit was that I was unable to detect the slightest sense of discomfort or embarrassment on the part of Antwan's mother and brothers, as if what I had just experienced is the way things are supposed to be. It seemed improbable that any human being could want to live like that, and yet I soon learned that they would not have it any other way.

The stress of my brief experience left me drained. The pain and shame in Antwan's face, however, awakened me to his challenges and served as evidence of the goodness within him. Determined to offer my friendship and help, I spent many hours with him. We would go to the gym, and he would accompany me in ministry visits and recreational activities. After he joined our mission's youth group, I had more time to spend with him. We also found a reading tutor who labored to help him overcome his learning problems, which had been compounded by years of neglect.

He finally graduated from high school with a diploma that he could barely read. Yet Antwan readily found a job at a local pizza chain. I marveled at his commitment to hard work and at the way he managed to hide his disabilities. Out of pure will, he found the strength to earn a living. There was something in Antwan that wanted to conquer the prescribed destiny of victimhood.

Antwan had his troubles with the law and made his share of mistakes. Growing up in a dysfunctional family means experiencing some trauma and acquiring some bad habits. In our long conversations he intimated how difficult it was not to be pulled into a life of crime and drugs. That life seemed exciting and attractive, even as he realized how devastating it ultimately would be.

The rest of the family was another story. To deal with them was exhausting and frustrating. For too long, many of us at the mission were part of a cycle of dependency that reinforced their victimization. Feeling sorry for them, many church members became enslaved by their constant requests for assistance and were cleverly manipulated with the instrument of pity. We paid bills, bought groceries, transported them, lent money, and absolved them from personal responsibility. All of it was done in the name of compassion and Christian love. All of it amounted to a well-intentioned charade. Contrary to my initial bout of environmental determinism—when my visit to the home led me to believe that healthier surroundings might be the solution to the family's problems—I eventually realized that the house was a window into their souls, the physical ugliness a manifestation of the spiritual decay within their hearts.

Relationships within the family were unnatural and strained. Fighting was the order of the day and repeatedly going to jail almost expected. Power resided in the label of dysfunction. Considered emotionally disabled by government decree, the two youngest brothers had to go periodically for medical appointments. The mother received monthly payments for them, and she admitted that she wanted to keep them labeled so that the money kept rolling in. The younger boys, Antwan being one of them, exerted influence over the household, demanding remuneration for their condition. Being official victims offered immense power to demand what was "owed" them. I have never observed the degradation of a family in perpetual crisis so manifestly as I did in Antwan's.

Eventually, the family disintegrated. One of the older brothers hanged himself from the trunk of a small tree in front of their house, ending a life of drug abuse and indignity that he could no longer endure. Another brother left home and fell into drugs, promiscuity, and continuous incarceration. The mother unexpectedly died soon after. Antwan continued to work consistently and tried to stay out of trouble, which he accomplished for the most part, with a few setbacks. His relationship with the rest of the family almost nonexistent, he eventually got married and left the area to live in New York City.

Was Antwan an agent with free will or just another victim who happened to fare a little better in life? Had the lives of his family members been determined by extrinsic factors in the macrosystems of an oppressive society that rigged the game and decided their fate? Were they doomed to existential despair unless and until the rest of us recognized them as victims of society?

EXPERT ADVICE IN VICTIMHOOD

The skepticism described in the third chapter has permeated our society, promoting attitudes that foster the creation and discourage the healing of dysfunctional families such as Antwan's. It is as if those engaged in empirical anthropology expect to discover the broken remnants of freedom as a material datum within the elements in man. The reality of transcendental freedom, however, cannot be grasped through scientific experimentation. It is only when man experiences himself as subject that the reality of freedom is knowable, as Karl Rahner put it, "in the depths of one's own existence."[2] I am inclined to believe—or better, to hope—that the allegiance between scientific technique and skepticism cannot forever resist the attack of man's "inner urgent need" for transcendence. It cannot forever suppress man's "deep sense of inner disquiet" with the numbing of pharmaceutical prescription or technological innovation. It cannot forever abate our "metaphysical uneasiness"[3] by pretending that it is just a dream, a chemical interaction, a curable malady.

As new deterministic theories spread, the pseudoscientific orthodoxy portraying free choice as inimical to the advances of science strengthens.

---

[2] Karl Rahner, *Foundations of Christian Faith: An Introduction to the Idea of Christianity* (New York: Seabury Press, 1978), 36–39.

[3] Gabriel Marcel, *Mystery of Being: Reflection and Mystery*, vol. 1 (South Bend, IN: Gateway Editions, 1950), 35.

Today, "[r]ationality is conceived in the direction of functionality, efficiency."[4] How easily the elite's deterministic attitude has filtered into the popular mind and how devastating its influence has been for black America. Immersed in deterministic visions, social workers, clinicians, community organizers, and do-gooders disseminate the ideas of a promising new world devoid of oppressive moral constraints. Radical, macro, structural, and "emancipatory" social-work theories, for example, describe traditional social work as a "victim-blaming and status-quo preserving enterprise" when the need is instead to focus on the "structural determinants of individual behavior and exhort the oppressed to fight for liberation and social change."[5] Wielding considerable authority as expert agents of collectivized compassion, they descend as a mighty army over local communities, affirming—either directly or subtly—that any thought of duty or personal responsibility is either an ill-conceived abstraction from social complexity or a cleverly crafted tool of oppression.[6]

Determinism imbues the body politic, starting from the ivory towers of the elite and descending into the abodes of the underclass. A new order of thought is slipping into the collective consciousness, simultaneously explaining away personal failures and absolving people from the obligations and demands of traditional morality.[7] A host of young troops indoctrinated in the new theories and ready to defend their newly acquired faith graduate from academic settings where determinism and victimhood are nurtured. Good and idealistic young people enter the bureaucracies of compassion only to experience frustration and settle for doing the minimum to keep

---

[4] Joseph Cardinal Ratzinger's phrase; see Samuel Gregg, *On Ordered Liberty* (Lanham, MD: Lexington Books, 2003), 35.

[5] Bob Pease and Jan Fook, eds., *Transforming Social Work Practice: Postmodern Critical Perspectives* (New York: Routledge, 1999), 8.

[6] A case in point is the response of social workers to the 1992 Los Angeles riots sparked by the Rodney King incident. According to John Hiratsuka,

> Social workers traced the roots of the crisis to a society that refuses to acknowledge race and class division, denies opportunities to those at the bottom and often pits struggling ethnic groups against each other. Many despaired of making U.S. leaders understand the seriousness of the problems that led to the nation's deadly riots and could do so again.

Hiratsuka, "L.A. Burning: Social Workers Respond," *NASW News*, 37 (July 1992) 3.

[7] Dalrymple, *Life at the Bottom*, chap. 7.

their jobs.[8] The agents of society who should be assisting families such as Antwan's are instead exacerbating the problems that they hoped to solve.

Being told that they are prisoners of desire, men learn to place responsibility for their misery everywhere but on themselves. In this conclusion, they find plenty of support from enabling experts who confirm their identity as "marionettes of happenstance."[9] The experts tell us that "social forces outside of individuals may greatly affect [their] ability to change their lives," *especially* for those of a "minority culture." Social workers and human-services providers must be cognizant of their own racism and how it affects their "clients." After all, they warn, human-services providers may be stressing too much the client's "intrapersonal (internal) factors."[10] Our humanitarianism leads us to help others, the experts say, but this compassionate stance is "mitigated by 'contradictions' in the American value system." This value system leads us to believe (erroneously, it is implied) that poverty is "somehow related" to improper behavior. Individualism that places responsibility at the feet of the person, and the exaltation of activity and work that causes us to suspect that welfare programs encourage nonwork behavior, are also problematic values.[11] Social workers, we are told, ought to help clients link to the labor movement and to political parties that represent the working class.[12] In short, we "help" people by turning them into leftist political activists.

Modern social-work practitioners and theorists provide us with new models to reinforce dubious presuppositions. One of these is the postmodern view that bases client assessment on the "socially constructed" nature of morality and "the need for empowerment of marginalized clients, the political nature of therapy, and a need for social justice."[13] According to one account

---

[8] Roland G. Meinert, John T. Pardeck, Larry Kreuger, *Social Work: Seeking Relevancy in the Twenty-first Century* (New York: Haworth Press, 2000), 10.

[9] Dalrymple, *Life at the Bottom*, 6.

[10] Ed Neukrug, *Theory, Practice and Trends in Human Services* (Pacific Cove, CA: Brooks/Cole, 1994), 200.

[11] Philip R. Popple and Leslie Leighninger, *The Policy-Based Profession: An Introduction to Social Welfare Policy for Social Workers* (Boston: Allyn & Bacon, 1998), 98.

[12] June Allan, Bob Pease, and Linda Briskman, eds., *Critical Social Work: An Introduction to Theories and Practices* (Sydney, Australia: Allen & Unwin, 2003), 56.

[13] Cynthia Franklin and Catheleen Jordan, "Effective Family Therapy: Guidelines for Practice," in *Social Workers' Desk Reference*, ed. Albert A. Roberts and Gilbert J. Greene (Oxford: Oxford University Press, 2002), 257.

in a major social work journal, "normalcy is a linguistic habit."[14] Another model is the multicultural, which "emphasize[s] race and culture and how these issues affect the presenting problems of clients."[15] We learn in *Human Behavior and the Social Environment* that some marginalized people "opt out of the competition" because they perceive that there is no opportunity for them, given the norms of society. Criminality is the result of system failure; the criminal becomes a victim who has lost hope and is cruelly taunted by the unreachable affluence around him.[16] According to this view, *freedom* is also a linguistic habit—a term used to explain our predetermined choices while furnishing the illusion of autonomy.

When men lose their inner freedom, they are vulnerable to external tyranny, and there is no more subtle tyranny than the one exerted by experts trying to help. The denial of personal guilt results in the victory of sin over our lives and the dimming of reason in the shadow of appetite. Pretending to be guiltless, men, transformed now into clients, attach their hopes to the exculpatory theories of those telling them that, after all, "You will not die" (Gen. 3:4). Penetrating into the mystery of the human condition, John Milton wrote in his epic poem of the death of reason when man descends into the servile condition of victimhood under the tutelage of tyrannical patrons:

> *Reason in man obscured, or not obeyed,*
> *Immediately inordinate desires,*
> *And upstart passions catch the government*
> *From reason, and to servitude reduce*
> *Man, till then free. Therefore, since he permits*
> *Within himself unworthy Powers to reign*
> *Over free reason, God, in judgment just*
> *Subjects him from without to violent Lords;*
> *Who oft as undeservedly enthrall*
> *His outward freedom: Tyranny must be,*
> *Though to the tyrant thereby no excuse.*[17]

---

[14] John Pardeck, John Murphy, and Jung Min Choi, "Some Implications of Postmodernism for Social Work Practice," *Social Work* 39 (July 1994): 343–46.

[15] Franklin and Jordan, "Effective Family Therapy," 257.

[16] Katherine S. van Wormer, Fred H. Besthorn, Thomas Keefe, *Human Behavior and the Social Environment: Macro Level; Groups, Communities, and Organizations* (Oxford: Oxford University Press, 2007), 148.

[17] John Milton, *Paradise Lost, Books XI and XII*, ed. A. W. Verity (Cambridge: Cambridge University Press, 1918), 35–36.

The involuntary manifestations of the client's oppressive status, or morally neutral "sickness," wreak havoc on those around them. The devastation for those who have been indoctrinated in the ideology of victimhood, however, is beside the point—a distraction from the task of changing social conditions by agglomerating victims and blaming society. After all, apologists of victimhood point out, the Eurocentric nature of our society and the ethnocentrism of the white majority negatively affect diagnoses of pathology. White practitioners, they say, do not take fully into consideration diverse ways of thinking, feeling, and behaving. Without ethnic-sensitive assessments, we confuse culture with pathology.

This is one dimension of the "quest for cosmic justice," as Thomas Sowell aptly names it. It is not a healthy reformism, of which society is always in need, but instead a refusal to accept the world as it is and an insistence that any possible defect (at least any with negative consequences for oneself) be remedied. One tragic consequence of this mentality is the epidemic of self-destructive behavior on the part of the young, who learn that discrimination explains everything and that being a victim pays. They learn that ordinary moral standards are an imposition and lead to a loss of authenticity. If the normal expectations of society are oppressive and the paradigm of cosmic victimhood is true, it is to be expected that uncouth comportment will be seen as a sign of recognition to be embraced rather than as disgraceful behavior to be avoided. They learn that their failures can be explained away as the result of the denial of access to opportunities by those who are "privileged" and have been given "advantages."[18] In such an environment, individuals such as Antwan who manage, at least temporarily and tentatively, to escape the victimhood trap are exceptional rather than normal.

THE DEMISE OF COMMON SENSE IN PUBLIC POLICY

Sociological determinism informs our public policy. Those with a stake in the maintenance and expansion of government bureaucracies feed on pathology and find a willing constituency among those who perceive the world in terms of victims and perpetrators. If men are not free, they are not responsible for their misdeeds and ought instead to be treated with pity for falling prey to tragic misfortunes. They are to be healed by those

---

[18] Thomas Sowell, *The Quest for Cosmic Justice* (New York: Free Press, 1999), 41–42; and idem., *Black Rednecks and White Liberals* (Jackson, TN: Encounter Books, 2006), 250–55.

who understand their powerlessness. Such enabling has produced a host of psychotherapeutic terms and treatments attempting to explain every human condition and every degrading act.

As Thomas Sowell has shown, the process of reallocating responsibility from the individual to society (with the state as its embodiment) has a four-stage pattern:

1. *The crisis.* A crisis is created through the manufacturing or selective utilization of data, giving rise to social outrage. Intellectuals often perform this function with the cooperation of the media.[19]

2. *The solution.* Government intervention is presented as absolutely necessary to solve the crisis.[20]

3. *The results.* They are to be measured not by evidence of positive change but by the very fact of allocating funds and creating structures to "attend the need."

4. *The response.* Evidence will no longer be considered if it points toward the reduction of funds or challenges the idea of government intervention. In fact, if things get worse—and they often do—greater resources are to be demanded, as "we have not yet done enough."[21]

Liberal historians, social theorists, and political philosophers bolster this narrative. Theda Skocpol argues that the history of social provision in the United States shows that the kind of targeted antipoverty programs that common sense would dictate "have generally been inadequately funded, demeaning to the poor, and politically unsustainable."[22] Weary of what he considers half-measures, another scholar insists that "the more realistic

[19] For a solid analysis of many such cases, see Mona Charen, *Do-Gooders: How Liberals Hurt Those They Claim to Help (And the Rest of Us)* (New York: Sentinel, 2004).

[20] A case in point is the welfare system before 1996. For a study of the conditions of the policy, see Michael D. Tanner, *The Poverty of Welfare: Helping Others in Civil Society* (Washington, DC: Cato Institute, 2003), chaps. 2–3; D. Eric Schansberg, *Poor Policy: How Government Harms the Poor* (Boulder, CO: Westview Press, 1996), chap. 17.

[21] Thomas Sowell, *The Vision of the Anointed: Self-Congratulation as a Basis for Social Policy* (New York: Basic Books, 1995), 8–30.

[22] Theda Skocpol, "Sustainable Social Policy: Fighting Poverty Without Poverty Programs," *American Prospect* 2 (Summer 1990), 59, 67.

approach would be to accept the need for more welfare and to reject continued fantasizing about day care and 'workfare' as miracle cures."[23] We are told that the system's *raison d'etre* is to help the poor, but families and bureaucrats are "disempowered and unable to effect lasting change in the macro system." The problem is that we do not have enough government funding "in a country whose conservative agenda clearly values spending for war preparation over spending for a child's life...."[24]

Under his "principle of redress," Harvard philosopher John Rawls asserts that "undeserved inequalities" must be accounted for by society.[25] As individuals do not decide their genetic endowment, we ought to at least compensate for the unfortunate inequalities of birth and for the social "*tyranny of skills.*"[26] These ideas of justice and equality have created a market for statistical explanations of disparity that attempt to prove the need for state action to correct "social injustice." Statistical disparities, it is thought, provide irrefutable proof that social structures continue to impede needed change. Under such a vision, equality needs to be imposed by third parties wielding "the power to control outcomes, [and] override rules, standards, or the preferences of other people."[27] Third parties will make sure that we right the wrongs of the prebirth lottery's assigning endowments; if nature does not produce a state of outcome equality, we will. With singular dexterity, the tragic misfortunes and depravities of men are traced all the way back to the human genome or to oppressive social arrangements.

What is proclaimed as collective justice can better be explained by what is termed in political economy as *public choice theory*, ably identified by Nobel-laureate James Buchanan as "politics without romance."[28] Collective entities do not make decisions; people do, and they have self-interested motives. We also know that, although certain interests are similar for all groups, other

---

[23] Gilbert Steiner, *The State of Welfare* (Washington, DC: Brookings Institution Press, 1971), cited in Neil Gilbert and Paul Terrell, *Dimensions of Social Welfare Policy*, 5th ed. (Boston: Allyn & Bacon, 2002), 82.

[24] Evan Imber-Black, *Families and Larger Systems: A Family Therapist's Guide through the Labyrinth* (New York: Guilford Press, 1988), 214.

[25] John Rawls, *A Theory of Justice* (Cambridge: Harvard University Press, 1971).

[26] Sowell, *Quest for Cosmic Justice*, 4–6, 40.

[27] Sowell, *Quest for Cosmic Justice*, 12.

[28] Anthony de Jasay, *Justice and Its Surroundings* (Indianapolis: Liberty Fund, 2002), 78–79.

interests are antagonistic to those of other groups. The reality of selfishness and the special pleading of particular interest groups ensures the troubling outcome that some of the benefits granted to one group will come at the expense of other groups.[29]

Politicians advance given positions and bureaucrats attempt to retain their livelihoods by enhancing the political desirability of certain public-policy options. Members of given groups perceive the possibility of some individual benefit and vote accordingly. Promised benefits to individuals or to a given block may take the form of direct payments (as with the well-known bailouts following the financial crisis of 2007–2008), better employment prospects, job security, more money for a certain kind of research, or any other tangible benefit.

Such subsidies often do not make anyone much better off than they would otherwise be, but they certainly entice. As Anthony de Jasay states in *Justice and Its Surroundings*:

> With the insights of public choice theory, it is easy to grasp how, for instance, even minority groups can obtain overt or covert transfers, that, by accepted modes of reckoning confer smaller benefits on them than the cost they impose on the community ... it is theoretically possible for literally each and every voter to be worse off thanks to the welfare state that each nevertheless keep voting for. What is more appalling still, each is perfectly rational to do so.[30]

Politics provide a mirage of benefit for those receiving a transfer and the appearance of minor loss to those being dispossessed of position, property, or wealth. At first glance, the exercise appears harmless. The transfers do not deeply affect the living conditions of those receiving benefit, but they give them a sense of comfort that only stimulates the demand for more.

Applied to minorities, the reliance on political markets increases their antagonism toward the mainstream and energizes the experts in their ongoing quest for perpetrators of injustice. Transfers offer a system with elements of rationality and calculation that, when united with moralistic appeals to social justice, are very difficult to counter but deeply detrimental to social harmony. In a society that seeks immediate gratification and ready tangible benefit, the politics of self-interest are hard to defeat.

---

[29] Henry Hazlitt, *Economics in One Lesson: The Shortest and Surest Way to Understand Basic Economics* (New York: Crown Publishers, 1979), 15.

[30] De Jasay, *Justice and Its Surroundings*, 79.

ONCE UPON A TIME

In *The Tragedy of American Compassion*, Marvin Olasky reveals an important generational contrast. "Until the 1960s, the public dole was humiliation. Soon, young men would be told that shining shoes was demeaning, and that accepting government subsidy meant a person 'could at least keep his dignity.'"[31] Up to that time, there was a social consensus defining deviance by relying on reason and tradition and not on emotion and the political advocacy of interest groups. The line of demarcation between acceptable and deviant behavior was clear and indispensable to the process of value transmission, to the formation of solidarity, and to the affirmation of moral standards. During the 1960s, societal mores began to change rapidly. Urging virtuous behavior and denouncing dependency became an affront against human dignity and personal autonomy; consequently, the loss of moral capital became a gain for political capital.

The new concept of human dignity as proscribing any kind of moral judgment on certain behaviors persisted and remains the dominant paradigm. It has established as mainstream the concepts of authenticity and entitlement, with government support and social engineering as its instruments. By redefining deviance as authenticity and normalizing dependency, contemporary thought has rejected the traditional concept of morality with a consequent corrosive effect on our culture. Conduct once regarded as shameful is now celebrated, with a host of sociological studies ready to justify the new approach.

The concept of deviancy, once commonly accepted, is now shunned by most sociologists. When morality is rooted in human contingencies, it changes along with cultural shifts. In fact, traditional morality is seen as a cultural construct created to oppress and marginalize those who are victims. In this view, human nature itself is pliable. From drug abuse to pedophilia and homosexual behavior, once-reprehensible acts are now destigmatized or seen as being in a state of transitory acceptance. The norm in sociology is that we can find either a medical/psychological or a social reason for every formerly defined deviancy and, accordingly, we can dispense with traditional norms of morality.

The media promote the new idea of deviance as a disease or a just rebellion against the tyranny of traditional morality. The "addict as expert" is a

---

[31] Marvin Olasky, *The Tragedy of American Compassion* (Washington, DC: Regnery, 1992), 168–69.

common theme of investigative reports. Episodes such as PBS's "Moyer's on Addiction: Close to Home" and its sequel, "The Hijacked Brain" deny the possibility of character defects or human choice in the decision to use drugs; such thinking is a kind of "moralizing" and must give way to the idea of genetic causality.[32]

VICTIMS AND PERPETRATORS: A DETERMINISTIC AVALANCHE

Curiously, the assumptions of cosmic justice take on a twist: Although individuals are seen as unequal in endowment, groups are presumed to possess equal potential. On this understanding, we must assume that mere agglomeration creates a balance of capabilities. Based on this predicate, and obviating other factors that may influence outcome, statistical disparity is seen *per se* as evidence that unjust discrimination has entered the picture.[33]

The history of affirmative action in the United States and around the world is an adequate exemplar of how government policies have been utilized to execute group-based cosmic justice.[34] Through "goals and timetables," enforced "representation" to ameliorate "disparate impact,"[35] quotas,[36]

---

[32] Anne Hendershott, *The Politics of Deviance* (San Francisco: Encounter Books, 2002), 15.

[33] Thomas Sowell, *Civil Rights: Rhetoric or Reality* (New York: Quill, 1984), 42–48.

[34] For a good historical account of affirmative action policies in the United States see Stephan and Abigail Thernstrom, *America in Black and White: One Nation, Indivisible* (New York: Touchstone, 1997), 171–80. On the same topic in international perspective, see Thomas Sowell, *Affirmative Action Around the World: An Empirical Study* (New Haven: Yale University Press, 2004).

[35] The story of "disparate impact" begins with the Civil Rights Act of 1964. Despite the rhetoric of those proposing changes in law that quotas would not be demanded, quotas began to develop almost immediately after the passing of the Act. The purpose of the law was to protect individuals from "disparate treatment," meaning individual discrimination. This, however, was reinterpreted from a protection against old-fashioned bias into an instrument for hiring members of a group by requiring a numerical inclusion regardless of the presence of evidence of actual discrimination. See Thernstrom, *America in Black and White*, 424–33.

[36] Quotas represent the total divorce of the spirit of the 1964 Civil Rights Act from its later implementation. See Stephan Thernstrom and Abigail Thernstrom, *America in Black and White: One Nation, Indivisible* (New York: Simon and Schuster, 1999), 425–35.

"race-norming,"[37] and other devices, affirmative action was transformed into a numbers game, enforcing collectivized justice and attempting to subvert structural oppression. In the vision of cosmic justice, individuals are thought of as tokens of a particular group, and individual benefit is derived from group identity without the slightest need to establish that they, as individuals, have been discriminated against.

Data that refutes a deterministic, causal link between genetic or social facts and outcomes is dismissed by appeals to the need to redress the evil effects of structural oppression.[38] What has been termed the *residual fallacy* is today accepted as dogma. If statistical disparity remains after certain nondiscriminatory elements are accounted for (or "controlled"[39]) it is safe to attribute the gap to a "soft" variable such as social discrimination or injustice. It is considered mean-spirited and unscientific to associate the persistence of a gap to any cultural difference, or worse, to individual *moral* causal variables.

Added to the residual fallacy, we find the *genetic fallacy* of discounting a phenomenon due to its cause or perceived cause. If a given pathology is acknowledged and traced back to racism and discrimination, it then disappears as a problem. Unless racism disappears, the problem is expected to remain. The genetic fallacy is one of the most valued among radicals and deconstructionists when it comes to racial issues, as the soft variable of the "legacy of slavery" can be invoked at will to explain every problem.

Most of the determinism in our policy discussions is of the soft kind. It expresses itself as a call to understand the "complexity" of a given situation

---

[37] See Sowell, *Affirmative Action Around the World*, 131. "Race-norming" relates to a system of quotas where different ethnic groups were grouped under separate rankings of test scores. Blacks will compete against other blacks only and whites against other whites. This system was banned by the Civil Rights Act of 1991. As Sowell explains, practices such as race-norming (which was clandestine) prove how difficult it is to eliminate affirmative action, as it can continue surreptitiously.

[38] Sowell, *Affirmative Action Around the World*, 32. As aptly stated by Sowell,

> Ultimately, of course, what matters are not such objective data but how the individuals involved feel and react. Here no one can say or rather, those who choose to make ringing denunciations cannot be conclusively contradicted by objective evidence, since objective evidence is irrelevant to how they feel."

[39] In the words of Sowell, "Most social phenomena are sufficiently complex with data on many variables being either unavailable or inherently unquantifiable that often such control is itself illusory." His example of studies pretending to "control" for education is especially instructive. See Sowell, *The Vision of the Anointed*, 37–40.

and to take into account discrimination. It is certainly true that reality is more complex than any theory can explain or any empirical analysis can demonstrate. This truism, however, is used selectively to reject *a priori* any conclusion at odds with a given accepted vision. By labeling a situation "complex," explanations at odds with determinism (whether biological or social) can be rejected as "simplistic." Those adopting so-called simplistic solutions can be immediately dismissed without an empirical demonstration of the falsity of their position. They are either naïfs who are misguided in their assessment, racists trying to protect white privilege, or "Toms" aiming to please the master.

Using that line of thought, serious problems can be denied if they can be described as coping mechanisms that help people challenge the evils of oppression. Andrew Billingsley, for example, argues that many features common among black American families but frowned on by traditional morality are culturally specific ways of coping and surviving; the black family is a "bundle of complexity" rather than a "tangle of pathology."[40] If someone argues that fatherlessness is a serious problem in the black community, he can be countered by the contention that single-mother families have often appeared as a response by oppressed populations to discrimination. Thus, fatherless families are an example of healthy adjustment.

The argument sometimes takes a different turn. In *Lost Fathers*, Dorothy Roberts states that fatherlessness is deemed to be a problem only because so many absent fathers are black: "Race influences the reason people think fatherlessness is a problem and the solutions proposed to address it. If missing fathers are the cause of society's ills, it is largely because black culture is considered the benchmark of social degeneracy and female-headed households are the emblem of that culture."[41] Similarly, if we can prove

---

[40] Andrew Billingsley, *Black Families in White America* (Upper Saddle River, NJ: Prentice Hall, 1968).

[41] Dorothy Roberts, "The Absent Black Father," in *Lost Fathers: The Politics of Fatherlessness in America*, ed. Cynthia R. Daniels (New York: McMillan, 2000), 145. Similarly, Michael S. Kimmel deflates the importance of fatherlessness in a section titled "The 'Problem' of Fatherlessness." There he states,

> Though father involvement may provide some benefits to children, family researchers Paul Amato and Alan Booth note that the effects are "far from overwhelming," and certainly not decisive for the wellbeing of children.... It turns out that high crime rates and fatherlessness are both products of a larger and more overwhelming problem: poverty.

that poverty is not in any meaningful way a function of individual behavior, there is no reason to demand more personal responsibility from the poor or attempt to distinguish between those who are truly struggling and those who are seeking enablers.

The worst feature of such deterministic explanations is that they objectify blacks. Blacks become static elements that react as chemicals do in the presence of certain agents. As George Gilder puts it, "Slavery, discrimination, and deprivation, it was said, have so abused the black psyche that all sorts of new ministrations and therapies are needed to redeem it; racism and unemployment still inflict such liabilities that vast new programs of public employment and affirmative action are required to overcome them." The reasonable inference from this premise, Gilder concludes, is "that even though blacks are not genetically inferior, science proves them to be so damaged by racism and poverty that they are inferior now."[42]

The implication is observable but remains unspeakable: Determinism makes us look inferior but we must not say it in public. Under the rubrics of such politically correct public discourse, academic work and public analysis must be conducted within strict political demarcations focusing on socially constructed impediments to black success.

Often, the reaction to characterizing racism as only *a* factor rather than *the* causal factor in blacks' lives is indignation, as if the suggestion erases racism completely. Scholarship has become an ideological battleground where activism trumps open discussion and where every problem is attributed to the complex apparatus of white supremacy. It has also become what McWhorter describes as a kind of emotional release or gesture with no intention of finding workable solutions; a preference for "acting up" instead of "acting toward."[43]

DETERMINISM AND DEPENDENCY THEORY

In *The End of History and the Last Man*, Francis Fukuyama tells of the growth of Marxism as an economic system in the Third World out of the appar-

Michael S. Kimmel, *The Gendered Society* (New York: Oxford University Press, 2000), 136.

[42] George Gilder, *Wealth & Poverty* (San Francisco: ICS Press, 1993), 75.

[43] John McWhorter, *Winning the Race: Beyond the Crisis in Black America* (New York: Gotham Books, 2006), 158.

ent failures of capitalism to produce sustainable economic growth. Abject poverty in the world's underdeveloped countries provided socialism with new life and permitted the leaders of leftist movements to continue to blame colonialism, neocolonialism, and corporatism for the economic disaster. Dependency theory appeared as an attempt by the left to blame the West for the failures of collectivism.[44] This was the vision that inspired the activism of Puerto Rican socialists such as my father.

The theory, developed in the late 1950s by economist Raul Prebisch, offers a consistent thread: external influences—political, economic, and cultural—explain the development of a state.[45] The poverty of the Third World is the direct result of the wealth of the West in a zero-sum game. Moreover, underdevelopment can only be addressed systemically.[46] The global capitalist system keeps Third World countries in a steady state of dependency. As the West controls the rules of the economic game, it maintains other countries in "perpetual backwardness."[47] Latin Americans, Marxist liberation theologian Hugo Assman claims, are "being kept in a state of underdevelopment."[48]

Radicals in the Third World advocated the violent overturn of the international system through revolutionary means. Cuba became the model for the radicals, the last hope for a Third World in need of detachment from a rigged system. One of dependency theory's most ardent proponents, Andre Gunder Frank, opened one of the movement's key works by stating that

---

[44] Francis Fukuyama, *The End of History and the Last Man* (New York: Simon and Schuster, 2006), 99.

[45] Osvaldo Sunkel, "National Development Policy and External Dependence in Latin America," *Journal of Development Studies* 6 (October 1969): 23.

[46] T. dos Santos, *La crisis de la teoría del desarollo y las relaciones de dependencia en América Latina*: Boletín del CESO, 3 (Santiago, Chile, 1968): 6

[47] Leninism introduced the concept of imperialism as a causal explanation for the trade imbalance between rich and poor countries. Lenin, contrary to Marx, taught that the class struggle contradictions between the proletariat and the owners of capital *within* given societies was not the one that would trigger the last great battle bringing about the synthesis of classless society. Rather, it was the more intense antagonism between the developed North and the underdeveloped South, as the North expanded its hegemony in search for labor and materials. See Peter Wade, *Race and Ethnicity in Latin America* (London: Pluto Press, 1997), 59.

[48] Hugo Assmann, *Theology for a Nomad Church*, trans. Paul Burns (Maryknoll, NY: Orbis Books, 1976), 45–46.

the historical process of underdevelopment "cannot be reversed ... until they destroy the capitalist class structure through revolution and replace it with socialist development."[49] Progress and innovation are not the engines of history; instead, exploitation of some by others explains all.

Dependency theory was an abject failure for two reasons. First, it misdiagnosed the reasons for the economic failures of Latin America. In reality, Latin America suffered from a precapitalist, feudal, and statist system akin to the one out of which capitalism first arose. These were societies committed to a status quo, favoring a landholding class and stifling economic dynamism. Second, it connected the Third World to another bloc, the Soviet one, with its stagnant and ineffective socialist economy.

A similar dependency theory exists among radicals interpreting black reality. Domestic racialist dependency theory argues that structural racism explains the economic disadvantages of blacks. The success of some is either an exception or a ploy; a tactic of the system to allow a few to lose their identity in the mainstream. The options available to blacks in a structure dominated by white privilege never provide real escape from subordination. Every institution in American society and every white person are, by definition, racist. For that reason, even "protectionist" policies such as affirmative action, although largely supported, remain a part of the structure of a system that dominates blacks.

As a result, white liberals who support an avalanche of government programs and initiatives addressing every conceivable aspect of life remain suspect to black radicals. Attempts to rescue or protect blacks without advocating meaningful systemic change demonstrate liberal complicity in a white supremacist conspiracy. The blame is placed squarely on the shoulders of a system dominated by whites and excuses blacks from responsibility. There is a radical Manicheanism in the approach: we are blameless and good; they are tainted and evil.[50] Yes, the state is the answer, in this view, but we must also change the system along the lines of Marxist analysis. The crucial step is the destruction of the white-dominated capitalist system

[49] Andre Gunder Frank, *Capitalism and Underdevelopment In Latin America* (New York: Monthly Review Press, 1967), 1, 19.

[50] See François Hubert Lepargneur, "The Theologies of Liberation and Theology," in James V. Schall, *Liberation Theology in Latin America*, trans. Msgr. Henry Cosgrove (San Francisco: Ignatius Press, 1982), 212, cited in Michael Novak, *Will It Liberate? Questions about Liberation Theology* (Mahwah, NJ: Paulist Press, 1991), 24.

and the inauguration of a socialist alternative suited to *people of color*. Our people, armed with a panoply of coercive powers, will control politics. The absorption of all of life and of social processes by the state is the answer and the radical error of racialism.

To dismantle white supremacy, some white leftists have tried to go beyond diversity policies to propose structural change and the development of "multiculturalist," "inclusive," and "antiracist" structures. Antiracism training organizations, such as *Crossroads Ministry*, operate under the deterministic concept of white racism. A Crossroads "Anti-Racism Training" workbook insists that "[e]very system and every institution in the U.S. (not including pre-existing Native institutions or 'resistance organizations') was originally created and structured legally and intentionally to serve white society exclusively." The same text states that "[Whites] are not born white. [They] are assigned a racial identity with all its trappings, rights and privileges. Life experiences then reinforce our assigned racial identity. Experience can also dismantle or call into question our identity." Additionally, racial determinism is of an essentialist kind: "We do not have a choice! So long as the systems in our society are designed to shape identity around race, we cannot avoid being affected; just as we can't avoid benefitting from it. This means that we are not free!... This does not mean that we consciously choose to be racist or even that we are self-consciously prejudiced against people of color."[51] Essentialism here is socially construed, embedded not in human nature but in the fabric of society.

Christian groups such as the Sinsinawa Dominicans, the Archdiocese of Chicago, the Episcopal Diocese of New Jersey, the Metropolitan Chicago Synod (ELCA), the Christian Reformed Church, and the National Council of Churches have been trained in and some have institutionally adopted this deterministic system of thought. As much as these white antiracists flagellate themselves with guilt, their understanding of racism continues to be dependent on white initiative. Liberation still comes only when the one in power, the one supposedly privileged, reverses the gain-loss calculus. White protagonism remains the antidote against racism.

---

[51] *Crossroads Anti-Racism Training* (workbook produced for workshop, September 10–12, 2014; in possession of author). Similar material can be found at Crossroads Antiracism Organizing and Training, http://crossroadsantiracism.org/training/workshops/.

Extreme racialists, however, do not waste precious time trying to redeem a lost system or going to antiracism workshops run by blue-eyed devils. They instead propose the total destruction of the white supremacy system by all means necessary, with Marxist racialists reducing the entire exercise to one of class struggle and anticapitalism. Some of them propose the separation of blacks from the system either by adhering to a radical sort of "salad bowl" essentialist multiculturalism or the strict separation of the races.[52] The key elements are racism and exploitation within the present system, and there is no need to accommodate.

These extremists conclude that institutionalized powerlessness is inevitable under the white supremacy system, adopting a sort of *internal colonialism theory* around the idea of entrenched poverty and despair within areas of high concentrations of poor blacks. Internal colonialism presents the inner city as the battleground where class/ethnic struggle shows the fully fledged binary nature of oppression; where class is submerged into ethnicity and vice versa, making the paradigm of domination more difficult to tackle. Inner-city blacks are not only dependent on a foreign white establishment (for whom ethnicity is more important than class) but are also dependent on being uplifted by middle-class blacks (for whom class is more important) who have escaped the slums, leaving their brethren behind.[53]

The success of some developing countries in Latin America and Southeast Asia has proven the weaknesses of dependency theory in the international realm. Dependency theory cannot account for why initially far poorer countries such as South Korea, Taiwan, Singapore, Hong Kong, and recently even Vietnam have done so much better with fewer resources than has Latin America. The way a given country or region responds to dependency is as important as the fact of dependency itself. Likewise, the improvement of the economic and social lot of black Americans within the mainstream has proven the decadence of racialist domestic dependency theory. The way we react to past and present discrimination is also as important as discrimi-

---

[52] The fourth point of the "Muslim Program" of the Nation of Islam is complete separation into a new state here in America or elsewhere; with the US government paying the bill to "supply our needs" for twenty to twenty-five years. See "What the Muslims Want" at http://www.noi.org/muslim_program.htm.

[53] See Peter Wade, *Race and Ethnicity in Latin America* (London: Pluto Press, 1997), chap. 4. Internal colonialism is described as the imposed domination and the institutionalization of powerlessness in the black ghetto. See Bob Blauner, *Still the Big News: Racial Oppression in America* (Philadelphia: Temple University Press, 2001), 67.

nation itself. The success of many ethnic groups in spite of heavy oppression demolishes the assumptions of internal colonialism and dependency theory.[54] Many such groups have shown that societal acceptance can come in the wake of a group's internal transformation.[55]

THE IRREDUCIBLE PERSON

Although some dependency theories attempt to present an alternative between individualism and structuralism, they do not escape the idea of race as the basic reality of human persons or systems.[56] A worldview characterized by mutually exclusive societies—white America on one side and black America on the other—is at the heart of racialist essentialism. Selen Ayirtman, a constructivist who denies the concept of essence, nonetheless accurately sees that "essentialism produces a false description of cultures by defining them not only as static in time and place but also as uniform. Essentialism falls short in addressing intra-cultural diversity and therefore fails to offer a suitable framework for a politics of difference."[57] As Ryan T. Anderson and Christopher Tollefsen argue, one of the primary reasons for the failure of varied modern secular philosophies is their inadequate theories of personal identity, and racialist essentialism fails precisely in this way.[58] The identity politics of racialism ends up narrowing the definition of black-

---

[54] What the success of other ethnic groups elsewhere demonstrates is the capacity of individuals and groups to transcend the circumstances of their existence. One need not demand a relative comparison of circumstances to demonstrate that radical transcendent capacity. Neither ought one to portray the reality of black America as so constrained as to impede that general expectation.

[55] For evidence of black American progress under the internalist paradigm see Sowell, *Black Rednecks and White Liberals*, 260–63.

[56] One example is Michael Eric Dyson's essentialist ideas about the "irreducible reality of race." See Michael Eric Dyson, *The Michael Eric Dyson Reader* (New York: Basic Civitas Books, 2004), 41–45.

[57] Selen Ayirtman, "Recognition through Deliberation: Towards Deliberative Accommodation of Cultural Diversity" (paper read at the Australasian Political Studies Association Annual Conference, September 2007, 24–26).

[58] Ryan T. Anderson and Christopher Tollefsen, "Biotech Enhancement and Natural Law," *The New Atlantis* (Spring 2008): 79–103.

ness to a certain immovable criterion that satisfies whoever creates it.[59] The abuse absorbed by black conservatives is an example of the alienating and divisive effects of the theory of racialist essentialism.

It is suspect to assign ontological reality to the construct of race; thus, it must be reducible. As John McClendon says, "race derives its ontological reality from social reality."[60] To assert that race is irreducible is to pretend to find race in the natural law instead of finding it in what is secondary in the human mind. In other words, there is no transcendent reality in nature where we can find ethnicity; all is rooted in social interaction, and men are not the arbiters of what is ultimate. Though some assign the label to race, what is truly irreducible is the person.

Modern, secularist understandings of law attempt to separate law and moral order from God, thus making natural law humanly mutable. Racialists want to change the system so that they can impose the "truth" of what they perceive as authentically black. Skeptics, on the other hand, also raise the issue of the uncertainty of the whole enterprise of knowing. They doubt the human capacity to attain knowledge of a reality that is independent of us. Utilizing Jacques Derrida's theory of deconstruction, Michael Eric Dyson contends that objective truth about the world is difficult if not impossible to decipher. Philosophy cannot convey objective truth; it is merely "part of the conversation."[61]

---

[59] Todd Gitlin, "The Rise of Identity Politics," in *Race & Ethnicity in the United States: Issues and Debates*, ed. Stephen Steinberg (Boston: Blackwell Publishing, 2000), 322:

> But there is a hook: For all the talk about the "social construction of knowledge," identity politics in practice slides toward the premise that social groups have essential identities. At the outer limit, those who set out to explode a shrunken definition of humanity end by shrinking the definition of blacks and women.

[60] John H. McClendon, III, "On the Nature of Whiteness and the Ontology of Race," in *What White Looks Like*, ed. George Yancy (New York: Routledge, 2004), 214. I am not saying that race has a natural ontological reality but that to find ontological reality in social reality points toward the assumption that there is no such thing as a natural law as traditionally understood.

[61] Michael Eric Dyson, *Open Mike: Reflections on Philosophy, Race, Sex, Culture and Religion* (New York: Basic Civitas Books, 2003), 54.

The human mind, however, is not first in the causal order, or in the ultimate order of being.[62] We must side with Russell Hittinger (citing Karl Barth) when he states that "[e]thics [is] a task of the Doctrine of God."[63] The Enlightenment's state-of-nature scenarios make man and his culture the ultimate reality with ontological independence; or as Hittinger puts it in his critique of this view, "The creator God exists, perhaps, but he does not govern."[64] What we must assert to be irreducible is the moral order and its first principles, at the heart of which is the ontological reality of the human person *qua* person. This is the way out of the determinist dead end.

---

[62] Russell Hittinger, *The First Grace: Rediscovering the Natural Law in a Post-Christian World* (Wilmington, DE: ISI Books, 2003), 9.

[63] Karl Barth, *Church Dogmatics* (Peabody, MA: Hendrickson, 2001), 2.1.36, cited in Hittinger, *First Grace*, 5.

[64] Hittinger, *First Grace*, 22.

5

GOVERNMENT, POVERTY, AND DEPENDENCY

"What shall we do with the Negro?" I have had but one answer from the beginning. Do nothing with us! Your doing with us has already played the mischief with us. Do nothing with us! If the apples will not remain on the tree of their own strength, if they are worm-eaten at the core, if they are early ripe and disposed to fall, let them fall!... And, if the Negro cannot stand on his own legs, let him fall also. All I ask is, give him a chance to stand on his own legs! Let him alone!

—**Frederick Douglass (1865)**

James and his younger brother were on the patio of their home, praying before eating their meal. They were interrupted by the screeching of truck tires in front of their house. Armed men piled out and rushed toward their home. James and his brother took off frantically in different directions. Looking back momentarily, James witnessed in horror and disbelief the last instant of his parents' lives. They were murdered for the crime of being ethnic Mandingos—a group targeted by fellow Liberians of other tribes.

James ran and ran, fleeing from a nightmare that had become real. When he stopped running, be began to wander aimlessly. There were many others in the same state of confusion, with the same deep sadness and blank stare. To avoid the danger of wild beasts, he slept high up in the trees. He thought often about ending his life.

He finally decided to give life one last chance. Risking capture, James went back to the city, where friends gave him temporary shelter. He snuck to the docks and inside a Canadian trade ship. Many days into the voyage and no longer able to endure the hunger, he revealed his presence to the captain. At once, he was chained like an animal. He found himself fettered like so many ancient African slaves were chained by other Africans, later to be sold to the white man as merchandise.

If you ever meet James, you will understand why the captain eventually decided to have pity on him. He is gentle and friendly and soon gained the trust of the crew; they decided to help him reach freedom and safety. Having arrived at port in Mexico, he found his way to the United Nations Center in Mexico City. After a short investigation, he was admitted as a refugee. In the midst of the pain of the loss of his loved ones, James began to build a new identity. He enrolled at a Mexican university to study Spanish and made many friends.

Even there, thousands of miles away, the shadows of the Liberian ethnic struggles fell upon him. Some men from a warring Liberian tribe were also in Mexico as refugees. These men were set on killing him for the same tribalistic reason that others were tearing apart their native land. In their animistic beliefs, they had a duty to avenge the death of their ancestors by killing James so as not to become prey to the angry spirits claiming the enemy's blood. Again, James had to say goodbye to new friends and renewed hopes. Eventually, he ended up in Florida and in our ministry.

James brought with him not only the sadness of personal loss but also an incredible desire to succeed, a burning drive that refused to allow the flame of life to dim. He immediately enrolled in school and began to volunteer at our center. For a long time, and without many knowing it, he slept in an abandoned, rat-infested furniture store close to the school because he did not want to be late to class.

Today, James is a graduate of Duquesne University, is happily married to his Mexican sweetheart, and is doing well. The poverty he experienced tells us much about the way in which many human beings live in many parts of the world, and that reality matters. It tells us even more about the kinds of beings we are and the reality of human dignity. James overcame the massive obstacles placed in his way and found success and fulfillment. That potential lies within us all. Too often, however, the character and expansiveness of government intervention have dampened rather than encouraged that potential.

IS THE STATE THE ANSWER?

One of the fundamental assumptions underpinning the treatment of social justice in America since the late 1920s is that the state is preeminent in ensuring the common good.[1] In effect, the boundless field of collective action moves toward collapsing the whole of social welfare into the affairs of the state. My many conversations with black leaders in local communities have made clear that for them this assumption is self-evident. To their minds, the possibility of creating a compassionate and moral society without the protagonism of the state is far-fetched if not inconceivable. At the same time, the failure of government to produce positive transformational change, especially among minorities, is also evident. Such evidence, however, fails to convince them that freedom and human industry can satisfactorily provide what collective action cannot. We ought to wonder why this assumption is so widespread.[2]

Good people shudder at the thought of the retreat of the great machine of government, believing that it would mean acute suffering for countless vulnerable people. A fear of the negative effects of the market prevents many from supporting a move toward decreased government intrusion. These effects—rampant individualism, greed, and consumerism—are thought to be pervasive and a necessary consequence of market economics absent

---

[1] For a supportive summary of the development of collectivism in America, see Alonzo L. Hamby, *Liberalism and Its Challengers: From F.D.R. to Bush* (New York: Oxford University Press, 1992).

[2] There is at this point a library of books that document the failures of the state to assure the common good. Among them are Abigail and Stephan Thernstrom, *America in Black and White: One Nation, Indivisible* (New York: Touchstone, 1997); Thomas Sowell, *The Vision of the Anointed: Self-Congratulation as a Basis for Social Policy* (New York: Basic Books, 1995); Thomas Sowell, *Black Education: Myths and Tragedies* (New York: McKay, 1972); Myron Lieberman, *Public Education: An Autopsy* (Cambridge: Harvard University Press, 1995); Gertrude Himmelfarb, *The Demoralization of Society* (New York: Alfred A. Knopf, 1995); and Robert H. Bork, *Slouching Towards Gomorrah: Modern Liberalism and American Decline* (New York: Regan/HarperCollins, 1996).

heavy government constraint.[3] Yet, interventionism does not necessarily respond to logical exigencies or a rational assessment of trade-offs between efficiency and security or between freedom and justice.[4] Instead, it seems to be something we fall upon as we begin to think that there is no other way.

Support for government intervention is rooted in the decisive influence of *progressivism* in American contemporary culture, an influence slowly but steadily moving through the body politic for most of the twentieth century.[5] Varied fields of knowledge and activity experienced a transformation from a "society-focused" interest toward a "government-focused" one. During the 1950s and 1960s, major works such as Graham Allison's *Essence of Decision* and Morton Halperin's *Bureaucratic Politics and Foreign Policy* shifted attention toward government as an independent and primary actor. American sociological debates and intellectual inquiry became dominated by neo-Marxist theories.[6]

In economics, interventionists believe that we possess an expansive set of choices and that economic inequities are caused by "society." Egalitarianism, the pursuit of equality as the good of highest priority, is assumed to be positive, without a thought as to its philosophical justifications. Inequalities can be resolved by the application of deliberate plans of action, which are geared toward assessing distribution, not production.

This progression seems to be a reaction to what are perceived as the only other alternatives—atomistic individualism and economic imperialism.[7] The expansion of the welfare system was the main attempt to create fairer

[3] See Anthony J. Santelli Jr. et al., *The Free Person and the Free Economy, A Personalist View of Market Economics* (Lanham, MD: Lexington Books, 2002), 111.

[4] For an excellent discussion of interventionism, see Ludwig von Mises, *Human Action: A Treatise on Economics* (San Francisco: Fox & Wilkes, 1996), 855–61.

[5] See Thomas Sowell, *The Vision of the Anointed, Self-Congratulation as a Basis for Social Policy* (New York: Basic Books, 1995), 104–19.

[6] Theda Skocpol, "Bringing the State Back In: Strategies of Analysis in Current Research," in *Bringing the State Back In*, ed. Peter G. Evans (Cambridge: Cambridge University Press, 1985), 4–5.

[7] Patricia Donohue-White et al., *Human Nature and the Discipline of Economics: Personalist Anthropology and Economic Methodology* (Lanham, MD: Lexington Books, 2002), 74. The authors define economic imperialism as "a growing desire on the part of all social scientists to use economic analysis to explain such human realities as family life, love and marriage, education and moral training of children, and charitable activity."

conditions through government intervention and redistribute income to avoid the perils of an unjust economic system. This effort is based on the assumption that much (or all?) wealth was not acquired justly—a kind of "social suspicion."

President Barack Obama is paradigmatic of this collectivist vision of redistribution of wealth through government action.[8] In an interview in 2001, Obama decried what he called the failure of the civil rights movement to move toward the redistribution of wealth, being content with *only* granting formal rights. Obama lamented that the Warren Court "did not break free" from "the constraints" the Founding Fathers established in the Constitution. The Constitution, he explained, provided negative instead of positive liberties and "tragically" the civil rights movement failed to demand the latter: "The Supreme Court never ventured into the issues of redistribution of wealth and more basic issues of political and economic justice in this society. And to that extent as radical as people want to characterize the Warren Court, it wasn't that radical."[9]

The perception that whites are in control of the economic system and benefit from it at the expense of people of color means that, for many who subscribe to this view, social suspicion necessarily degenerates into *racial suspicion*. There is then a causal relationship between the effects of capitalism and liberal democracy and the reality of racial oppression.[10] Racism is a complication of the pathology of a capitalist society, an additional symptom

---

[8] For a detailed examination of Barack Obama's redistribution policies see Peter Ferrara, "Obama's Huge Tax Hikes Will Ruin Weak Economy," *Human Events* (October 10, 2008). See also the report done by the Tax Policy Center at http://www.taxpolicycenter.org/publications/urlprint.cfm?ID=411693.

[9] The Supreme Court under Chief Justice Earl Warren (1953–1969) oversaw an unprecedented expansion of the scope and power of the federal government. The interview was conducted by Chicago Public Radio in 2001, while Obama was an Illinois state senator and a law professor at the University of Chicago. (It has been available online at various times and in various places but its location has not been stable enough to permit a durable citation.)

[10] Not all racialist socialists agree with the reducibility of race into theories of class. Theologians such as James Cone identify the problem of race as inherent in the very fabric of Western civilization and present it as a scourge even after capitalism has been defeated. James H. Cone, *The Black Church and Marxism: What Do They Have to Say to Each Other?* (New York: Institute for Democratic Socialism, 1980), 8.

arising from class struggle, and its remedy is to be found in the rearrangement of the economic system.

In *The Clash of Orthodoxies*, Robert P. George warns against the temptation for judges to engage in "usurpative acts" in areas where they may be strongly inclined one way or the other. Even if the judge pursues an end that he deems just, he must exercise restraint and self-discipline.[11] Collectivists, in contrast, believe that humility in interpreting the Constitution and restraint from engaging in esoteric readings of the founding document are contrary to true justice. The Court is to serve as a super legislature, enacting judgments from "fringe areas" in the Constitution. This contradicts the intention of the framers, who established limits on the power of the state precisely because they did not want to "break free from the essential constraints" that a truly free civil society places on government power. The framers understood well what Lord Acton meant when he said that power tends to corrupt. They rejected rule by men with grandiose designs.

There is a pernicious belief among many on the left that the federal government has always come to the rescue of blacks, and they in turn react to government initiative.[12] Far from bringing about the promised economic and social success, the interventionist policies of the last fifty years have produced moral decay and the acceptance of squalor. Managing poverty and helping people be comfortable in their misery has become the main task of welfare. In effect, social science scholars tell us to simply get over it and accept welfare as a necessary reality. "There are many things about welfare that can be improved," one social work textbook concludes. "However, we need to recognize that in a large, rapidly changing, urban, postindustrial society, we will always need a large welfare system. In other words, welfare is simply a condition with which we should make peace."[13]

---

[11] Robert P. George, *The Clash of Orthodoxies* (Wilmington, DE: ISI Books, 2001), 199–200.

[12] When I refer to "the left" I am referring to any collectivist concept of social processes. The left, then, can be found in the thought of people across the partisan spectrum, from Communists to Republicans.

[13] Philip R. Popple and Leslie Leighninger, *The Policy-Based Profession: An Introduction to Social Welfare Policy for Social Workers* (Boston: Allyn & Bacon, 1980), 175.

POVERTY: THE "ARISTOCRACY OF APPETITE"

This attitude, as Thomas Sowell observes, has rightly given modern liberalism a bad name. "The War on Poverty," he observes,

> represented the crowning triumph of the liberal vision of society and of government programs as the solution to social problems. The disastrous consequences that followed made the word *liberal* so much of a political liability that today even candidates with long left-wing track records have evaded or denied that designation.[14]

Even so, the assumptions on which collectivist liberalism is built not only remain but are rapidly gaining force. James H. Cone's description is paradigmatic of the way liberals frame the issue:

> America is a nightmare for the poor of every race. In this land of plenty, there are nearly 40 million poor people who are trying to survive with little or no resources for their emotional and physical well-being. The Washington-based Community for Creative Nonviolence has estimated that as many as 19 million Americans might be homeless in less than fifteen years.... This nation can find the scientific, technological, and financial resources to build spaceships to explore other planets, but it cannot provide food and shelter for its poor citizens.[15]

This statement illustrates all the cleverness and political power of the radical attack on America. First, it exaggerates the plight of the poor and the vagrant.[16] Writing in 1991, Cone was expressing a widely held position about the number of homeless in America. During the Reagan years, the plight of the homeless became an effective political attack against a conservative

---

[14] Thomas Sowell, "War on Poverty Revisited," *Capitalism Magazine* (August 17, 2004).

[15] James H. Cone, *Martin & Malcolm & America: A Dream or a Nightmare* (New York: Orbis, 1991), 317.

[16] Although I will generally use the designation *homeless* here, it is important to notice that this terminology might imply an externalist causal assumption. A *vagrant* is a person in a situation of poverty who wanders from place to place. This definition focuses on the objective situation of the person in view. *Homelessness* tends to convey the idea of dispossession, of someone deprived of what ought to be his.

ascendancy.[17] Yet the number of homeless individuals in America has been exaggerated. There is simply no reliable information placing the number of homeless persons in the millions.[18]

We may ask similarly: Is poverty in America a nightmare? First, we need to clarify what we mean by *poverty*. Poverty in the United States is rarely an abject condition similar to what we encounter in many other countries in the world. Indictments of poverty in America concern *relative* poverty.[19] Most of the things we Americans—rich and poor—take for granted are attainable only by the wealthy in most of the world.

James's story perfectly illustrates this reality. "When I was in Liberia," he once told me, "I had nothing, I had to walk everywhere, and yet I was never late anywhere. But once I was able to buy a car here in America I began to struggle to be on time." Our consumerist society and the expansion of the margin of human choice tempt us to lose ourselves in competing options. They distract us from living as we ought to live. In a country of taken-for-granted wealth, there is need to cultivate our spirit, exercise the virtue of gratitude, mobilize ourselves toward productive effort, and refuse the strong pull of victimization. Poverty in the economic sense ought to always be understood through such a spiritual and cultural prism.[20]

---

[17] Washington Talk, "Washington Talk; The Homeless Become an Issue," *The New York Times* (February 7, 1987):

> Estimates on their number differ widely, from 250,000 to as high as three million. Whatever the correct number, a bipartisan effort is under way on Capitol Hill to provide immediate emergency aid for the homeless, and all this week events involving public officials and private groups in the capital have focused attention on the issue.

[18] See Christopher Hewitt, "Estimating the Number of Homeless: Media Misrepresentation of an Urban Problem," *Journal of Urban Affairs* 18 (December 1996): 431–47. Hewitt affirms that media bias and faulty research exaggerated the number of homeless in the 1980s. A fair number was between 300,000 to 500,000 homeless nationwide.

[19] Of course there are individuals in material need in America and they deserve our help. Exaggeration about the plight of the poor, however, makes it difficult to discern who is most in need and who is most deserving of support—not to mention that resources are consequently diluted.

[20] The reality of a spiritual and personal dimension to poverty calls us not to lose sight of personal responsibility but it does not deny that, at times, systemic processes make it difficult for the working but struggling poor to advance.

Self-interest leads to the sublime only indirectly by creating habits in the direction of virtue. There is thus a kind of purpose, a reason behind virtuous action, and even behind religious fervor. The doctrine of "self-interest properly understood," as Tocqueville called it, leads people not to get used to their poverty and to strive for a better life.[21] In America, he observed, the virtues cultivated could be placed in the service of self-interest, thus moving individuals to a better life economically and to a more joyful life spiritually. Men are thus seen as unified wholes where both the spiritual and the physical merge in a beautiful harmony of being.

However, there is danger in the pursuit of self-interest: "Love of comfort has become the dominant national taste. The main current of human passions running in that direction sweeps everything along with it." Still, placed in the context of a democratic people who are cultivating virtue, even if only indirectly, such passion for comfort remains controlled by reason as "love of comfort appears as a tenacious, exclusive, and universal passion, but always a restrained one."[22] In other words, the American ethos offered virtue in the context of self-interest both as a restraint on passion and an incentive toward effort.

We are now getting closer to what poverty really is. Dependency on government intervention has become a substitute for the human incentive to succeed, and comfort can be achieved without the need for the strenuous effort that once led toward virtue. Virtue was already a hard sell, even in the context of self-interest properly understood. Now, under a welfare and entitlement mentality, virtue as a tool to succeed appears as nonsense, for comfort can be acquired without effort.

The old aristocracy, Tocqueville observed, showed "haughty contempt for the physical comforts they [were] actually enjoying" and the poor got used to their poverty and "despaired of getting [comfort]," not knowing much about what it really was. Now, the poor very well know comfort and desire it very much, and an enabling system allows for its easy acquisition. Those struggling for a better life are often disheartened by the spectacle of the success of the indolent. A new aristocracy has been created, an aristocracy of appetite, where unbridled desires consume all in a ravaging quest for

---

[21] Alexis de Tocqueville, *Democracy in America* (1835; repr., New York: Bantam, 2000), 531.

[22] Tocqueville, *Democracy in America*, 532–33.

never-attained satisfaction. Now we can see clearly what poverty really is: *the unrestrained appetite for comfort, acquired without effort, which leads directly to vice.*

COMPASSION AND INTERVENTIONISM

As we have seen, government interventionism has become the standard response to poverty and want. *Compassion*, however, literally means "suffering *with*" another. This definition speaks of closeness and encounter. True compassion moves me to recognize that I am personally obliged to give myself to you as you walk the path of a journey that only you are called to make—but not alone. I am there to share in your struggle, not necessarily to eliminate it.

Human struggle is the means for finding oneself. By passing through the fires of adversity, a person is refined. Compassion will intervene to prevent despair, but it is not opposed to struggle. When I see you faltering, when I see you weak-kneed and stumbling, I come to hold you and love you and help you. With the same compassion, I will let you go. It is *your* life and *your* responsibility.

When relief and compassion are collectivized, we transform compassion from a moral encounter into a bureaucratic function. John Paul II recognized the problem. "By intervening directly and depriving society of its responsibility," he wrote, "the Social Assistance State leads to a loss of human energies and an inordinate increase of public agencies, which are dominated more by bureaucratic ways of thinking than by concern for serving their clients, and which are accompanied by an enormous increase in spending."[23]

Welfarism co-opts the language of empathy to become a kind of counterfeit compassion, but bureaucracies cannot love nor can they discern the deeper human need. A welfare system fails where collectivist economics fail: *at the point of knowledge.* Just as socialism lacks a coherent way to establish price, welfarism and bureaucracy fail to assess true need.

Bureaucratic intervention is now included in the order of ethics and morality when it does not belong there. The common ethical explanation is that redistribution of wealth is commanded by the gospel. Through the enactment of public policy, we have created a series of programs that "take care of the poor"; thus, it is our responsibility to extract resources from some and transfer those resources to others. Father Robert Sirico describes the error:

---

[23] Pope John Paul II, Encyclical Letter *Centesimus Annus* (1991), no. 48.

The problem here is the slick move from personal ethics to public policy. What is required of us as individuals may or may not translate into a civic policy priority. In the case of the welfare state, it is possible to argue that it does great good (though I would dispute that). Whether it does or does not, however, a government program effects nothing toward fulfilling the Gospel requirement that we give of our own time and income toward assisting the poor.[24]

As government bureaucracies tend to grow exponentially, the temptation is to provide increased evidence of an ongoing need, not to eliminate the problem whose very existence justifies offices, budgets, and jobs, and even launches political careers. Indeed, government utilizes methods that exaggerate economic poverty to justify demands for increased government intervention; such exaggerations are the bread and butter of its bloated existence.

One such method is the most common and the most erroneous: poverty rates. Originally developed by Mollie Orshansky in 1963, this threshold is updated each year by the Census Bureau and is utilized mainly for statistical analysis. A different and simplified version of the threshold is known as *poverty guidelines*, issued each year by the Department of Health and Human Services and utilized to determine eligibility for a number of federal programs. These are proxies that provide a snapshot of a specific point in time but affect policy decisions covering longer periods. As economics professor Eric Schansberg points out, there is a difference between falling within a given category described as *poor* and actually *living in poverty*. As the threshold applies only to reported wages or reported cash income (to the exclusion of assets, subsidies, and other monetary and in-kind government transfers), it does not provide reliable information concerning the actual economic status of individuals and families.[25]

By providing a standard numerical demarcation, these proxies use an absolute benchmark that pegs individuals to a place in a distribution—a level in a numerical hierarchy.[26] The problem is evident when considering

[24] Robert Sirico, "Mandated Giving Doesn't Come from the Heart," *Religion & Liberty* 17 (Fall 2007).

[25] D. Eric Schansberg, *Poor Policy: How Government Harms the Poor* (Boulder: Westview Press, 1996), 6–9.

[26] See Deborah A. Stone, *Policy Paradox and Political Reason* (Glenview, IL: Scott, Foresman, 1988), 72.

the aggregation of individuals at different life stages into a given poverty rate without regard to context. For example, younger people often enter the workforce at a lower income level only to rise above that level shortly thereafter. Their momentary poverty seldom acts as a hindrance to their later success. At other times, married individuals studying at elite universities but reporting minimal income are counted as poor although their poverty will normally be only a temporary step toward lucrative careers. Another group included is middle-class families in a low-income year, whose situation is, nonetheless, economically stable and bound to improve.

In Liberia, James was poor in monetary terms but he had a wealth that did not correlate with his economic condition. In a society lacking any meaningful mobility and mired in ancestral tribal rivalries and intractable corruption, his spiritual wealth could not spark the engine of economic and social progress. In America, he was still poor, but no longer the prisoner of poverty. He was immersed in economic activity full of meaningful possibilities. Energized by this environment, he achieved much. No deterministic explanation does justice to what is created by the merger of personal determination and social possibility.

Once Upon a Time

Massive government intervention did not elevate the poor from their condition nor is it the answer to the problems of those who persistently remain on the bottom rung of the economy in our still-mobile society. It is an affront to those who make great sacrifices to posit that their success is due to the interventions of government. A brief historical account can demonstrate this truth.

The 1601 English or Elizabethan Poor Law had a great influence on America's system of caring for the poor. In the colonies and then in the early United States, relief was given in the form of food, clothing, and even monetary provisions. The Poor Law was supposed to consolidate and centralize disparate earlier laws and was considered a transition from the punishment of the poor to their correction.[27] Relief was focused primarily on supporting those who could not help themselves, as most beneficiaries were the widows, the children, the sick, and the elderly. Veterans as well

---

[27] See A. L. Beier, *The Problem of the Poor in Tudor and Stuart England* (Lancaster, UK: Lancaster Papers, 1983); and Steve Hindle, *The State and Social Change in Early Modern England* (London: Macmillan, 2000).

as civilians seriously affected by the events of the War of Independence were also recipients of help. A minority of recipients were unemployed and able-bodied men, who were resented by most segments of society for seeking support. The resentment was so widespread that it became a factor in the transition of government assistance from outdoor relief to poorhouses: "Poorhouses were seen as superior to outdoor relief both because they were less expensive and because they provided a deterrent to able-bodied people's applying for relief."[28] Victims of misfortune, illness, accident, and sudden loss of employment were considered "deserving" recipients of aid, but it was important to keep the system from being taken advantage of by the "undeserving." Living conditions in poorhouses were intentionally difficult, and rules had to be kept in the strictest fashion. Poorhouses were intended to weed out vagrants and reinforce the idea of the undesirability of dependency.

Although counties and townships were the primary administrators of government aid, private charities were very important in caring for the poor.[29] Alexis de Tocqueville wrote about the great compassion of the American people: "Besides the permanent associations that are established by law under the names of townships, cities, and counties, a vast number of others are formed and maintained by the agency of private individuals." The principle of subsidiarity was ingrained in the very fiber of the American people. "The citizen of the United States," Tocqueville continues, "is taught from his earliest infancy to rely upon his own exertions in order to resist the evils and the difficulties of life; He looks upon social authority with an eye of mistrust and anxiety, and he only claims its assistance when he is quite unable to shift without it."[30] Early on, as Marvin Olasky recounts, charities utilized "work tests" to distinguish among those seeking relief: "When an able-bodied man came to a homeless shelter, he often was asked to chop

---

[28] Michael D. Tanner, *The Poverty of Welfare: Helping Others in Civil Society* (Washington, DC: Cato Institute, 2003), 14.

[29] Local governments always had some degree of involvement in relief, but federal intervention is another matter. National relief efforts grew gradually but were almost universally opposed. For example, in 1794, James Madison strongly opposed a welfare bill in the House. See Michael D. Tanner, *The End of Welfare: Fighting Poverty in the Civil Society* (Washington, DC: Cato Institute, 1996), 33–34.

[30] Tocqueville, *Democracy in America*, 218.

wood for two hours or to whitewash a building; in that way he could provide part of his own support and also help those unable to chop."[31]

With the end of the Civil War, demand for relief on the part of widows, orphans, and veterans increased. The mostly informal charity work prevalent before the war gave rise to the more organized efforts of benevolent associations and philanthropists and later to the creation and expansion of the state-led welfare system.[32] By the close of the nineteenth century, collectivism was gradually infiltrating the American understanding of the role of government in charity work. "The rise of modernism and progressivism," Michael Tanner recounts, "caused many Americans to believe that 'experts' were required to solve most problems and that only government could provide the needed expertise.... Now government was seen as a problem solver."[33]

These experts had more in mind than just helping the poor; they were pressing for a new kind of society, in line with Marxist theories about social processes. Writing in 1920, Owen Lovejoy, president of the National Conference of Social Work, presented social work as a field of service based on the conviction that men are warranted in working for something corresponding to a divine order on earth, a "social faith" that could cure the ills of society.[34] Radicals within the social workers' network, together with trade unionists, feminists, and other activists laid the groundwork for what later became the New Deal.[35]

Earlier, charity workers appealed to civic groups such as local associations or ethnic groups. When all these efforts failed, charity workers focused on establishing bonds of togetherness with the needy, bonds that could last many years. Charity workers were expected to exhibit a "personal willing-

---

[31] Marvin Olasky, "Effective Compassion: Seven Principles from a Century Ago," in *Transforming Welfare: The Revival of American Charity*, ed. Jeffrey J. Sikkenga (Grand Rapids: Acton Institute, 1997), 43.

[32] For a good history of these transitions see Robert A. Gross, "Giving in America: From Charity to Philanthropy" in *Charity, Philanthropy and Civility in American History*, ed. Lawrence Jacob Friedman and Mark Douglas McGarvie (New York: Cambridge University Press, 2003), 29–48.

[33] Tanner, *Poverty of Welfare*, 16.

[34] See Owen Lovejoy, *The Faith of a Social Worker* (New Orleans: Proceedings of the National Conference of Social Work, 1920).

[35] Michael Reisch and Janice Andrews, *The Road Not Taken: A History of Radical Social Work in the United States* (Philadelphia: Brunner-Routledge, 2001), 57–58.

ness to be deeply involved." The goal of charity work was not to connect people to programs or to create programs; in fact, the goal was to help people avoid them.[36] Now, charity workers went from engaging in the tiring but effective task of contacting families and friends to bypassing such bonds in an attempt to solve immediate problems.

Welfare programs began as local government initiatives and eventually moved up to the state and federal government levels. County and city programs such as mothers' pensions were gradually adopted by state governments. By 1933, the state was also involved extensively in the care of the elderly.[37] The Great Depression brought about the greatest government intrusion in public charity since the founding of the nation, an intrusion for which we are still paying.[38]

BLACKS AND WELFARE

The incipient welfare system was a government-driven bureaucracy assisting mostly white people. White widows and white children received most of the attention and services.[39] "Most public welfare programs, particularly in the South but throughout the country as well," Tanner tells us, "refused to provide benefits to African Americans."[40] Fraternal organizations were created by blacks as a response to their exclusion from government-led programs. Among these widely diverse private organizations were the Masonic Lodges, the Elks, and the Loyal Order of Moose.[41] The work of these fraternal organizations was remarkable both in terms of their effectiveness and of the numbers they served. Nearly 30 percent of adult black

[36] Marvin Olasky, *Renewing American Compassion: How Compassion for the Needy Can Turn Ordinary Citizens into Heroes* (Washington, DC: Regnery, 1997), 50, 59.

[37] Tanner, *Poverty of Welfare*, 17–19.

[38] See Lawrence W. Reed, *Great Myths of the Great Depression* (Midland, MI: Mackinac Center, 2008 [1981]).

[39] "No fewer than 96 percent of the people receiving 'Mothers' Pensions' before the creation of Aid to Dependent Children (ADC) had been white." John McWhorter, *Winning the Race: Beyond the Crisis in Black America* (New York: Gotham Books, 2006), 116.

[40] Tanner, *Poverty of Welfare*, 19.

[41] See Joe William Trotter, "African American Fraternal Organizations in American History: An Introduction," *Social Science History* 28 (Fall 2004): 355–66.

males in the South were thought to be Masons and hundreds of thousands of blacks belonged to black fraternal organizations and women's auxiliary groups.[42] These fraternal societies stressed brotherhood, thrift, self-help, and self-mastery. Most fraternal societies shunned economic class distinctions within their ranks and stressed personal values and behavioral standards. Good character, entrepreneurship, and a strong work ethic were expected of anyone wishing to belong.

The history of fraternal associations is one of self-reliance and self-help—a remarkable story of strength in the face of oppression. Writing in 1908, Amos Warner stated, "blacks shared a palpable dread of being assisted, especially when they think an institution will be recommended." Another commentator agreed: "[S]eldom does one find a Negro begging on the streets. The members of the race possess in high degree the quality of human kindness, and are ever ready to help their fellows in times of need."[43]

Need during the Great Depression grew exponentially. There was a concerted call for increased federal intervention as both private charities and state and local governments seemed overwhelmed by the demands of the crisis in the economy. When Franklin Delano Roosevelt was elected, he wasted no time increasing the role of government. After only ten weeks in office, he signed the Federal Emergency Relief Act and eventually created a host of programs that dramatically changed the face of charity work and the welfare state for decades to come.[44]

New Deal welfare programs are often highlighted as being critical for the uplifting of blacks, but even during that period of increased government involvement, blacks did not immediately fall into dependency on welfare. In fact, during the 1930s, Roosevelt placed Southern whites in charge of New Deal programs, which basically assured black exclusion. Roosevelt was a remarkable politician, and his New Deal efforts were focused primarily on the needs of Southern whites—not on blacks, as many blacks could not vote during the 1930s, while white Southerners were crucial to Roosevelt's political

---

[42] Tanner, *Poverty of Welfare*, 20.

[43] David T. Beito, *From Mutual Aid to the Welfare State: Fraternal Societies and Social Services, 1890–1967* (Chapel Hill: University of North Carolina Press, 2000), 26.

[44] Tanner, *Poverty of Welfare*, 22–26.

prospects.[45] In the agricultural South, blacks were especially crushed by the Depression, yet they remained excluded from most New Deal initiatives.[46]

Other New Deal programs were also limited in their impact on blacks. The Civilian Conservation Corps provided employment for young men coming from unemployed families and became one of the most popular New Deal programs. By setting a ten percent quota for blacks, however, the Corps failed to meet the needs of many black families affected severely by unemployment. Emergency relief programs were relatively more accessible to blacks. In other words, blacks got the rhetoric of civil rights and some handouts and whites got the government loans and the jobs. "Excluded from the programs that might have put them on the road to steady work and self-reliance," says Alan Keyes, "many blacks instead were herded toward the welfare trough of dead-end dependency."[47]

The unprecedented growth of the welfare state in the 1960s and early 1970s brought American practice into line with the welfare spending of most European socialist economies.[48] In 1965, social spending in our country amounted to 24 percent of the government budget, but by 1975 it had grown to 42 percent, and by 1995 it stood at 55 percent. Between 1965 and 1986, per capita social welfare spending measured in constant dollars grew by 107 percent for children and 191 percent for elders.[49] By 1971, 90 percent of people eligible for Aid to Families with Dependent Children (AFDC) were enrolled, and a new black elite of public officials invested in the perpetuation of the patronage of dependency had formed.

---

[45] Nancy J. Weiss, *Farewell to the Party of Lincoln* (Princeton: Princeton University Press, 1983), 39–40, 48.

[46] See Harvard Sitkoff, *A New Deal for Blacks: The Emergence of Civil Rights as a National Issue*, vol. 1, *The Depression Decade* (New York: Oxford University Press, 1978), 35.

[47] Alan Keyes, *Masters of the Dream: The Strength and Betrayal of Black America* (New York: Harper Perennial, 1996), 113. Similar efforts were made in my native Puerto Rico where the Puerto Rican Emergency Relief Administration ("La Prera" as we called it) made possible the distribution of free food items while most people still remained unemployed and dependent. To this day, dependency on government relief is scandalously widespread on the island.

[48] Neil Gilbert and Paul Terrell, *Dimensions of Social Welfare Policy* (Old Tappan, NJ: Pearson Higher Ed, 2013), 34–35.

[49] Paul W. Newacheck and A. E. Benjamin, "Intergenerational Equity and Public Spending," *Health Affairs* 23, no. 5 (2004): 142–46.

"Ironically," writes John McWhorter, "at the very time that long-term welfare dependency was becoming a norm rather than a stopgap in black communities, black poverty and unemployment were decreasing.... Thus, welfare was not expanded to arrest a downward trend in blacks' progress."[50]

A new concept of welfare that surfaced in the 1960s allowed for unlimited and lifelong dependency. "Welfare had once been a low-profile affair, offering a temporary safety net to people who found themselves in dire straits," McWhorter observes. "But now, 'welfare' referred to a well-publicized bureaucracy eagerly courting even people who had been getting by on their own, and after it got people onto the rolls, unconcern with when or even whether they left.[51]

Conceived as a basic institution of society, welfare became, in the words of Gilbert and Terrell, "a distinct pattern of activities serving not as a safety net to catch the victim after all else has failed but rather as an integral and normal 'first line' function of modern industrial society." Welfare is now often viewed as a form of reparations for past offenses and the inherent injustices of market economics. As welfare is now seen jointly with other basic institutions in society, it "carries none of the stigma of the 'dole' or of 'charity.' It is seen instead as a primary means by which individuals, families, and communities fulfill their social needs."[52]

Some insist that we ought not to focus on blacks on welfare, as most people on welfare are white. Although in aggregate numbers that is correct, that statistic fails to account for the high number of blacks on welfare relative to their proportion of the population. In 1961 blacks were about 10 percent of the population but 43 percent of those on welfare.[53] In the early 1970s, blacks comprised 43 percent of AFDC recipients.[54] In 1994, more than 37 percent of welfare recipients were blacks.[55] Even today, forty-six

---

[50] McWhorter, *Winning the Race*, 117.

[51] McWhorter, *Winning the Race*, 121.

[52] Gilbert and Terrell, *Dimensions of Social Welfare Policy*, 14.

[53] McWhorter, *Winning the Race*, 116.

[54] Martin Gilens, *Why Americans Hate Welfare* (Chicago: University of Chicago Press, 2000), 124.

[55] See *Overview of Entitlement Programs: Background Material and Data on Programs Within the Jurisdiction of the Committee on Ways and Means, U.S. House of Representatives* (U.S. Government Printing Office, 1994), https://books.google.com/books?id=6B7 sAAAAMAAJ&focus=searchwithinvolume&q=.

states have disproportionate numbers of African-American children in their child welfare systems.

The transformation of welfare catalyzed an explosion of dependency previously absent from the black community. William Julius Wilson observes:

> Despite a high rate of poverty in ghetto neighborhoods throughout the first half of the twentieth century, rates of inner city joblessness, teenage pregnancies, out-of-wedlock births, female-headed families, welfare dependency and serious crime were significantly lower than in later years and did not reach catastrophic proportions until the mid-1970s.[56]

Stephen Goldsmith is exactly right when he says, "Welfare did not make work unnecessary—it made work irrational."[57] If a community has the task of providing benefits directly, why bother to get a job? Ironically, the truth was well stated by one who did much to further the progressive agenda, Franklin D. Roosevelt: "Continued dependence on relief induces a spiritual and moral disintegration fundamentally destructive to the national fiber. To dole out relief in this way is to administer a narcotic, a subtle destroyer of the human spirit."[58]

CONFRONTING ASSUMPTIONS THAT GET IN THE WAY

When Jesse Peterson graduated from high school, he headed to California where he soon got involved with drugs. After working all kinds of odd jobs, some friends told him all he needed to do was go to the nearest welfare office and claim to be a drug addict and money would come. He did and instantly he was given plenty:

> My take was $300 a month, plus rent money, food stamps, and vocational training. I was amazed at how easy it was. Every month, the money rolled in. The first effect of this generosity without any kind of accountability was that I stopped even trying to work. And, of course,

---

[56] William Julius Wilson, "From The Truly Disadvantaged: The Inner City, the Underclass, and Public Policy," in *The Blackwell City Reader*, ed. Gary Bridge and Sophie Watson (Malden, MA: Blackwell Publishers, 2000), 261.

[57] Cited in John McWhorter, *Winning the Race: Beyond the Crisis in Black America* (New York: Gotham Books, 2006), 129.

[58] Cited in Mona Charen, *Do-Gooders: How Liberals Hurt Those They Claim to Help (And the Rest of Us)* (New York: Sentinel, 2004), 89.

since I was not working, I started partying more. I started experimenting with drugs and sex, and descended into a pit of irresponsibility and laziness. It nearly destroyed me.[59]

Peterson behaved rationally, according to the incentives in place. After all, we are told by the experts that he was simply utilizing a normal basic community to fulfill his social needs.

The great error of the new concept of the welfare state is at its root anthropological: It normalizes and affirms dependency, triggering destructive behaviors and awakening every craving of our base instincts. The next time someone criticizes "welfare queens" having babies to get more money, we ought to remember that the normalization of dependency is the product of the new elite's desecration of a black history of self-reliance, self-help, and fraternal encounter. The interests, customs, and values springing from a history of self-reliance are now mostly forgotten.

Some claim that, although dependency and other vices are admittedly a large part of modern inner-city life, it was always so. We certainly need to avoid nostalgic descriptions of idyllic black communities where all lived in utopian harmony before they somehow degenerated into nests of incivility, promiscuity, and violence. Likewise, however, we cannot avoid concluding that the situation has indeed gotten worse. As McWhorter points out, "A poor neighborhood is one thing, but a war zone where drug vending, drug addiction, early child-birth, absent fathers, unemployment, violence, and murder are all norms is another."[60]

The root of the problem lies in faulty collectivist assumptions that warp the very nature of the state and its intended purpose. The discussion about welfare, unfortunately, has been settled by the left and by most of those on the right: Welfare is here to stay; we just need to amend it to make it work better. I disagree. A return to black self-help through the creation of institutions focusing on entrepreneurship and effective compassion is a more humane answer to the plight of the poor, and the success of such an alternative is antithetical to the existence of a federal government welfare institution. Should we abandon the idea of a safety net at the federal level? Yes! It does not work.

---

[59] Jesse Lee Peterson, *From Rage to Responsibility* (St. Paul: Paragon House, 2000), 9.

[60] McWhorter, *Winning the Race*, 22–23.

To challenge accepted thought is a daunting task. Those invested in the welfare plantation system control the language of "compassion." Some of these fit Booker T. Washington's timeless description of cynical opportunists: "There is a class of colored people who make a business of keeping the troubles, the wrongs, and the hardships of the Negro race before the public. Some of these people do not want the Negro to lose his grievances, because they do not want to lose their jobs."[61]

Even among those of manifest good will, it is difficult to break out of the statist paradigm. Many now speak against dependency only in the cause of promoting it further. A neutral language about welfare and dependency makes them appear to be "moderate" while they continue to vie for more government intervention. Not long ago I had a conversation with an officer of a national organization that was coming into town to "organize people for justice." After a long talk during which she agreed with every point I made concerning personal responsibility, she asked me to consider joining the efforts to demand justice from the state and public officials, meaning more government funding.

In America, collectivism is now "the black agenda." Every politician seeking national office must support that agenda and must make a required appearance at an NAACP convention trying to convince them that he is the best candidate to advance it.

The history of American blacks tells us that they do not need the government to rule their lives. The conditions necessary to recapture that history of self-reliance, however, do not seem available due to the power and control exerted by a collectivist leadership. Where does the solution lie? It does not lie in categorical measures. To call for the immediate elimination of welfare at all levels is a pipe dream. Yet, to return welfare initiatives to the states seems feasible. Admittedly imperfect, welfare reform has nonetheless been a success, and we must continue to highlight that victory and push for transferring all authority over welfare decisions to local governments.[62]

---

[61] Emma Lou Thornbrough, ed., *Booker T. Washington* (Englewood Cliffs, NJ: Prentice-Hall, 1969), 69.

[62] Even at the local level the principle of subsidiarity applies. The care of the poor is better met at the nongovernmental level, with government only as a secondary aid.

The Surrender of Individuality

The expansion of earmarked entitlements has contributed to what Gertrude Himmelfarb calls the "pauperization of the poor."[63] This kind of distributive equity is defended on the assumption that certain major divisions in society—race, gender, or ethnicity—outweigh individual characteristics in determining distribution and assuring equality. The human person is thought to be incapable of transcending his environment or his race to move forward in life. Racial, ethnic, and gender identity, as well as any kind of infirmity or special condition, totally define the person. Intervention by the state becomes the great equalizer by redistributing "fair shares" to such groups.

Unfortunately, such shares demand the surrender of our individuality. The benefits derived from this kind of entitlement are limited and their effects on the culture are often detrimental. In truth, the alienation of members of minority groups can be traced to some degree to the failures of earmarked, group-based policies.[64] It is ironic that racialists are offended when someone points out the existence of pathological behavior among minorities (there is nothing distinctive in these detriments, they insist), but when it comes to assigning funds and distributing benefits, they trumpet concepts such as "disparate impact," which emphasize the distinctive challenges facing favored minorities.

What is truly fair? While many government policies inflict disproportionate harm on blacks, these effects are often overlooked.[65] Nonearmarked policies (programs not specifically designated to benefit a particular group) are ignored by leaders in the minority community due to their lack of political value. What is fair and important is understood as that which is assigned through a political process to specific groups of people or to individuals based on group characteristics. The G.I. Bill, for example, benefited blacks immensely, but it offered no political benefit to black politicians; thus, it is

---

[63] The pauper is not only poor but is also dependent, having entered a state of hopelessness and incapacity. Gertrude Himmelfarb, "Welfare and Charity: Lessons from Victorian England" in *Transforming Welfare*, 27.

[64] Sowell, *Civil Rights: Rhetoric or Reality* (New York: Quill, 1984), chap. 4, 86–90.

[65] Walter Williams has detailed the detrimental effects of licensing laws on blacks. These laws tend to be ignored by black leaders simply because challenging them does not carry political benefits for those leaders. See Walter E. Williams, *The State Against Blacks* (New York: McGraw-Hill, 1982).

rarely mentioned as an important policy contribution to black progress.[66] While some do benefit from group-specific policies, the majority experience increased alienation and the feeling of having been "left behind." The outcome of this situation is an intensification of social tensions and a heightened demand for further governmental action. The collectivist monster feeds on itself.

One of the stated goals of earmarked social policy is to ameliorate the effects of social structures at the root of differences among groups, assuring in that way the equalization of outcomes. At the heart of the problem, we find an error of anthropology, a failure to grasp the reality of human dignity discussed above. The unrepeatable and unique human person is sidestepped in favor of agglomerated identity.

To provide real equality, collectivists believe, we must pursue an equality of opportunities *and* results. As Thomas Sowell points out, equality of opportunities has a unique meaning for collectivists. They define it as "equalized probabilities of achieving given results."[67] The idea of fair shares, coupled with group-based earmarked policy, produces in the individual a vision of what is just that inevitably spells one word: *entitlement*. If it is fair to create by governmental engineering equalized probabilities by offering to some groups certain benefits at the expense of others, then I, as a member of a lower-stratum group, am entitled to such a benefit. The exercise of compassion and justice becomes a matter of politics rather than of morality. Redemption is achieved through structural change brought about by persons willing to surrender their individuality for the benefits promised by the new machine. Yes, "rage against the machine," but only in the cause of creating another.

WELFARE AND VICTIMHOOD

The bureaucratization of welfare has also perpetuated the damaging ideology of victimhood. Historically, blacks experienced victimization through slavery and segregation. Today, unfortunately, a rational assessment of the meaning and present effects of this troubled history has been replaced by a

---

[66] Sowell, *Civil Rights: Rhetoric or Reality*, 86.

[67] Sowell, *A Conflict of Visions*, 123 [emphasis mine].

political approach to rights based on mere plausibility and political rhetoric.[68] Victimization as a *fact*, or as a present possibility, however, is different from victimization as an *ideology*. The ideology of victimization permeates government action, social interaction, and intellectual inquiry and contributes to the acquisition of victimhood as an identity.

We are told that black powerlessness is the direct result of the oppressive activity of the dominant white group. White America is guilty of "racism, classism, ableism, heterosexism, regionalism, sexism, ethnocentrism and ageism."[69] In this view, if we are to understand the reality of oppression and the need for state power to remedy it, we must understand the nature of American society as prejudiced.[70] In the classic account of the ideology of victimhood, William Ryan coined the phrase "blaming the victim" to reject the proposition that the personal behavior of the presumed victims has much to do with their condition. Ryan called it "a brilliant ideology for justifying a perverse form of social action designed to change, not society, as one might expect, but rather society's victim."[71]

The field of social work is permeated with "blaming the victim" assumptions. Herbert and Irene Rubin, for example, tell us that "blaming the victim is a form of social control that disempowers by denying people a legitimate focus for complaint." They deplore the fact that "people often blame themselves for the bad things that happen to them."[72] William Brueggemann

---

[68] See Sowell, *The Vision of the Anointed: Self-Congratulation as a Basis for Social Policy* (New York: Basic Books, 1995), 124.

[69] See Karla Krogsrud Miley, Michael O'Melia, and Brenda DuBois, *Generalist Social Work Practice: An Empowering Approach* (Boston: Allyn & Bacon, 2004), 89.

[70] See Philip R. Popple and Leslie Leighninger, *The Policy-Based Profession: An Introduction to Social Welfare Policy for Social Workers* (Boston: Allyn & Bacon, 1998), 98. There we read:

> In fact, many policies, such as affirmative action and minority scholarships, are often proposed specifically for this purpose [to ameliorate the effects of societal racism, sexism, etc.]. On the other hand, individuals and groups often oppose social welfare policies and, although they generally don't admit this, the reason for the opposition is often directly a result of racism and sexism.

This is the kind of explanation social workers get in their training to "help minorities."

[71] William Ryan, *Blaming the Victim* (New York: Vintage Books, 1976), 78.

[72] Herbert J. Rubin and Irene S. Rubin, *Community Organizing and Development*, 3rd ed. (Boston: Allyn & Bacon, 2001), 81. Social workers are very active in minority

states that "institutional deviance" is responsible for individual problems: "We concentrate on the social deviant, but fail to look at the conditions that may cause people to become deviant." According to Brueggemann, victim blamers shift responsibility from the capitalist system to the individual, or they may blame the anointed reformers—"socialists, pacifists, union organizers, social activists, community organizers, and civil rights activists"—instead of blaming capitalist oppressors. They may also target a minority group—gays, the poor, blacks—as blameworthy for a given social ill.[73] The initial step in empowering and helping the oppressed, Rubin and Rubin instruct us, "takes place as people recognize that they are victims of problems that are shared by many others." Through "consciousness-raising sessions" people come to realize that "their problems are caused by a broader social structure and occur because they rebound to the advantage of others."[74]

It is possible to take a more balanced approach. As sociologist Orlando Patterson explains, "To hold someone responsible for his behavior is not to exclude any recognition of the environmental factors that may have induced the problematic behavior in the first place. Many victims of child abuse end up behaving in self-destructive ways; to point out the link between their behavior and destructive acts is in no way to deny the causal role of their earlier victimization and the need to address it."[75]

Some scholars who blame society for individual misfortune point to low self-esteem as a by-product of victimization. "Persons who experience blame, shame, and stigma," the authors of *Generalist Social Work Practice* say, "often assimilate this negativity into their self-image.... In general, feelings of powerlessness increase, often resulting in low self-esteem, alienation, and despair."[76] Richard Delgado has posited that similar harmful effects of low self-esteem spring from the social stigmatization of minorities and result in varied intra- and interpersonal pathologies. From the inability to

---

communities and, paired with police officers, are often the first line of connection with government structures. As "professional caregivers" they have a deep influence in the lives of their clients and in molding the culture.

[73] William G. Brueggemann, *The Practice of Macro Social Work* (Belmont, CA: Brooks/Cole, 2002), 41–43.

[74] Rubin and Rubin, *Community Organizing and Development*, 89.

[75] Orlando Patterson, "A Poverty of the Mind," *New York Times*, March 26, 2006.

[76] Karla Krogsrud et al., *Generalist*, 90.

form relationships and the failure to become good parents to high blood pressure, these maladies and more are traceable to racial stigmatization.[77]

But this theory does not fit the evidence. As Orlando Patterson demonstrates, studies on self-esteem amply show that, while up to the 1960s African-Americans exhibited low levels of ethnic and individual self-esteem, that trend has been reversed:

> Nearly all African Americans now feel no sense of "racial" inferiority whatsoever when comparing themselves with Euro-Americans or any other ethnic group. And in reference to personal (individual) self-esteem, not only do African Americans of all classes have a healthy sense of self-esteem, but numerous studies suggest that, especially among the working and lower classes, Afro-Americans often score higher than their Euro-American counterparts on tests measuring self-esteem.[78]

The black underclass exhibits higher "self-regard" but lower "feelings of personal efficacy." Afro-Americans experience a lower sense of internal control but high self-esteem. It seems as if the identity of victim has been internalized, with individuals accepting personal failure as a result of external forces. This pattern is corrosive to the fabric of a people. Individuals tend to devalue areas where they personally fail as such failure can be easily attributed to external forces. If my educational attainment is low, then it is because of white oppression, and I need not pay much attention to my education—after all, I cannot be expected to excel until "whitey" fixes the problem.[79]

As Patterson shows, the problem is no longer that individuals feel bad about themselves but that they exhibit a "sense of positive regard ... from their commitment to blaming the system.... Lower-class Afro-Americans, with the full support of their leaders and professional psychologists, have come to respect themselves because they have no autonomy."[80] When individuals see important areas of self-development as unimportant and abandon a commitment to improve them, the results are devastating.

---

[77] Richard Delgado and Jean Stefancic, eds., *Critical Race Theory: The Cutting Edge* (Philadelphia: Temple University Press, 2000), 131–33.

[78] Orlando Patterson, *The Ordeal of Integration: Progress & Resentment in America's "Racial" Crisis* (New York: Basic Civitas, 1997), 88.

[79] Patterson, *Ordeal of Integration*, 89.

[80] Patterson, *Ordeal of Integration*, 90–91.

INTERVENTIONISM AND THE CONTRADICTIONS
OF DETERMINISM

Calls for government intervention in black America are often based on political agendas rather than on scientific assessment. They preeminently appeal to a distorted view of compassion and to a particular vision of the world and of causality focusing on structures as the primary culprits for individual and group pathologies. This vision entails a moral assessment of those who dare to disagree with the need for government action—what Thomas Sowell has called "a vision of differential rectitude."[81] Ronald Walters, for example, characterizes blacks who oppose interventionism as inauthentic tools of white nationalists, as opportunists, and as traitors to the race because they have abandoned the collectivist ethos allegedly brought to America by the slaves.[82] In *The Failures of Integration*, Sheryl Cashin offers some thoughtful reasons against separate residential black enclaves, but she also makes sure we do not mistake her for "some black conservative or neoconservative trying to be provocative to gain attention or career advancement." She is instead "a progressive Democrat who cares passionately about the state of inequality in this nation," a "race woman" who "enjoy[s] and thrive[s] in the

---

[81] Sowell, *Vision of the Anointed*, 5. For example, Robert Eisner, past member of the leftist National Jobs for All Coalition, states that conservatives simply do not care for people:

> Most conservative economists do not really care about the deficit. They advocate balanced budgets because their real desire is to cut government spending, particularly on the "social programs" they abhor.... [D]eficit paranoia ... is used to justify depriving the American people of their health care, their education and all of the public investment on which their future depends.

Robert Eisner, "Why the Debt Isn't All Bad: Balancing Our Deficit Thinking," *Uncommon Sense* 9 (February 1996), http://www.njfac.org/pubs.html.

[82] Ronald Walters, *White Nationalism, Black Interests: Conservative Public Policy and the Black Community* (Detroit: Wayne State University Press, 2003).

company of black people."[83] Black conservatives, she implies, are uncaring opportunists who are indifferent to the fate of their people.[84]

This "crisis of interventionism," which Ludwig von Mises thought was coming to an end in 1949, is alive and well more than two decades after the collapse of communism.[85] The black community is a place where the crisis is clearly visible as there remains distrust of economic freedom and the market. The tactics of "eternal supplication" and "eternal protest" are transforming the community into a collectivist haven. The distrust of economic freedom triggers a distrust of those African-Americans who, becoming successful, abandon the idea of the primacy of government initiative. Those who move away from inner cities or express an independence of consciousness that refuses to avow the black liberal consensus immediately become suspect.

The great contradiction of deterministic interventionism is that it relieves blacks of the daunting task of being what they already are, human persons with the dignity of free and volitional beings. Determinism, if taken seriously as an explanatory proposition, also excuses the supposed victimizer from any kind of moral blame. If affirming the dignity of persons called to live worthy and autonomous lives is blaming the victim, then we remove any moral claim against the perceived oppressor who is also a victim of predetermined antecedent factors. Both victim and victimizer are tokens in an inevitable game of fate; they are linked by the same cord of cosmic victimhood.[86]

---

[83] Sheryl Cashin, *The Failures of Integration: How Race and Class are Undermining the American Dream* (New York: Public Affairs, 2004), 160.

[84] Actor Joseph Phillips has experienced the same hatred:

> "Sell-out!" "Uncle Tom" "Set in fetchit!" I have been called it all and so often that it all tends to bleed into one long ugly name and one not even all that clever. It matters not how highbrow the conversation or how many letters follow the name of the accuser. Proponents of race preferences will eventually get down and dirty and challenge black opponents of race preferences, race pride, and will call white opponents racists.

Joseph C. Phillips, *He Talk Like a White Boy* (Philadelphia: Running Press, 2006), 243.

[85] See Ludwig von Mises, *Human Action*, 4th ed. (1949; repr., San Francisco: Fox & Wilkes, 1996), 855–57.

[86] See Patterson, *Ordeal of Integration*, chap. 2.

POLITICAL MARKETS, OUR DEMISE

The new liberal/radical consensus represents a betrayal of the virtues connected to the entrepreneurial initiative and Christian principles that ignited the black community's fight for civil rights. Personal responsibility becomes a bit of rhetoric instead of a genuine conviction. We are said to have only one choice. Liberation theologian J. Deotis Roberts proclaims, "Whites always have a choice; they can always become 'square' and join the mainstream. Our only choice is resistance! Resistance! Resistance!"[87]

If oppression by a hierarchically structured society condemns us to perpetual marginality, political action that demands structural change must remain the answer to social problems. "The reason why Black theology is 'political,'" Roberts explains, "is that the one-on-one approach is inadequate and unattractive to any black man who is aware of the serious and insidious character of racism."[88] In such an understanding, there can be no space for concepts such as merit, equal treatment, or achievement. Equality of results is the goal, even as it can only be achieved by demoting individual responsibility. Process equality, the very kind that the civil rights movement strove for, is perceived as oppressive—a process embedded in a hierarchically structured society configured to maintain the status quo of white dominance.[89]

In political markets, the actors (constituents, elected officials, bureaucrats) are not only benevolent "do-gooders," but they are also interested parties, similar to economic market actors. Political markets, however, differ from economic markets in a number of ways. Economic markets involve transactions of benefits between actors who must make economic calculations of mutual benefit, while political markets involve the confiscation of property from one actor to benefit another based on a centralized political calculus. The confiscatory power of the state becomes the instrument of coercive exchange.

[87] J. Deotis Roberts, *A Black Political Theory* (Louisville: Westminster John Knox Press, 1974), 142.

[88] J. Deotis Roberts, *Liberation and Reconciliation: A Black Theology* (Louisville: Westminster John Knox Press, 2005), 34.

[89] Thomas Sowell has observed: "If you have always believed that everyone should play by the same rules and be judged by the same standards, that would have gotten you labeled a radical sixty years ago, a liberal thirty years ago, and a racist today," John Perazzo, *The Myths that Divide Us: How Lies Have Poisoned American Race Relations* (New York: World Studies Books, 1999), 321.

Here the problem of price or economic calculation is at hand: How does one measure success? In economic calculation, in spite of the fact that we cannot know future changes in incentives for future economic actors, we must assess the economic value of a transaction or of any other activity. As Ludwig von Mises says in *Human Action*, "If a hydroelectric power station is to be built, one must know whether or not this is the most economical way to produce the energy needed. How can [we] know this if [we] cannot calculate costs and outputs?"[90] Redistributive political markets are inherently irrational. They neglect economic calculation in favor of political expediency. Political planning is no planning at all, for it removes from primary consideration the economic calculus needed to make sound decisions.[91]

Political markets cannot allocate economic resources in a rational way because, for the most part, they disregard the human actor. The clever reasoning of blaming oppression or discrimination for the condition of some can never become a rational calculation helping us to make sound economic—or moral—decisions. Political calculation is not like entrepreneurship. The entrepreneur takes chances and calculates risks with profit or loss becoming the measure of his success. In the absence of economic calculus, the feasibility of achieving success is lost. In fact, in political markets, the continuation of the allocation of resources depends not on success as indicated by profit but on *failure*, indicative of a need for further allocation of resources. By placing the fate of black America in political markets, we guarantee failure. As political markets move wealth around through the hands of a noneconomic intermediary, the state bureaucracies are paid regardless of success.[92]

The welfare state created by political markets insults the very human beings it attempts to rescue by depriving them of the power to shape their destiny. We become wards of the state when we rely heavily on political markets. This stands in contrast to the discharge of moral obligation in true charity, which preserves the humanity of both giver and recipient. Individuals in desperate situations of need deserve to receive assistance from those with the resources to help. To remove from the gift a moral element of voluntarism deprives individuals of the opportunity to make

---

[90] von Mises, *Human Action*, 700.

[91] von Mises, *Human Action*, 833.

[92] See D. Eric Schansberg, *Poor Policy: How Government Harms the Poor* (Boulder: Westview, 1996), 37–39.

"self-constitutive choices" to "shape themselves as the persons they should be."[93] A limited role of the state in assisting the poor does not contradict the true superiority of private charity, but excessive reliance on political markets is a grave mistake.

It is common to hear that "a hungry man is not free." The catchy phrase is used to justify government intervention to alleviate human need as a way to activate citizens toward bettering themselves. If we help people to have all their basic needs met, the argument goes, they will in turn have the presence of mind to rise above their peculiar circumstances. Minorities, especially, will see their status exponentially improved by at least a token of "reparations" for past injustices. The Great Society experiment was predicated on such a theory of human action. Forgotten in this vision are the concepts of incentives and achievement. There is a great difference between avoiding want and achieving success.

I have seen how a failed anthropology disguised as compassion hurts the poor. I have seen how charities hand out free items to people after making donors feel so guilty for their success that they turn over whatever is asked. I have seen the avalanche of people pressing against each other to get the handouts and noticed that the recipients realize no genuine material or spiritual benefit from the experience.

I am far from idolizing the market. If I were to assert that markets completely abolish human passions and permit only rational calculations, I would be courting utopia as much as those who dream of a socialist heaven-on-earth. In his determined defense of markets, von Mises failed to find a place for morality and wrongly concluded that "any examination of ultimate ends turns out to be purely subjective and therefore arbitrary."[94] In his vision, we choose to attach intrinsic value to an end and our means are valuable only in a derivative sense, valued by their utility. In other words, von Mises believed that there is nothing like an *ought* built into human nature.

One school forgets the process in favor of an ever-elusive end built on the foundation of erroneous anthropology, and the other elevates contingency

---

[93] Christopher O. Tollefsen, "Welfare Rights vs. Welfare States," *Public Discourse*, November 21, 2008.

[94] von Mises, *Human Action*, 96. If ultimate ends are not discernible, human action is merely transitive and we can assert, in Humean fashion, that human action does not affect our character, only the external world. We do not shape ourselves by the choices we make and thus human action has nothing to offer besides its utility to meet our wants and desires. See Gregg, *On Ordered Liberty*, 43–44

while eschewing the ontological reality of values. The answer to this false dichotomy lies in economic markets that are imbued both with a respect for the dignity of persons and with a recognition of the ontological nature of values. It lies in the recognition of what each system misses: the true nature of man and the true nature of value.

In black America, however, enthrallment to political markets overwhelms in scale any countervailing idolatry of the market. Lost in the noisy clanging of the great machinery of the state, the quiet protest of human dignity cannot be heard. When it raises its voice, it is asked to take a number, sit, and wait for its turn in the long line of an agency of bureaucratized assistance.

A Return to Civil Society and Subsidiarity

In his 1971 introduction to a German edition of F. A. Hayek's masterpiece, *The Road to Serfdom*, Milton Friedman spoke of the state of the collectivist impulse at the time:

> Now and then, the promotion of collectivism is combined with the profession of individualist values. Indeed, the experience with big government has strengthened this discordant strand. There is wide protest against the "establishment," an incredible conformity with the protests against conformity; a widespread demand for freedom to "do one's own thing," for individual lifestyles, for participatory democracy. Listening to this strand, one might also believe that the collectivist tide has turned, that individualism is again on the rise.[95]

A similar observation is likewise applicable to our time. While radicals support an expansive role of government in the economic and social realm, they are comfortable with radical individualism in the moral sphere. It goes unrecognized that eventually the individualism they support will collapse under the weight of the statist machine. The more the state intervenes, the more the margin of choice disappears.

Is the tradition of liberty strong enough, and are the inefficiencies of collectivism evident enough to contain the tide of interventionism? Or, has the animus of the American people toward statism been so weakened that they are now willing to permit the collapse of the whole of society into the affairs of the state? I fear that we are far along in the process of the

[95] F. A. Hayek, *The Road to Serfdom* (1944; repr., Chicago: University of Chicago Press, 1994, xi.

subtle but steady surrender of freedom. David Hume's eighteenth-century observation that it is "seldom that liberty of any kind is lost all at once" is still compelling.[96] In 359, Saint Jerome complained of the advance of the Arian heresy within the Christian world: "The whole world groaned and marveled to find itself Arian." We may be close now to an updating of his words: "The whole world yawned and scratched to find itself in serfdom."

When Karl Marx called on all the workers of the world to rise up from their pitiful existence and rebel against the tyranny of capital in a last and decisive revolutionary battle, he never thought that the best chance for the triumph of the collectivist faith was by way of incrementalism. The socialist idea lives in the consistent and unchecked growth of the state. Is not the very idea of responding to every normal downward market fluctuation with increased government intrusion an admission of the state's superior knowledge? In the name of regulation, oversight, and efficiency, the realm of civil society recedes ever more.

Ironically, this development is taking place with the blessing of institutions that were once vigorous champions of that civil society. Michael D. Tanner has shown that many charities are no longer private philanthropic ventures but virtual arms of the state. Standing to lose significant funds if charity work is privatized, they have become ready advocates of government intrusion and expansion. Tanner furnishes examples: "Federal, state, and local governments, provide nearly two-thirds of the funding Catholic Charities USA uses to operate its nearly 1,400 programs. Goodwill Industries receives half of its funding from government. The Jewish Board of Family and Children Services receives 75 percent of its funding from the government."[97] By depending so much on government, large charities have become the best advocates of government expansion in the name of "helping the poor."

This situation is a departure from the principles that inspired the formation of these religious institutions. In the past, charity was based, in fact if not in theory, on the Catholic principle of *subsidiarity*. Subsidiarity focuses on the individual human person as the primary reality within the basic communities of society. Although it reflects the perennial wisdom of human social

---

[96] David Hume, *The Philosophical Works of David Hume*, vol. 3 (London: 1826), 12.

[97] Tanner, *Poverty of Welfare*, 98. See also Brian C. Anderson, "How Catholic Charities Lost Its Soul," *City Journal* (Winter 2000).

interaction, Pope Pius XI first gave the principle of subsidiarity its modern formulation in the encyclical *Quadragesimo Anno* (1931).[98]

Within Catholic social teaching, subsidiarity was a response to the collectivism of fascism and communism. It establishes that social institutions are not mere instruments of the state. These institutions possess their own spheres of influence and must possess the necessary freedom to fulfill their responsibilities. "Just as it is wrong to take away from individuals what they can accomplish by their own ability and effort and entrust it to a community," Pius writes, "so it is an injury and at the same time both a serious evil and a disturbance of right order to assign to a larger and higher society what can be performed successfully by smaller and lower communities."[99]

As we learn from political philosopher Jacques Maritain, the state, as one of society's communities, has as its basic reasons for existing the codification and administration of the law, the promotion of the common good, and the maintenance of public order.[100] However, the state is not a synonym for society—the whole of the social order. Individuals do not belong to the state, nor is the state the primary object of individuals' allegiance.

The principle of subsidiarity is not just a negative postulate that warns against interference by the state. On the positive side, the state must promote the common good by providing assistance to other basic communities in cases of crisis or when individuals are "unable or unwilling" to act for themselves. Distributive justice, after all, demands that the members of a political community have access to the means for a dignified existence. Such interventions, however, are to be "as brief as possible."[101] Additionally, distributive justice does not automatically mean government intervention and group entitlement.

In fact, the primary characteristic of a state that promotes justice is not the creation of a welfare state or a safety net. The temptation to find government-driven solutions to promote the common good must be carefully assessed according to the dictates of general and commutative justice. The excesses, abuses, and errors of bureaucratized compassion are testimony

---

[98] See Russell Shaw, ed., *Our Sunday Visitor's Encyclopedia of Catholic Doctrine* (Huntington, IN: OSV Books, 1997), 650.

[99] Pope Pius XI, Encyclical Letter, *Quadragesimo Anno*, no. 79.

[100] Jacques Maritain, *Man and the State* (Chicago: University of Chicago Press, 1951), 12.

[101] Pope John Paul II, Encyclical Letter, *Centesimus Annus*, no. 48.

against entitlement becoming the formal mechanism for justice and compassion because they injure true justice in the name of "social" justice.[102] We must move away from what Bertrand de Jouvenel describes as the "loose modern habit" of calling just "whatever is thought emotionally desirable."[103]

Subsidiarity prevents the inordinate use of state power as the primary means of equalization because the state plainly has no authority to intervene indiscriminately into the affairs of lower structures in society. If any government structure has a primary responsibility to intervene under certain stringent conditions, it must be the governmental entity closest to the individual as he actually lives his life. Thus, *reciprocity*, not entitlement, is the means toward the end of communal harmony. Reciprocity involves a mutuality of respect and recognition among the various basic structures in society.

In contrast, humanitarian intervention under state solidarism is "top-down" with the state directing. This inclination reflects what Russell Hittinger lucidly describes as "the instrumentalist description of civil society."[104] Even though there is no clear constitutional ground for such a vision of the state, a normative shift through the redefinition of the concept of state action has taken place. Statism offers a *residualist analysis*: The state decides which activities can be better accomplished by civil society while it reserves the right to change its mind. If the state concedes space to other communities, the state can take it away. Many policy discussions in America occur under this residual and instrumental assumption; civil society must justify why the state ought *not* to control this or that activity.

A return to social solidarity properly understood is essential as it shifts the future of the black community from political to social and moral markets. Civil society is not a lingering social tool to accomplish certain tasks or check the powers of the state. The question is not, for example, whether or not the state can better educate children. It is instead: What social order, what community within society, has as its constitutive purpose the education of children? Civil society is not simply a cushion to soften the advances of the

---

[102] Stephen J. Grabill, Kevin E. Schmiesing, and Gloria L. Zuniga, *Doing Justice to Justice* (Grand Rapids: Acton Institute, 2002), 34–36.

[103] Bertrand de Jouvenel, *The Ethics of Redistribution* (Indianapolis: Liberty Fund, 1990). 18.

[104] Russell Hittinger, *The First Grace: Rediscovering the Natural Law in a Post-Christian World* (2003; repr., Wilmington, DE: ISI Books, 2007), 269.

tyranny of the state but a community that possesses a rightful basic association and plays a given perfecting role.

This is not to say that certain instrumental reasons for civil society do not exist, only that they do not constitute the basic reasons for its existence. The common good is realized first in individuals by virtue of sharing a common human nature: a share in a common status (human), common perfections (such as health and knowledge), and common utilities (such as food and technology). Second, the common good is realized through cooperation in common activities.[105] Every time a higher structure intervenes unnecessarily in such common activities, society loses some of its harmonic constitution.

Civil society exists because in the collaborative interaction of free individuals society is perfected. As Hittinger observes, it would not be better for us all if we were to subcontract the rearing of our children or the feeding of the hungry to a third party—whether the state or any other entity—simply because we have been convinced by experts that such activity is thus maximized. In Romans 12:2, Paul tells us: "Do not be conformed to this world, but be transformed by the renewing of your minds, so that you may discern what is the will of God—what is good and acceptable and perfect." To rediscover the true place of civil society and begin to bring about a retreat of the collectivist behemoth from our midst, the reform must begin in our minds. We need to begin again to believe that a compassionate, loving, and effective charitable society is possible without the government's domination of the effort.

Our participation in the good completes our being. We are subjects called not only to be successful but also to be faithful—faithful to our call as persons and faithful to our personal commitment to each other. We are called not only to collaboration and effectiveness but also to *communion*.[106] This communion is actualized among men by the free and voluntary encounter of individuals through their respective basic communities by helping each other and loving each other. A return to the values of cooperation in free associations is the answer to racial antagonism and the path to social harmony.

---

[105] Hittinger, *First Grace*, 277–79.

[106] Hittinger, *First Grace*, 180–81.

CHARITY WORK AND THE HUMAN PERSON

Charity has come to mean "to give to."[107] This giving is open and distant and downplays the individuality of persons by creating monolithic classes of people. Giving things to people has become the feel-good alternative to a rational and intelligent assessment of the needs of the poor. When we make emotions the primary criterion for charity work, we assume a distorted notion of human nature and run counter to the precepts of natural law. Practical reason allows us to discover the true human good in an action, helping us to pursue the good in the everyday affairs of men. It demands both our taking seriously what is good and our courage to pursue the good even when our emotions incline us otherwise. Dehumanizing bureaucratization is inevitable if meeting purely biological needs is the primary criterion of charity work and the distribution of goods ignited by emotions is its basic element.[108]

It may seem valid to assume that if people are given things, that activity in itself alleviates need in an immediate way. Only by an intelligent assessment of needs, however, can we value persons in their integrity and encourage the development of the capacities necessary for individuals to rise above poverty and break the cycle of dependency. A collectivist welfare system based on group entitlement is a byproduct of the lack of attention to the uniqueness of every person and to the courage that each instance of life demands from us. Entitlement becomes a safe but amoral exercise that lacks the nerve to risk failure and instead stamps the exercise with a quantifiable "can't miss" label. When charity focuses on the offering of things to alleviate the specific physical needs of the moment, immaterial human goods are neglected.[109]

The provision of benefits through bureaucratic entitlement cannot help people deal with the tensions of life. It cannot assist them in making choices to fight isolation and achieve the communion that is the deeper human need.

---

[107] See Robert Sirico, "Compassion and the Rise of the Welfare State" in *Transforming Welfare*, ix.

[108] We can define bureaucracy as the action of public power in society by the adoption of deliberate patterns of organization for the pursuit of distribution.

[109] Human goods are important as reasons for action. They are reasons for action because they constitute intelligible aspects of the fulfillment of persons and communities. Only God, however, is the *Summum Bonum*, or absolute good. When man grasps the intelligibility of a good, it can serve as a principle for action directing us to pursue a certain path; but it can never exhaustively fulfill the human person. See John Finnis, *Natural Law and Natural Rights* (Oxford: Oxford, University Press, 1980).

This kind of system is often degrading and alienating, yet it can produce the illusion that we are being compassionate: I pay my taxes and the state takes care of the poor. It ignores, however, the important element of *bonding*. As Marvin Olasky reminds us: "Charity volunteers a century ago usually were not assigned to massive food-dispensing tasks but were given the narrow but deep responsibility of making a difference in one life over several years." Olasky points out that today, by contrast, "Some failed programs spend a lot of money but are too stingy in what is truly important: treating people as human beings made in God's image, not as animals."[110]

Direct assistance through the distribution of goods creates an immediate appearance of success by providing charities with measurable data. This kind of activity, however, tends to ignore that human reality goes beyond simple materiality; it neglects the fact that "human beings are spiritual subjects capable of reasoning, understanding, responding, and acting. Though humans are located in the natural realm as finite living beings, as persons, they are capable of transcending the dynamism immanent to biological life by maintaining a relationship to the world and other persons in acts of understanding, creativity, and self-determination."[111]

A further dimension of the problem of bureaucratization is the lack of a clear rationale on which the gift can be modified to meet individual needs. Bureaucracies tend to codify statutes and regulations to meet general criteria. Frustration and apathy build in sincere charity workers who begin to see themselves merely as functionaries. A great interpersonal barrier is erected between the functionary, who experiences the lethargy and monotony of paperwork, deadlines, and quotas on a daily basis, and the client who perceives the system as impersonal and who often lashes out in frustration at the functionaries.

The need for a stronger affirmation of individuality as the only way out of the cycle of dependency and poverty seems obvious. More and more individuals and their families need to take control of their lives and their communities without depending even on local charities or intermediary

---

[110] Olasky, "Effective Compassion: Seven Principles from a Century Ago" in *Transforming Welfare*, 43.

[111] Patricia Donohue-White et al., *Human Nature and the Discipline of Economics* (Lanham, MD: Lexington Books, 2002), 13.

"leaders."[112] Entrepreneurship, the individual's discovery of the best use for his capacities for personal and community betterment, is the way out of poverty.[113]

In black America, this task—empowering the individual to escape the mire of dependency and soar into the liberating air of self-reliance—should be our chief priority. We need only go to inner cities around the country, where clusters of offices and agents of the state administer their palliatives, to witness the plague of dependency. As race consciousness reigns, and government action remains the preferred instrument of social justice, this segment of our community continues to suffer the ravaging effects of collectivism.

---

[112] The Second Vatican Council clearly states what is needed:

> A sense of the dignity of the human person has been impressing itself more deeply on the consciousness of contemporary man, and the demand is increasingly made that men should act on their own judgment, enjoying and making use of a responsible freedom. The demand is likewise made that constitutional limits should be set to the powers of government, in order that there may be no encroachment on the rightful freedom of the person and of associations.

Second Vatican Council, *Declaration on Religious Freedom* (Boston: St. Paul Books & Media, 1965), 5.

[113] Hayek said:

> The successful use of this entrepreneurial capacity (and, in discovering the best use of our abilities, we are all entrepreneurs) is the most highly rewarded activity in a free society, while whoever leaves to others the task of finding some useful means of employing his capacities must be content with a smaller reward.

F. A. Hayek, *The Constitution of Liberty* (Chicago: University of Chicago Press, 1960), 81.

6

INTOLERANT TOLERATION

---

*Real selves, after all, face the complexities of
the modern world and, mind you, they do not
recruit the notion of complexity as a proxy for
wordier renditions of the same old blowing the
whistle on whitey.*

—**John McWhorter**[1]

Once, during my college days, one of my friends proposed to me what I
considered a "socialist-lite" alternative for Puerto Rican independence.
I laughed at him. I considered any qualification of the hard-line socialist view
to be the soil from which heresies grow. Consequently, as I waited for the
taxicab in the city of Aguadilla, I delighted in making him look like a fool.

"I cannot accept your ideas," I told him. "You don't understand! The
only option is to destroy this society to the ground and, from its ashes, build
the just socialist society."

"I'm not sure of that, Ismael," he kindly began, "what about ..."

I interrupted him in a tone of exasperation. "You are not a socialist—
'friend,'" I ended sarcastically.

Later, I felt terrible about the way I had mocked him. I have asked God
to place me again before him so that I can ask for forgiveness, so that I can

---

[1] John McWhorter, *Winning the Race: Beyond the Crisis in Black America* (New York:
Gotham Books, 2006), 387.

ask him to appreciate the leap in understanding that I had not yet achieved on that long-gone day.

At the time, however, I only escaped my emotional discomfort by focusing on the scenic majesty of the land. The route from San Juan to Mayagüez always took the Aguadilla turn, and, as you follow it, the surroundings offer no ordinary attraction. When I recently traveled that route again, the incident with my friend pricked my memory. This time, the picturesque beauty offered an opportunity for pure admiration rather than emotional avoidance. As I descended toward the Guajataca turn, the green mountaintops followed by the indigo splendor of the ocean took my breath away. To the left, the rain forest mountains seemed impregnated with color and life. In their outline, I am convinced, we can glimpse what God had in mind when making paradise. At times, if you listen carefully with your soul, you may hear the Arawakan cries of the Taino people wafting on the sea breeze of the evening while you admire the landscape filled with Puerto Rican flora: yagrumos, alelís, palm trees, and giant ferns. Then, to your right, you can delight in the majestic plain, and a little further, in the crystal blue of the Atlantic heaving in an eternal affair with the sparkling foam. Don't let its appeal fool you, however, as the expansive ocean splendor hides raging tidal currents beneath it, as if they have witnessed the spilled blood of the Taino people under the brutal blade wielded by Spanish hands.

Taking one of those notoriously steep curves on the way to Isabela, I always feel as if the car is about to tumble down into the nothingness beneath. The long ride and the fear are symbolic, I think, of the perilous leap away from the idea of socialism; symbolic of the ecstasy and turmoil experienced when a socialist has second thoughts. Measuring the distance from one ideological pole to its opposite gives me a sense of falling into that depth, of losing myself. Such is the grip by which revolution holds true believers. To abandon the idea of revolution is death, and worse, betrayal.

In the early morning hours of November 7, 1944, a train packed with electors going back home to vote in their districts was traveling from San Juan to Ponce. At each stop on its way, new passengers boarded as it approached the city of Aguadilla. The engine deviated at the Jimenez Station in Aguadilla to switch conductors. Although the new one had no experience with passenger trains, José Antonio Román was supposed to finish the trip all the way to the southern city of Ponce. It must have been around 2 a.m. when the train sped down the hill section known as Cuesta

Vieja hauling six passenger cars with hundreds of commuters. Derailing, the train exploded.

The newspaper *El Mundo* described the incident: "The machine suffered a terrible explosion as it derailed and the impact was so great that three wagons were converted into fantastic wreckage. Sixteen people died and almost fifty were injured."[2] Although attributed to the conductor's error of driving at high speed, some Nationalists believed that it was a revolutionary act against imperialism on election day. My father seemed to have knowledge about his brother Guango being somehow involved in the incident. He rarely mentioned this, as if hiding some secret reserved only for the friendly ears of true revolutionaries. Was this only Nationalist and Communist propaganda to foster their respective causes, or was there some truth in the rumor? After all, Nationalist leader Pedro Albizu Campos, by then in prison, called the ballot the "coffin of the Puerto Rican nation."[3]

This possibility strengthened my commitment to the cause. Nothing could interfere with a revolutionary's commitment. This may be why my father grew so detached from his family, as if coming too close to us was adulterous. I can see him standing, agitated, while my mother sat at the table and contended with him. "Revolution is my life," he said. "You see these children [pointing toward us]; if I could offer their lives right now for independence and revolution, I would do it without hesitation!"

I can remember Mom crying at this remark. We tried to console her. Deep inside, however, I proudly agreed with Dad.

But that was long ago. How my metamorphosis must have pained him! By the early 1990s, my passion for socialism fading, I had become a stranger to him, and he could not take it. No rejection from past comrades could compare with the sadness of my father's disappointment in me. Close to the end, we ceased to discuss politics at all and dreaded to bring up anything touching on ideology. In a way, this neglect ripened the reward of a few deep conversations on other matters, especially related to faith. The antipathy toward my new ideas, however, never allowed for an encounter at the level I had hoped for.

---

[2] Haydee E. Reichard de Cancio, *La Tragedia del 7 de noviembre de 1944* (The Tragedy of November 7, 1944) *El Nuevo Día*, Por Dentro Sección, December 7, 1996, 116.

[3] The speech is available at http://www.youtube.com/watch?v=f3oszOEBt5s&feature=related.

What I have learned about collectivism is that it is moralistic and all encompassing, admitting no real compromise or partial commitment. Revolution sweeps your life like a Caribbean hurricane, tearing apart everything in its path. It offers a posture of moral justification and, as a reward, anoints your superiority. But reward comes at the expense of reality. The revolutionary dream denies the truth of a fallen and imperfect world where self-alienation, division, error, sin, and inequality exist. We do not possess the capacity to eliminate the imperfection that is part of human nature. It is only in accepting reality that an ocean of authentic possibilities opens before us.

Resistant to both close personal relationships and to intellectual challenge from his son, my father was, I eventually realized, unlikely to accept the deep encounter that I desired. The closest I felt to him was while reading his only letter to me, wherein he expressed his love and admiration for what I had accomplished and thanked me for a previous letter I had sent him. I always knew he loved me, even though he never verbalized it. After all, I was the most radical of his children, the one who could always understand. The great fear of *totally* losing him by forsaking the dreams of revolution, I am thankful, never materialized, and his letter was enveloped in that truth.

My relationships with other radicals were another matter. Those who switch sides in the political and social contests of their time always pay a price in lost friendship, and my experience is no different. Puerto Rican socialists reading this account will despise me even more. For black leftists, consternation is an understandable reaction; what is worse is outright dismissal. From their perspective, I simply cannot understand their reality; I am not one of them.

DUALISM AND BLACK REALITY

In the diverse history of dualism, two strands and two men stand out: the soul-body dualism of Plato and the mind-body dualism of Descartes. In *Meditations on First Philosophy*, Descartes described two substances in man: body and mind. This radical separation of mind and body allows for a separation between the physical body and consciousness. Although closely aligned to our body, the mind is the true self.[4]

---

[4] Rene Descartes, *Meditations on First Philosophy*, Second Meditation, 16. For a detailed explanation of Descartes' dualism, see Robert P. George and Christopher Tollefsen, *Embryo: A Defense of Human Life* (New York: Doubleday, 2008), 64–66.

The determinism of race aligns well with such mind-body dualism. It is possible, in the view of some black thinkers and activists, that a person of African descent may have the physical traits and family history of an African-American, yet may not be a true black person because he lacks black consciousness—that is, acceptance of the predominant liberal-radical consensus. If one strays from the consensus, one ceases to *think as* a black person. In addition, as true self is consciousness, one indeed becomes a nonperson by lacking a true black consciousness. There is, of course, a hierarchy of offenses against true self, with some being foundational and others being derivative. Having the wrong ideology is worse than belonging to the wrong political party, and both of these may be worse than, say, crossing the line and marrying a white person.

I often experience the force of this dualism at gatherings of black community leaders. I am initially regarded as a brother—one of the family—regardless of my Puerto Rican ancestry. In fact, some American blacks make it a point to affirm my blackness as "we all got in the boat." It is only as they learn my strong disagreements with the black radical-liberal consensus that they want to throw me out of the boat.[5]

We must reject this dualism. Blacks are essentially individual human persons from the moment of conception until the moment of death. They possess a capacity for love, rationality, and consciousness, as any other human being does, by being members of the human species. It is precisely the wondrous reality of our uniqueness as unrepeatable beings that constitutes our dignity, regardless of whether we agree with certain politics. Dualism errs in proposing that the subject performing mental acts is different from the subject performing physical acts. In reality, however, there is a full integration of body and mind in the acts we perform.

It is crucial to notice that historical oppression against blacks occurred against human beings who possessed certain *physical characteristics*. As Glenn Loury explains, race "is a mode of perceptual categorization people use to navigate their way through a murky, uncertain social world." Such "informa-

---

[5] The treatment afforded Supreme Court Justice Clarence Thomas by fellow blacks is perhaps the most egregious instance of this phenomenon. Black intellectuals and celebrities have said the following, among other things, of Thomas: "ethnically, Thomas has ceased to be an African American"; he is a "virulent Oreo phenomenon"; he is a "handkerchief-head, chicken-and-biscuit-eating Uncle Tom." Cited in John Perazzo, "Affirmative Acton: Facts & Myths," *FrontPage Magazine*, January 9, 2002.

tion hunger" is not a normative but a cognitive function of human agents who "will notice visible, physical, traits presented by those whom they encounter in society: their skin color, hair texture, facial bone structure, and so forth."[6] Dualistic racialism simply inflicts another injury on those who possess those physical traits by allowing an anointed few the right to determine their racial identity based on a subjective criterion: agreement with their politics.

We have seen how, in the name of toleration, certain viewpoints are excluded from respectable public (or even private) discussion. Although my focus has been on the experience of black Americans, the phenomenon can be seen across Western civilization. This *ideology* of toleration—as distinct from the *practice* of tolerance, which is indeed a good thing—is extremely dangerous. It is the ground from which tyranny easily grows. It is also deeply rooted in Western liberal philosophy and culture, which helps to explain how it has become so pervasive. This problem lies at the heart of much dysfunction in black America and prevents the necessary solutions from being implemented.

EQUAL CONCERN AND RESPECT?

A secularist understanding of basic individual rights is supposed to be independent of any specific concept of the good—whether individual or communal.[7] Individual rights under this kind of antiperfectionism[8] derive not from what is good but from an *abstract right* of individuals to be treated with "equal concern and respect."[9] Whatever an individual devises as good for himself, whatever he appropriates as worthy, whatever content of moral significance an individual imparts to his actions, must be treated by the

---

[6] Glenn Loury, *The Anatomy of Racial Inequality* (Cambridge: Harvard University Press, 2002), 17.

[7] Robert P. George, *Making Men Moral: Civil Liberties and Public Morality* (Oxford, UK: Clarendon Press, 1993), 83–84.

[8] Antiperfectionism rejects the idea that the state has a role in helping people live valuable lives by promoting certain standards of morality and excellence. The state must be neutral in terms of what constitutes a good life.

[9] George, *Making Men Moral*, 85. The abstract right of equality, as George asserts, is assumed as if by intuition.

law with equal concern and respect, regardless of whether his actions are *objectively* degrading.

A purported "right to moral independence" guarantees a right to perform *any* "self-regarding" or "private" act. Tolerance of vice becomes a virtue. This theory is inconsistent with its own requirement of neutrality; it is not neutral on its strong *moral* support for "toleration" and "autonomy."[10] After all, what value can we assign to autonomy if the state shuns from policy-making consideration morally valuable options?[11] In a secularist society, the only value affirmed is freedom from constraint. The desire for freedom, however, is a sign of contradiction. Joseph Cardinal Ratzinger (the future Pope Benedict XVI) wrote in 1986:

> In man's desire for freedom there is hidden the temptation to deny his own nature. Insofar as he wishes to desire everything and to be able to do everything and thus forget that he is finite and a created being, he claims to be a god. "You will be like God" (Gen. 3:5). These words of the serpent reveal the essence of man's temptation; they imply the perversion of the meaning of his own freedom. Such is the profound nature of sin: man rejects the truth and places his own will above it. By wishing to free himself from God and be a god himself, he deceives himself and destroys himself. He becomes alienated from himself.[12]

Samuel Gregg rightly observes that "[s]o-called neutralists invariably have strong convictions: it is simply that their convictions are different" from those held by religious believers.[13] It is not neutral to defend a specific

---

[10] As aptly stated by Samuel Gregg, the absolutizing of tolerance is incoherent:

> If people really believe that the meaning of tolerance is tolerating, then they ought to tolerate even intolerance. Likewise, if one really considers the best foundation for tolerance is to avoid having any strong beliefs, then one should not have a strong belief that intoler-ance is wrong. Thirdly, if you truly believe that when you do have strong beliefs you should refuse to express them, then your tolerance amounts to nothing less than self-emasculation.

Samuel Gregg, *Morality, Law and Public Policy* (Sydney: St. Thomas More Society, 2001), 21.

[11] Joseph Raz, *The Morality of Freedom* (Oxford: Oxford University Press, 1986), 395.

[12] Congregation for the Doctrine of the Faith (Joseph Ratzinger, Prefect), *Instruction on Christian Freedom and Liberation* (1986), no. 37.

[13] Gregg, *Morality, Law, and Public Policy*, 22.

good such as autonomy while rejecting as illegitimate the advocacy of other goods, such as truth. Secular liberals try to limit the realm of public life "by stigmatizing as 'superstitious' or 'irrational' the strong claims of religious persons." What in fact happens is that a secularist faith, with its own myths and metaphysical assertions, is enthroned in the body politic as the basis for an "overlapping consensus" under which all citizens are supposed to act.[14] The allegedly neutral state extends the consensus beyond individual choice into culture. We soon discover that freedom from constraint is not the only value endorsed by the so-called neutralists.

The multiculturalism affirmed by secularists supposedly accepts every cultural pattern without consideration of the values affirmed; all cultures are equally acceptable and deserve their niche within a kaleidoscope of competing concepts of civilization. In reality, however, multiculturatism is a radical rejection of Western values. The only barbarians are in the West. Multiculturalism, as an expression of secularist neutralism, is a well-executed campaign against Western civilization's "dead white men" and against traditional Christianity. As Christianity and Western civilization are so intertwined, to discredit one is to undermine the other. Autonomy is asserted against *certain* truths and cultural claims, not against *every* comprehensive claim. After all, William Galston notes, "no form of political life can be justified without some view of what is good for individuals."[15] Neutrality is impossible. Every person embraces and promotes a particular worldview, but some are more forthright about it than others.

OF BABIES AND SLAVES

Comments by President Barak Obama during the 2008 presidential campaign are a good example of the advocacy of a specific concept of the good masquerading as neutral political theory. During an exchange between presidential candidates at Pastor Rick Warren's Saddleback Church, Obama affirmed that he could not change the faith understanding of those who think life begins at conception. "If you believe that life begins at conception and you are consistent in that belief," he said, "then I can't argue with you on

---

[14] Gregg, *Morality, Law, and Public Policy*, 24–26.

[15] William Galston, *Liberal Purposes: Goods, Virtues, and Diversity in the Liberal State* (New York: Cambridge University Press, 1991), 79.

that because that is a core issue of faith for you."[16] This kind of comment fails to do justice to the pro-life position and exemplifies the cleverness of the pseudo-neutral paradigm that is so common today.

Obama presented the pro-life position as inherently religious and thus alien to discussions of public policy. In fact, the question here is one of basic justice and scientific evidence, both of which vindicate the pro-life position. The injustice of the act is established independently of religious affirmations and is confirmed by science—the very criterion of the secularist liberal principle of legitimacy. What we must not forget in examining these kinds of arguments is that if we renounce the idea of objective value and ban believers from the public square, there is nothing that may prevent the violation of the rights of individuals. If government declares the child in the womb, the Jew, or the slave a nonperson, and we have banished normative arguments for human rights, what then?

Framing the matter as he did, Obama made pro-life believers look like religious fanatics while pro-choice advocates appear as reasonable people using scientific data.[17] The net effect is that the arguments of religious believers, even if defended without recurring to religious claims, are ruled out of consideration. What would be the state of black America if Martin Luther King had agreed with such a "liberal consensus"? On May 17, 1957, King stood on the steps of Washington's Lincoln Memorial to deliver his first major speech. At that momentous event, he appealed to the Christian faith as the comprehensive system of thought, thus moving forward a mass movement for justice. In effect, he made it clear that in its moral admonitions of justice the Christian faith not only stirs the individual soul but also places demands on the state. His words still reverberate with the power that galvanized a social movement:

> I conclude by saying that each of us must keep faith in the future.
> Let us not despair. Let us realize that as we struggle for justice and

---

[16] See http://www.cnn.com/2008/POLITICS/08/16/warren.forum/#cnnSTCVideo.

[17] In truth, sophisticated pro-choice figures such as Naomi Wolfe and Judith Jarvis Thompson have abandoned the scientific debate on abortion in favor of metaphysical theories of personhood and ideas such as "justifiable homicide"; they have recognized that there is no longer any good scientific argument against the pro-life position that a new, distinct human being exists from the moment of conception. See Judith Jarvis Thompson, "A Defense of Abortion" in *The Rights and Wrongs of Abortion*, ed. Marshall Cohen (Princeton, NJ: Princeton University Press, 1974), and Naomi Wolfe, "Our Bodies, Our Souls" *The New Republic*, October 16, 1995, 26–35.

freedom, we have cosmic companionship. This is the long faith of the Hebraic-Christian tradition: that God is not some Aristotelian Unmoved Mover who merely contemplates upon Himself. He is not merely a self-knowing God, but an other-loving God forever working through history for the establishment of His kingdom. And those of us who call the name of Jesus Christ find something of an event in our Christian faith that tells us this. There is something in our faith that says to us, 'Never despair; never give up; never feel that the cause of righteousness and justice is doomed.[18]

A secularist understanding not only vitiates public discourse by unjustly banning believers from engaging in it; it also places society at the mercy of destructive behavior. Pro-choice positions on abortion, slavery, and racism are dangerous ideologies built on historicism, constructivism, and conventionalism. As these theories deny that there is a determinate human nature and that there is such a thing as a God (or, at least, if there is one, that his existence has anything to do with ordering our lives together), rights can exist only if *we decide* they do. If all knowledge is socially constructed, contingent on convention and experience, then truth and human rights are whatever we make them to be. If we confer them, they pertain; if we refuse them, they are gone.[19] Those who are ready to do the bidding of such comprehensive liberalism built on the absolute sovereignty of human choice are stepping onto perilous ground.

Multiculturalism rests on such unstable ground. Misusing the obvious fact of diversity of mores, multiculturalists present natural-law thinking and the truth claims of Western civilization as impositions on the rights of others. Each culture is entitled to its own truth, they say. Multiculturalism prefers that we put up with everything rather than assert any claim of priority, with some multiculturalists vying for more than mere toleration of different cultures. They want celebration, recognition, entitlement, and separation.[20]

---

[18] Martin Luther King Jr., "Give Us the Ballot," Address at the Prayer Pilgrimage for Freedom, http://mlk-kpp01.stanford.edu/index.php/encyclopedia/documentsentry/doc_give_us_the_ballot_address_at_the_prayer_pilgrimage_for_freedom/.

[19] Robert P. George, *The Clash of Orthodoxies* (Wilmington, DE: ISI Books, 2001), 153–54.

[20] For a good discussion of multiculturalism and secularist neutralism, see Charles Taylor, *Multiculturalism: Examining the Politics of Recognition* (Princeton: Princeton University Press, 1994).

Stephen A. Douglas proclaimed the same doctrine of the sovereignty of the will on the issue of slavery. He was the pro-choice advocate insistent on protecting the right to choose regardless of the content of the choice.[21] The Lincoln-Douglas debates offer an instructive example of the philosophical and practical foundations of both the secular neutralist position and the principled natural-law position. Lincoln articulated an understanding of slavery that is still operative today concerning every issue of human life and dignity:

> That is the issue that will continue in this country when these poor tongues of Judge Douglas and myself shall be silent. It is the eternal struggle between these two principles—right and wrong—throughout the world. They are the two principles that have stood face to face from the beginning of time; and will ever continue to struggle. The one is the common right of humanity and the other the divine right of kings.[22]

Instead of the divine right of kings to choose as they please and impose mandates on their subjects, we have today the divine right of personal choice imposing on all the acceptance of every degrading choice in the name of tolerance and autonomy. In following that lead, not only does the state use compulsion against people of a certain economic status, but it also ostracizes through positive law and societal reproach people who hold certain beliefs.

When truth claims are shunned, the whole character of the community and of individuals within the community is distorted. That was Martin Luther King Jr.'s point concerning the system of segregation. "There are two types of laws: just and unjust," he wrote. "To put it in the terms of St. Thomas Aquinas: An unjust law is a human law that is not rooted in eternal law and natural law.... Hence segregation is not only politically, economically and sociologically unsound, it is morally wrong and sinful."[23]

---

[21] Douglas's Kansas-Nebraska Act passed by Congress on May 30, 1854, repealed the ban on slavery in the territories of Nebraska and Kansas (the Missouri Compromise of 1820) under the rubric of popular sovereignty.

[22] Debate at Alton, Illinois, October 15, 1858, in *Collected Works of Abraham Lincoln*, vol. 3, ed. Roy P. Basler (New Brunswick, NJ: Rutgers University Press, 1953).

[23] Martin Luther King Jr., "Letter from Birmingham Jail," in *A Testament of Hope: The Essential Writings and Speeches of Martin Luther King, Jr.*, ed. James M. Washington (San Francisco: HarperCollins, 1991), 289.

Courage—the courage of Lincoln—is needed.[24] A morally indifferent conscience, one where values are eschewed, is insufficient to establish a legal right precisely because certain acts are so degrading and militate so strongly against basic human goods that they erode human dignity and the common good.[25] Its protests to the contrary notwithstanding, our present secularist society is anything but neutral. It is precisely our desire to respect the equality and dignity of individuals that motivates certain acts to be criminalized and certain assumptions to be called into question. As we cannot give absolute moral content to what we choose, absolute rights to moral independence do not obtain; in short, autonomy is not independent of truth. Neither can we give equal moral status to every comprehensive system of thought, or more accurately, to every cultural expression.

Under the cover of neutrality, we have become accomplices in a true black holocaust. If justice anywhere is a threat to justice everywhere, then abortion is a greater injustice against the black population than against any other group of people in America. Currently, African-Americans make up 13 percent of America's population, but 30 percent of all abortions are performed on black women.[26] Alveda King, niece of the late Martin Luther King Jr., has said, "Over 150 years [after the end of slavery] an entire class of Americans is still treated as nothing more than property. Our laws regard babies living in the womb as non-persons. It's a tragedy and a disgrace."[27] In the words of Dolores Bernadette Grier, "Yesterday, they snatched the babies from our arms and sold them into slavery. Today, they snatch them from our womb and throw them in the garbage."[28] A neutral liberal theory cannot protect the rights of persons, cannot take us out of bondage, cannot

---

[24] Ramesh Ponnuru, *The Party of Death: The Democrats, the Media, the Courts, and the Disregard for Human Life* (New York: Regnery, 2006), chap. 7.

[25] George, *Making Men Moral*, 95.

[26] "Fact Sheet: Induced Abortion in the United States," July 2014, Guttmacher Institute, http://www.guttmacher.org/pubs/fb_induced_abortion.html.

[27] See http://www.christianpost.com/article/20080611/alveda-king-links-abortion-slavery.htm. It is worth noting, too, that the early twentieth-century movement to promote birth control (including abortion) was in many respects a eugenic movement that specifically targeted people of color. See Angela Franks, *Margaret Sanger's Eugenic Legacy: The Control of Female Fertility* (Jefferson, NC: McFarland, 2005).

[28] See "Statements by Black Americans on Abortion," November 5, 2008, http://www.priestsforlife.org/library/document-print.aspx?ID=142.

stop the murderous hand of the abortionist, and cannot prevent the abuses of majorities trampling on the basic rights of all.

DETERMINISTIC LIBERALISM, NEUTRALITY, AND THE "RADICALISM OF FEAR"

Comprehensive liberalism does not want competitors. As comprehensive liberalism has established itself as the *modus vivendi* of American society, it is easy to see how its defenders equate liberalism with mainstream thought. The modern liberal idea is defended as a pragmatic response to the fear of social turmoil resulting from the clash of incompatible comprehensive systems.[29] Because comprehensive liberalism proclaims itself neutral and pluralistic, its comprehensive views are offered as the needed alternative to extreme views.

The exclusion of other comprehensive views establishes *convention* as the basis for rights and public debate. By disallowing the public discussion of comprehensive views, conventionalists deny that positive law can embody universal propositions. This agnostic attitude inevitably leads to cynicism in public life. If, on the matter of rights, the law is reduced to opinion and power, then the tendency of the populace—and, in particular, those most genuinely concerned with the common good—is to withdraw from involvement in the affairs of society. The law becomes a burden that we learn to tolerate. Even more, conventionalism encourages a sort of probabilism where liberal opinion triumphs even if the contrary opinion has better reasons behind it. Power is enthroned as the tool to adjudicate competing rights; nevertheless, power resides in the status quo of liberalism.

The fact of pluralism is indeed a social reality that must be confronted. Multiculturalism in its varied forms is one attempt to articulate a response to pluralism, but it is a dead end. It is under the multiculturalist paradigm, clustering individuals into groups or classes, that modern liberalism understands diversity and offers redress to the sins of the past. Thus, we hear of "black truth" and "white truth" of how "blacks think" or "Hispanics think." The task of redressing the balance from racial oppression toward harmony has taken the turn of balkanization. The commendable task of correcting

---

[29] See Robert P. George, *In Defense of Natural Law* (New York: Oxford University Press, 2001), 201–2.

the absurd historiography that dismissed racial oppression has devolved into the use of history as a weapon.[30]

"Pluralist multiculturalism" has given rise to an even more alienating multicultural strand that Diane Ravitch calls *particularist multiculturalism*; an identity politics that confuses ethnicity with culture and is based on the inheritance of a kind of "cultural DNA."[31] To counter Eurocentrism in the curriculum, for example, we are offered the pseudo-history of Afrocentrism, one extreme giving way to another. It is not balance that is offered as a solution but a historical mythology to heal wounded self-esteem and to invent physiological and psychological differences between blacks and whites.[32]

Political theorist Jacob Levy has proposed one solution to balkanization: he calls it a "multiculturalism of fear." Levy tries to offer a balanced approach between cultural essentialism, on the one hand, and the preservation of ethnic communities with the enervation of cultural identities, on the other. A multiculturalism of fear aims to prevent the evils associated with tribalism and ethnic antagonism. Under this social arrangement, ethnic identities are not celebrated but only acknowledged, as individuals experience emotional attachments that must be recognized while kept at bay.[33]

An entire ideology built on the fear of social upheaval may be understandable in some parts of the world, but is it necessary or desirable here in America?[34] Are we to place America in the category of an ethnic state where land distribution, economic resources, and social recognition are fought for in political struggles among clearly defined ethnic groups?

---

[30] Arthur M. Schlesinger Jr., *The Disuniting of America* (New York: Norton, 1992), chap. 2.

[31] Diane Ravitch, "Multiculturalism: E Pluribus Plures," *American Scholar* 59 (Summer 1990): 339.

[32] Schlesinger, *Disuniting of America*, 63–65.

[33] Jacob T. Levy, *The Multiculturalism of Fear* (Oxford: Oxford University Press, 2000), 38. There is much to be praised in Levy's account and in his desire for ethnic harmony. Yet, I believe that once a given separate status is recognized in law, it inevitably asserts itself further until celebration is accomplished. From there, we only get more particularity.

[34] Even in societies such as Rwanda it is not readily obvious that insisting on ethnic identity and rights of ethnicities solves the problem of violence. In fact, such competition for benefits based on group rights may trigger increased tensions, resentments, and upheaval.

We must also reject the monoculturalism of fear predicated by the Euro-racialists, which attempts to avoid any non-Western cultural expression out of fear of balkanization and the loss of social cohesion.[35] Neither ideology should have any place in the American milieu. These fears are fueled by a kind of radical cultural antagonism that exists only because some people say it does and not because there actually are such radical demarcations among us.[36]

A nation born in plurality, America was not first and foremost an ethnic haven for those of common ancestry but was instead a nation conceived in an idea, a set of values with cultural significance. The encouragement and celebration of ethnic separatism is antithetical to the idea of America. The multicultural left is less preoccupied with diversity and inclusion because its defense of ethnicities is secondary to its opposition to the idea that America represents. Its radical view of America as oppressive is what is at the heart of its opposition to assimilation into American culture.[37]

Akin to the concept of the multiculturalism of fear is another twist in the complex nature of comprehensive liberalism: a *radicalism of fear*. By insisting on the inherent racism of American society, radicals present forceful activism as a necessary tool to prevent ethnic annihilation. In rejecting the

---

[35] *Social cohesion* is one of those terms that, like obscenity, is hard to define, but we know it when we see it. One good working conventional definition is the presence of shared values and feelings of togetherness in a human group. See Jane Jenson, *Mapping Social Cohesion: The State of Canadian Research* (Ottawa: Canadian Policy Research Networks, 1998), 17. A different definition is that of Dick Stanley:

> the willingness of members of a society to cooperate with each other in order to survive and prosper. Willingness to cooperate means they freely choose to form partnerships and have a reasonable chance of realizing goals, because others are willing to cooperate *and share the fruits of their endeavours equitably*. [Emphasis mine]

The insistence on equality and diversity is common in definitions of social cohesion and denotes an ideological bent toward collectivist understandings of justice and equality. See Dick Stanley, "What Do We Know about Social Cohesion: The Research Perspective of the Federal Government's Social Cohesion Research Network," *Canadian Journal of Sociology* 28 (2003).

[36] Peter Wood, *Diversity: The Invention of a Concept* (San Francisco: Encounter Books, 2003), 23–31.

[37] David Horowitz, "Conservatives and Race," in *Left Illusions: An Intellectual Odyssey* (Dallas: Spence, 2003), 197–98.

possibility or desirability of multiculturalism without the celebration and legal recognition of difference, the radicalism of fear prescribes the imposition of a particularist understanding of ethnicity.

Under the guise of responding to continued and expanding oppression, and negating any meaningful racial progress, the radicalism of fear utilizes violence and shame to advance its objectives of restructuring society on the lines of collectivism and separatism. This radicalism has hijacked modern liberalism in the cause of introducing the very divisiveness liberalism fears. Michael Eric Dyson, for example, views "aggressive minority students" at colleges and universities as "authentic." He believes that liberals on campus ought not appeal to the virtues of civility and tolerance to impede their anger; after all, these virtues are but a continuation of exclusionary practices and an attempt to fit blacks into a mold prescribed by the mainstream:

> As minorities speak for themselves—in tones, perhaps more harsh, more insistent, and less patient, *less civil* or *less tolerant*—their views are seen sometimes, even by those who have formerly spoken for them, as unacceptable. Thus the competition of racial virtues at times appears inevitable: civility and tolerance as the highest priority for even liberal whites, agitation and disobedience as a means to liberation deployed by excluded blacks.[38]

As a result, anger and violence become the preferred tools to continue without interruption "the struggle" radicals see as necessary for liberation. Of course, the black struggle for justice in America was not primarily about upheaval but instead about standing in dignity, courage, and civility to demand just deserts. It was an appeal for inclusion in the structures of society precisely to enjoy the exercise of civic values. That in the past some appealed to certain values by obviating others (as in calling for patience while forgetting about justice) does not make such virtues forever suspect.

Today, a confirmation of black progress is the willingness of institutions to include black voices in a civil and tolerant discourse. To continue purposeless anger is to deny the inroads paved by the sweat and blood of those who preceded us in the struggle. Where is the evidence that white liberals were not expecting blacks to defend themselves or speak out once some doors opened? Were not those black people who were ready to exert their

---

[38] Michael Eric Dyson, *Open Mike: Reflections on Philosophy, Race, Sex, Culture and Religion* (New York: Basic Civitas Books, 2003), 59–60.

influence on the affairs of the Republic the ones who initiated and moved forward the civil rights movement? The insinuation that white liberals were surprised by black assertion says more about our view of blacks than about white liberals. It portrays those black Americans who paid with their lives to open opportunities as passive recipients of liberal white magnanimity.

On the contrary, whites are the ones who now often remain in public silence. I have seen white liberals and conservatives repeatedly genuflect at the altar of guilt and fear. The actual problem is that radicals, at heart, *reject* tolerance and civility toward those who disagree with them. So convinced are they of the truth of radicalism that they see no need to allow space for dissenting voices. That is why many black radicals on campus use their "agitation and disobedience" not to open a space for their voices but to silence contending ones.[39]

THE DIVISIVE MYTH OF AFROCENTRISM

Standard textbooks for training social workers take the ideas of the Afro-centric worldview for granted.[40] The *Clinical Assessment for Social Workers* asserts that a "common cultural value among U.S. blacks is an 'Africentric' worldview that is rooted in and incongruous with the dominant Eurocentric culture."[41] We are also told that "while standardized measures may pass the test of high reliability and stability, they can be culturally biased when used with ethnic-minority groups." Minorities are placed in a totally different universe, responding to a different morality, possessing different biological

---

[39] For extensive accounts of the radicalism of fear on campus, see Dinesh D' Souza, *Illiberal Education: The Politics of Race and Sex on Campus* (New York: Vintage Books, 1992); and David Horowitz, *The Professors: The 101 Most Dangerous Academics in America* (New York: Regnery, 2006). See also Joseph C. Phillips, *He Talk Like a White Boy: Reflections on Faith, Family, Politics, and Authenticity* (Philadelphia: Running Press, 2006), 243–45.

[40] See Jerome H. Schiele, *Human Services and the Afrocentric Paradigm* (New York: Haworth Press, 2000); Geoffrey L. Greif and Paul H. Ephross, *Group Work with Populations at Risk* (Oxford, UK: Oxford University Press, 2005), chap. 16; Lisa Schreiber, "Overcoming Methodological Elitism: Afrocentrism as a Prototypical Paradigm for Intercultural Research," *International Journal of Intercultural Relations* 24 (September 2000): 651–71.

[41] Cathleen Jordan and Cynthia Franklin, *Clinical Assessment for Social Workers: Quantitative and Qualitative Methods*, 2nd ed. (Chicago: Lyceum Books, 2003), 354.

composition, and even deserving different diagnostic expectations. The so-called experts in the multicultural myth have even devised different "tribe-specific" or Afrocentric tools, with subjective measures designed to assess "the impact of societal oppression on psychological functioning."[42]

Any idea or worldview that challenges Afrocentric notions is a "back-lash" from white supremacists who resist change. Diane Ravitch, because she questions the validity of Afrocentricity, is a "resister" who "conceal[s] her true identity as a defender of white supremacy."[43] Another critic, Mary Lefkowitz, becomes "the leader of a Jewish onslaught" for the same reason.[44] If you are not white and still reject Afrocentrism, you are "a special problem." Either you are truly ignorant and see yourself as "a cop[y] of the Europeans" or you "seek to be appointed overseers on the plantation."[45] For the most part, the engagement of Afrocentrists with their challengers is a full-frontal assault on their integrity—a rhetorical strategy that avoids dealing with the issues by instead attacking personal motives or character.

The Reverend Jeremiah Wright, who gained notoriety during President Obama's first presidential campaign, has repeated a line of thought that deserves condemnation.[46] During one of his sermons, Wright stated his belief that black children's brains, being eminently African, are wired dif-

---

[42] Jordan and Franklin, *Clinical Assessment*, 360–70.

[43] Molefi Kete Asante, "The Afrocentric Idea in Education," *Journal of Negro Education* 60, no. 2 (1991): 173–74.

[44] Tony Martin, *The Jewish Onslaught: Despatches from the Wellesley Battlefront* (Dover, MA: Majority Press, 1993), 30, cited in Mary Lefkowitz, *Not Out of Africa: How Afrocentrism Became an Excuse to Teach Myth as History* (New York: Basic Books, 1996), xii. See also James Michael Brodie, "Feel Good History: Scholars Debate Afrocentrism," *Black Issues in Higher Education* (April 18, 1996).

[45] Molefi Kete Asante, "Afrocentricity: The Theory of Social Change," http://www.assatashakur.org/forum/pan-afrikanism-afrocentricity/1437-afrocentricity-theory-social-change.html.

[46] Wright has many supporters on the left and among American blacks. Among white leftist believers, Tony Campolo is paradigmatic:

> Rev. Wright's words may seem harsh and his style may be strident, but that just may be the way that those of us in the white establishment react. For his African-American brothers and sisters, there may be a different reaction. Many of them will hear him as an angry prophet in the tradition of ancient Israel. To we [sic] white folks, Jeremiah Wright sounds threatening. But we might ask ourselves if we deserve

ferently than are those of whites. Harvard professor Stephan Thernstrom was right to comment that this kind of statement is patently offensive. In fact, it mirrors the racist ideas of southern social scientists of the nineteenth century.[47] Yet Wright's comments are not unique. Over twenty years ago, Arthur Schlesinger provided ample evidence of the prevalence of such views among black educators and sociologists.[48] A whole movement was created to teach black children the so-called Ebonics language and exempt them from certain expectations due to alleged psychological, genetic, and cultural differences.

Afrocentrism is cultural nationalism of a reactionary kind, responding to perceived attacks from Europeans. Its adherents, for the most part, perceive themselves as belonging to a different nation, a Pan-African nation in Diaspora throughout the world. As we can see, a necessary element of Pan-Africanism is disconnection from the mainstream. Separatism within Pan-Africanism, however, has not always been advocated in the formal sense of secession; instead, it vies for recognition, respect, and power.[49] Its mythology has contributed to the idea of particularist multiculturalism by insisting on the existence of a single "African Cultural System" that needs to be adhered to as a way to fight the ingrained and pernicious Eurocentric indoctrination of Western civilization.[50]

---

to be threatened." Tony Campolo, "What Is Liberation Theology?" *The Washington Post* (April 2008)

[47] Thernstrom, in private correspondence with the author, stated:

I found that an especially appalling and disgusting claim, and yet many who alluded to the speech did not have the same reaction. If you really believed this, of course, you would have to favor strictly segregated schools. Moreover, any employer who wanted to hire people with mathematical or other scientific skills would properly view black job applicants with considerable skepticism. *Brown v. Board*, after all, rested on the premise that black and white children did not have different capacities for learning, and should therefore be taught in the same schools.

[48] Schlesinger, *Disuniting of America*, 63–65.

[49] Stephen Howe, *Afrocentrism: Mythical Pasts and Imagined Homes* (London: Verso, 1998), 87–88.

[50] Molefi Kete Assante, *Afrocentricity*, rev., exp. ed. (1988; repr., Chicago: African American Images, 2003), 1–2, 20.

To use Étienne Gilson's formulation, some distinguish in order to unite while others distinguish in order to divide.[51] Social-work students may learn that what are termed African-American family patterns "for the most part are more humanistic and have greater validity than the hollow values of middle-class American society."[52] Blacks are more "person oriented and whites more financial gain oriented." This perceived contrast, although admittedly built with "little rigorous comparative research" to sustain it "points to an important, perhaps pervasive cultural contrast, one that may distinguish large segments of the African American community from the politically and economically dominant white world."[53] These theories drip with victimhood: If my culture is objectively superior but the inferior one dominates, it seems logical to conclude that the latter does so by force.

It is difficult to imagine the creation of an "overlapping consensus" that is readily acceptable to all citizens yet ignores the reality of an overarching American culture and tradition. It could be argued that precisely because different cultural views exist we need a "neutral" liberal theory—one where we can accept both Afrocentric and Eurocentric myths (to use Afrocentric dichotomies). This claim ignores the falsity of such pretended neutrality. Our society assumes ideological multiculturalism as a given, instead of granting the reality of multiculturalism *as a fact* while allowing open discussion of the meaning of true pluralism.

In assuming ideological multiculturalism, we renounce the idea of a true American culture able to serve as a standard of traditional values and around which we can develop a consensus. One of the fundamental errors of Afrocentrism and of radical multiculturalism is similar to the fundamental mistake of right-wing racialists: the conflation of race with culture. Because Western civilization originated in Europe, in this view, America must remain white-dominant—as, apparently, nonwhite individuals are genetically or ethnically incapable of accepting the great contributions of Western culture. Black racialists use the same method: If you are a "person of color" then you must adopt a non-Western cultural identity. Black and white racialists are joined at the hip in their ideology of racial determinism.

---

[51] Étienne Gilson, *God and Philosophy* (New Haven: Yale University Press, 1941), 71.

[52] Barbara B. Solomon, *Black Empowerment: Social Work in Oppressed Communities* (New York: Columbia University Press, 1976), cited in James W. Green, *Cultural Awareness in the Human Services* (Boston: Allyn & Bacon, 1999), 196.

[53] Green, *Cultural Awareness,* 196.

INCLUSIVE MONOCULTURALISM

It seems to me that *inclusive monoculturalism* is a better description of the set of ideas under which an overlapping social consensus may be feasible. The concept embraces a variety of cultural expressions and even compatible comprehensive views within the framework of American political, social, and economic institutions, while retaining the foundational features of our Western civilization heritage. Inclusive monoculturalism is not neutral with respect to culture but affirms the primacy of Western civilization in the formation of our sociopolitical ecology. As individuals from other cultures enter the mainstream of American life, some of their cultural mores may find a place in our midst *if* they are compatible with the American principles of human dignity, rule of law, constitutionalism, democracy, tolerance, and the basic ethical tenets of the Christian faith.[54]

This embrace of other cultures, however, cannot be absolute. Only those aspects of cultures (and of their corresponding comprehensive views) compatible with traditional mores based on our Western cultural heritage are to be accepted as consistent with what philosopher Robert P. George calls a "reasonable moral agreement ... on fair terms of cooperation" among citizens.[55] In other words, only contributions true to type are to be embraced and included in the creation of an American culture that continues to adapt without losing its essential features. American culture is seen in a *foundational* rather than in an *essentialist* fashion. This means that American culture is not viewed as unalterable but as providing a set of cherished basic beliefs.

Inclusive monoculturalism recognizes the need for what Joseph Raz labels "social forms," offering recognition to certain values affirmed through the polity's formal institutions. Public affirmation of a unifying cultural commonality provides a framework of expectations and affirms society's commitment to certain values. Making a social commitment to a given culture provides a boundary within which the value of autonomy is affirmed. That commitment will shape people's cultural options and offer intelligibility to the country's cultural life. As these cultural commitments are social choices, autonomy is not suppressed by providing a boundary.[56]

---

[54] By basic ethical tenets I mean basic understandings of the human person captured in documents such as the Declaration of Independence—which was mostly successful in reflecting an anthropology consistent with Christian natural law.

[55] George, *In Defense of Natural Law*, 200.

[56] Raz, *Morality of Freedom*, 164–67.

There is, however, a *private* moral pluralism that affirms the existence of diverse valuable forms of life. One can affirm the goodness of certain private cultural expressions and the possibility of eventually incorporating them (or not) into the general culture without having to accept *every* cultural expression. This is not akin to relativism as it recognizes that there may be unworthy cultural expressions.[57]

Individuals in their private affairs are free to practice other particular cultural expressions. They are also responsible for their preservation, as the state neither discourages them nor presses for their inclusion. As individuals live their lives in free association with others, certain new expressions will become part of our heritage without any attempt by the state to direct these impulses. Other compatible expressions will remain among those who continue to value them without necessarily expanding their sphere of recognition. No ethnic group or race is enthroned over others.

Education under Inclusive Monoculturalism

Students in publicly funded schools and universities ought to learn extensively about other cultures as those cultures really are. There should be no teaching of ideology under the guise of teaching about cultures. Nativism as a system of thought that attempts to demean other cultures must disappear from the curriculum because to affirm your country's culture does not entail denigrating other cultures, especially as cultures are always encountering each other and shifting. The dogma of innate superiority is a tool of oppression as much as the *a priori* assertion of cultural equality is. Even so, cultures are not equal and historical competition demonstrates the superiority of certain cultures.[58] Learning about other cultures demands respect and honesty in the task of appreciating the features, beliefs, values, social patterns, human behavior, and history of diverse civilizations.

This important learning exercise ought to be performed by students who are intensively taught about the features of their republican and democratic society and about the Western heritage that formed it. They are to explore other ideas *as Americans*. If freedom and democracy are to be foundational

[57] On the idea of pluralistic perfectionism and autonomy see George, *Making Men Moral*, 162–73.

[58] Thomas Sowell, *Race and Culture: A World View* (New York: Basic Books, 1994), chap. 8.

to the teaching of history, students at all levels ought to learn about how America is their beacon in spite of the twists and turns of our history. The inculcation of national identity must continue to be an important, although not the exclusive, purpose of the teaching of history and the communication of values.[59]

Black history, as an integral part of Western civilization, must be an important component of an American history class that is honest about the past. The contributions of black Americans and other minorities ought not to be portrayed as marginal wherever they were more than that, and the horrid chapters of our racial history must not be skipped or minimized. But a study of our history that is more of an indictment than an honest examination is dogma, not inquiry. Schools and universities must treat every subject as assisting in the creation of a unified civil worldview that transcends group differences and serves as a key to participation in building our civilization.[60] Social science departments in publicly funded colleges and universities need to have a balanced faculty and academic curriculum, trying the best they can to offer various ideological points of view.[61]

By treating black history as a component of American history, we avoid the compartmentalization of culture—a dissection that only increases tension and divisiveness. Multicultural ideologies can be examined in the classroom to assess their merits but they should not become institutional policy. Clubs, fraternities, and sororities that discriminate based on race must be eliminated. Academic departments discriminating against scholars who differ ideologically must be dismantled in order to create balanced ones. Such radicalism and divisiveness now pervading the academic world in no way helps to create a climate of tolerance and commonality; on the contrary, it separates students into tribes.

---

[59] Education in national identity must emphasize the founding of a new experiment in human social interaction, an experiment in ordered liberty that is expressed through a set of institutional arrangements. See Gregg, *On Ordered Liberty*, 45–47.

[60] Diane Ravitch and Maris Vinovskis, *Learning from the Past: What History Teaches Us about School Reform* (Baltimore: Johns Hopkins University Press, 1995), 113.

[61] See for example, Barry Mehler, "African American Racism in the Academic Community," *The Review of Education* 15 (Fall 1993).

INCLUSIVE MONOCULTURALISM AND CHRISTIANITY

Inclusive monoculturalism values freedom and autonomy as much as it values the ethical tenets of the Christian faith. These tenets find their basic expression in the Golden Rule, which instructs us to treat others as we would have them treat us, and in the commandments to love God and to love our neighbor. Resisting the recognition of any denomination as the state's national church remains foundational, but faith itself is not confined to the private sphere. In our cultural proposal, Christianity is recognized as deeply entwined in the fabric of the culture and the country.[62] In essence, the contest is between those who defend the power of the mind to autonomously *create* its own rule and establish its own protocols and those who believe in the power of the mind to *discover* objective truth and the duty of man to live by it. Today, as ever, the issue is *what truth is*. If we are to engage that formidable issue, we simply cannot dispense with the natural law.

This proposal does not insist on the acceptance of religious authority or revelation as the basis for consensus; instead, it merely recognizes the need for Christian ethics to fill the empty shell of procedural democracy. We must affirm that "the secular public square, properly understood, is a Christian legacy and one that requires an ongoing Christian presence to remain true to itself."[63] People of faith, as well as secularists, must present their views in language that is accessible to all. At the same time, public reason cannot be accepted as a device to exclude certain views because religious people adhere to them. Principles of natural law are considered natural, "because, and only because," as John Finnis observes, "they are rational ... and thus accessible to beings whose nature includes rational capacities."[64] Here I must

---

[62] See Larry Schweikart, *48 Lies About American History (That You Probably Learned in School)* (New York: Sentinel, 2008), 69–74. The recognition of Christianity as a formative value ought not descend into a propagandistic affirmation of America as a Christian nation that fails to appreciate the complexity and variety of influences that shaped it. It is simply an examination of historical facts and an appreciation of some foundational natural-law principles.

[63] Nick Spencer, *Doing God: A Future for Faith in the Public Square* (London: Theos, 2006), 38.

[64] John Finnis, "Abortion, Natural Law, and Public Reason" in *Natural Law and Public Reason*, ed. Robert P. George and Christopher Wolfe (Washington, DC: Georgetown University Press, 2000), 78.

join Jacques Maritain in asserting that "[t]he philosophical foundations of the Rights of man is Natural Law. Sorry that we cannot find another word!"[65]

At present, we are not preventing other faiths or comprehensive views from having a place in the public square, nor are we excluding and bullying them in the manner that modern liberalism excludes Christianity. Inclusive monoculturalism is neither chauvinist nor relativist; it is not neutral nor oppressive. It is, however, uncompromising with regard to the human person *qua* person as understood by the natural law tradition. Inclusive monoculturalism stands on the side of the central tradition of natural law accepted by Aristotle,[66] Thomas Jefferson, Thomas Aquinas, and Martin Luther King Jr. It affirms as foundational the Declaration of Independence and realizes that every human person, across the spectrum of diverse mores and ways of existence, participates, through reason, in the eternal law of God.[67] Such participation is the foundation of our shared humanity, the grounding of rights, and the precondition for social cohesion.

The choice before us is not between the constraints of a given comprehensive doctrine and the safety of unachievable neutrality. The choice is between the affirmation of a given, albeit inclusive, culture and the expansive, yet shallow, sea of relativistic multiculturalism. An inclusive theory of culture built on the virtues of traditional Christian ethics and the values of the American founding grounds the concept of rights on morality, not

---

[65] Jacques Maritain, *Man and the State* (Chicago: University of Chicago Press, 1951), 80.

[66] In book 1 of his *Politics* and in book 7 of the *Nicomachean Ethics*, Aristotle speaks of slavery. There he argues that slavery is the natural condition of some, not simply a social construct. Greeks naturally rule over barbarians. The barbarian is one incapable of self-rule but, unlike mere beasts, cognizant of such need to be ruled. Here is not the place for a detailed discussion on the great debate about Aristotle's view of slavery. The key is that our sensibilities are anachronistic. I agree with Orlando Patterson on this matter:

> I think far too much, in the way of moral judgment, has been made of Aristotle's comments on the institution. What he has left us is a first-rate sociology of it, written from the viewpoint of someone who, like nearly everyone else in his day, assumed that it was essential for economic and social life.

Orlando Patterson, *Freedom in the Making of Western Culture* (New York: Basic Books, 1991), 162.

[67] Thomas Aquinas, *Summa Theologiae* Ia IIae Q. 91, art. 2.

on convention. Such a theory can affirm as always valid condemnations of injustice, violence, irrationality, and prejudice. It can also affirm goods of human nature such as life, play, beauty, knowledge, self-determination, integrity, authenticity, religion, patriotism, friendship, and self-fulfillment.[68] There is certainly space in a constitutional, representative democracy for informal encounter and informal recognition of varied cultural expressions consistent with inclusive monoculturalism. As ethnic identities are neither essential nor static, and individual identity is formed by varied "identities," the best way to respect persons is to confer on them, *as persons*, formal rights. Individuals ought to have the space to develop as they see fit within their communities, while society holds tight to the values of a Western tradition that respects certain goods of human nature that transcend the particularities of culture.

By expanding the basic understanding of what is reasonable, we increase the diversity of voices in the public square. "None of the Founders," says Mark Noll, a leading scholar of American religion, "interpreted the First Amendment as prohibiting religiously grounded arguments for general public policy."[69] Freedom of religion was never intended as freedom *from* religion but rather as protection for the free expression of diverse Christian views without the establishment of a state church. Three years after signing the Declaration of Independence, Thomas Jefferson presented a bill before the Virginia Assembly on the matter of religious freedom. The bill clearly explained that religious liberty simply meant that individuals are free to believe or not believe and that they may not be coerced, punished, or unduly burdened by governmental impositions to join any given church. Any coercive actions, he wrote, "are a departure from the plan of the holy author of our religion, who being lord of both body and mind, yet chose not to propagate it by coercions on either as was in his Almighty power to do, but to extend it by its influence on reason alone."[70]

---

[68] Grisez and Shaw, *Beyond the New Morality*, 64–75.

[69] Mark A. Noll, *A History of Christianity in the United States and Canada* (1992; repr., Grand Rapids: Eerdmans, 2003), 148.

[70] Edwin Scott Gaustad and Mark A. Noll, *A Documentary History of Religion in America: To 1877* (Grand Rapids: Eerdmans, 2003), 230–31.

FIGHTING TILL THE END

We cannot deny that the world is changing in ways that those committed to a traditional Judeo-Christian worldview would say is not for the best. In spite of the demise of communism, the West seems unable or unwilling to assert truth claims and recoils at the thought that, after all, we were right. Intellectuals in the West have simply ceased to believe in the values of our civilization. They seem bored with orthodoxy—or at least with the Judeo-Christian type—and excited by the new orthodoxy of secularism. Friedrich Hayek noted this intellectual shift generations ago: "The mood of [Western] intellectual leaders has long been characterized by disillusionment with its principles, disparagement of its achievements, and exclusive concern with the creation of 'better worlds.'"[71]

Bristling with ideas of collective victimhood, secularist orthodoxy continues to overshadow and weaken free-market economies and societies once committed to the Judeo-Christian worldview. It is tempting to think that the secularist barbarians have already won the clash of civilizations.[72] Seemingly, we are no longer slouching toward Gomorrah—we have become Gomorrah.

In reality, it may be the other way around. In spite of the apparently overwhelming and combined efforts of major media and state power, the paradise of determinism has not arrived. The socialist project, ably dissected by Joshua Muravchik,[73] has created nothing but devastation. The little utopias of socialism have disintegrated and the only thing left is the stench of the dead they left behind. From Robert Owen's nineteenth-century utopian communities to the failures of democratic socialism and from the horrors of the Gulag to the debacle of Third World socialist experiments, theories grounded on determinism have failed to bring about heaven on earth.

RESOLVING THE TWONESS

Abraham Lincoln criticized the *Dred Scott* decision precisely on the grounds that the framers of the Constitution established the principle that all men are created equal—even if this principle, as a right, was not at the time enjoyed

[71] F. A. Hayek, *The Constitution of Liberty* (Chicago: University of Chicago Press, 1960), 2.

[72] James Kurth "The Real Clash," *The National Interest* 3 (Fall 1994), 3–15.

[73] Joshua Muravchik, *Heaven on Earth: The Rise and Fall of Socialism* (San Francisco: Encounter Books, 2002).

by all. Our Declaration of Independence recognizes the foundational principle of "the Laws of Nature and Nature's God" in part because there are certain understandings of rights and culture that are rationally superior to others—rationally superior, for example, to any understanding that rejects the ontological reality of rights.[74]

Inclusive monoculturalism recognizes the diversity of expressions and ways of life compatible with a respect for human goods. It sits squarely on the side of principles that better secure rights across the spectrum of human social existence. Furthermore, it understands well what it means to be an American. America was a nation "conceived," an idea for the ages, a departure from the evolving nations of Europe or the tribal identities of non-Western cultures and nations.[75] Other nations are tied to long-evolving cultures and, at times, long lines of genetic preservations. Neither whiteness nor blackness can ever define America. America is defined by the values we hold dear, the ones we conceive in our minds and decide to accept.

Blacks, more than any other group, have a right to make that choice, being members of a group forcibly brought here. It is precisely that nonvolitional violent act that reveals how profoundly American is the decision that blacks make to become Americans. The existential *twoness* that Du Bois described is resolved in the affirmation of individual dignity, in the existential imperative of self-affirmation by making the choice to be an American—a choice that has already been made by the great majority of us. There is thus no more authentically American group than blacks. "Even where Afro-Americans appear to be very different," says Orlando Patterson, "closer examination reveals that they are merely emphasizing, sometimes to extremes, certain values and traditions that are very American."[76]

This is why Paul Johnson is correct in calling America the greatest of all human adventures. It has been an arduous and difficult adventure, one where grievous wrongs have mixed with magnificent accomplishments and where unreason and hate have worked alongside goodness, justice, and love. Johnson asks whether America has risen from the injustices of its origins,

---

[74] George, *Clash of Orthodoxies*, 155.

[75] David Horowitz, *Left Illusions: An Intellectual Odyssey* (Dallas: Spence, 2003), 196.

[76] Orlando Patterson, *The Ordeal of Integration: Progress and Resentment in America's "Racial" Crisis* (New York: Basic Civitas Books, 1997), 182.

and the answer is yes. Has America become an exemplar for humanity? The answer again is yes.[77]

In the opening of his *Confessions*, Saint Augustine gave us one of the most powerful lines in all of Western literature: "Our hearts are restless until they rest in Thee, O Lord."[78] While traveling in the far country, we hear the echo of God's voice calling us to himself—calling us to turn back from our wandering in the darkness of a life lived without a sure destination. Regaining our senses and our memory, we take painful steps toward the Promised Land. Refusing to be misled by intemperate calls to refuse our destiny, we finally arrive where we belong, and that place is not Africa. Turning back from the diaspora of our minds, which calls us to follow other paths of self-recognition, we realize that the land of milk and honey was always here in our midst. Our restless search for a resolution to our twoness gives way to peaceful acceptance that America, after all, is home.

---

[77] Paul Johnson, *A History of the American People* (New York: Perennial, 1997), 4.

[78] Augustine of Hippo, *Confessions*, bk. 1.

7

AMERICA THE RACIST?

---

*Blacks now increasingly experience a
sense of alarm, a turning back of the
clock, a renewed sense of apartness,
of being outsiders in a hostile world.*

—**Robert Charles Smith**
We Have No Leaders

As a long term member of the NAACYMN[1] and, as an African American Catholic, I feel that it is my right to bring to your attention the negative feelings and attitude of Mr. Hernandez in regard to American blacks of all races and ethnic cultures." The letter, dated October 14, 2003, and addressed to the bishop of my diocese, was from the presiding chair of the Florida Conference of Offices of Black Catholic Ministry. I will never forget the day. As I read the letter, a torrent of anger engulfed me. I sat there at my desk stock-still, trying to calm down. I could not believe that anyone would accuse me of sentiments so utterly foreign to me.

Upon reflection, I understood that I should have anticipated it. Racialists long ago recognized the power of racial shame, and it was seldom exercised with a moderate hand. Deviating from the norms of racialist understandings of history and identity means social death.

---

[1] The National African American Catholic Youth Ministry Network.

THE ENEMY WITHIN

When I received the letter, I had been the director of a diocesan Office of Black Catholic Ministry for only a couple of months. Just a few weeks before the letter's arrival I had my only encounter with its author. In a five-minute phone conversation, she welcomed me and expressed a commitment to help me secure funds for the office so that I could pay its dues to the Florida Conference of Offices for Black Catholic Ministry.

At the time of the call, I was assumed to be a "brother," aligned with the vision of blacks as victims of a racist country. By the time of the letter a few weeks later, I had been excommunicated from the racial brotherhood. The change of heart was "due to the fact," the letter explained, "that the majority of [the Florida Conference's] literature contains concerns of racism which has had, and is still today having a direct and devastating effect on the black community."[2] In her view, I was insufficiently sensitive to these concerns of racism. I was summarily rejected and my office decreed "non-participating."

The charge was made, as she put it, "in light of my disinterest" in racial injustice. I had, she observed, "'very acutely disregarded" the United States bishops' pastoral letters on racism. These charges were made without ever engaging in dialogue with me about these matters. I had never privately or publicly stated any opinion about the Catholic bishops' views on racism or about their pastoral letters on the subject. Even so, she claimed that I had contradicted the bishops in my "public and private words."[3]

I can only assume that the "public words" were articles that I had published in various newspapers in which I expressed opinions like those contained in this book: that racism is not the preeminent obstacle to progress for American blacks and that affirmative action is not an effective means

[2] Letter to the author, October 14, 2003. This separate letter to me, which announced her decision to attack my standing as an official in black Catholic ministry, contained a copy of the letter she sent to several bishops and other Catholic leaders (quoted in the first paragraph above).

[3] It may be relevant to note that, even if my views were in tension with those expressed by the bishops in their pastoral letters, there is still no ground for the charge that I contradicted Catholic Church teaching. As a general rule, judgments of fact and policy recommendations contained in pastoral letters from the national conference of bishops are intended to be prudential assessments derived from official teaching, not definitive declarations that are binding on the faithful. The most recent pastoral letter that I was accused of violating was published in 1984—nineteen years before my "offense."

for overcoming it. These opinions were evidently considered to be heresy, contrary to the teachings of the Catholic Church.[4]

A common error manifested in many American religious institutions as they attempt to deal with racism is to assert that fighting racism demands specific political positions on issues such as affirmative action and welfare. That there may be a range of acceptable prudential choices in dealing with racial issues is implicitly denied. The fact is that one can stand side by side with another person in the binding principle that racism is evil and, at the same time, be far apart in one's analysis of specific policy and social issues. The question of the relative importance of racism as a force in contemporary American society is an example of an empirical question that can be disputed among individuals who still share a basic set of values.

My refusal to toe the line on liberal, race-based policies not only set me apart from most American blacks, it also separated me from most blacks who shared my own faith. (Black American Catholics, it has sometimes been said, are a "minority within a minority." My conservative views make me a minority within a minority within a minority.) My long record of full commitment to serve blacks in active ministry in blighted areas of southwest Florida was deemed unimportant. My black ancestry, my happy marriage to my beloved wife—a proud African-American woman—and my (two, at the time) beautiful black children did not matter either. I refused to accept my place in the plantation of victimhood and that made me a pariah.

When I read the accusatory letter I felt the dagger of shame piercing through my heart, and I wept. I cried because shame works on your emotions. It is intended to demoralize the enemy and send him into silence. It attempts to eliminate your views from public debate and allow the gatekeepers of blackness to pretend that you and your ideas do not exist. Few openly dare to resist the powerful pull of group identity. The racialists are aware of this reality, and I am not the only one to notice that they draw here on an ancient stratagem, articulated long ago in a different context by the Roman historian Tacitus: "Segregate the freed, and you will only show how few free-born there are."[5]

---

[4] As for the "private words," since I had never spoken with the official about these matters, I must suppose that some acquaintances communicated to her opinions that I had expressed in conversation. It is likely that they also apprised her of the newspaper articles.

[5] Tacitus, *Annals*, trans. Michael Grant, p. 13.27 cited in Orlando Patterson, *Freedom in the Making of Western Culture* (New York: Basic Books, 1991), 228.

The fear of losing group identity in a perennial battle of "us against them" makes those who dare to challenge the received liberal/radical orthodoxy the "enemies within," Krug barely tolerated and at the same time reviled.[6] Rejection is a ritual that expresses a strong desire for group affirmation and solidarity in "the struggle." The ultimate rejection of those who will not conform to the received wisdom is akin to the rite of slaughter, the sharing in a cannibalistic feast that cements communal solidarity.

RACISM EVERYWHERE

America remains a racist country that cannot be redeemed.[7] Racism is not receding but transmogrifying and the task of communion described in the previous chapter is impossible. These are the claims of black intellectuals who consistently portray racism as intractable and essential to understanding the core of the society that they sometimes call "Amerikkka."[8] The definition of racism has been altered from a moral, attitudinal, and *individual* concept into the idea of a pervasive *institutional* phenomenon, a structural device difficult to prove

---

[6] The term derives from the customs of the Tupinamba tribes of the Amazon. Prisoners of war were at times admitted to the group as "enemies within" whose lives were momentarily spared, sometimes even to the point of apparent acceptance within the tribe. Eventually, they were freed, recaptured, abused, brutally murdered, and eaten. The need for group affirmation against an external enemy from which the slave initially came was a powerful reason for warfare, enslavement, and the cannibalistic slaughter of the slave. The internal enemy threatened the harmony of group commonality, and his presence harmed the institutional group identity by offering definition and solidarity. Eventually, the tension had to be relieved through the destruction of the enemy within. See Orlando Patterson, *Freedom in the Making of Western Culture*, 14.

[7] This fit-all explanation is not new. In his *Writings* (1903), W. E. B. Du Bois had identified the "color line" as America's major problem. In his autobiography *Dusk and Dawn* (1940; repr., New York: Schocken Books, 1968), he exhibited the same pessimistic attitude toward America in spite of great progress. Du Bois ended up losing faith in America, becoming a Communist, and even abandoning the country.

[8] The satiric misspelling still lives in the culture, especially in rap music. "Gangsta Rap" performer Ice Cube's album *Amerikkka's Most Wanted* is an indictment against American society for the conditions of the ghetto underclass. In another example of how racialists on the left and the right are two sides of the same coin, the Ku Klux Klan also uses the word to assert its belief in a racist America.

but more politically useful.[9] By defining racism as institutional, there is less need to demonstrate causation and verify its effects using specific instances. White supremacy, says bell hooks, "continue[s] to shape perspectives on reality and to inform the social status of black people."[10] White supremacy is so internalized in attitudes and systems that it is an inextricable part of what America is.

Michael Eric Dyson claims that "[f]rom the very beginning of our nation's existence, the discursive defense and political logic of American democracy have spawned white dominance as the foundational myth of American society."[11] Andrew Hacker speaks of the agony of black Americans' having to explain to their children "that they will never be altogether accepted, that they will always be regarded warily, if not with suspicion or hostility."[12] Derrick Bell posits that "racism is an integral, permanent and indestructible component of this society."[13] Worse, there is little hope for improvement. Bell contends that "our careers, even our lives, are threatened because of our color," and Carl Rowan asserts that "racism remains a terrible curse in this society ... and nothing in sight suggests that the curse will soon vanish."[14] Even—or especially—those who have enjoyed extraordinary success in this nation offer derision rather than gratitude in return. Emmy-award winning singer Alicia Keyes says that she "sees lies in that flag."[15] This is the vision articulated by the black activists and intellectuals who maintain great influence over many blacks in America.

---

[9] Robert C. Smith, *Racism in the Post-Civil Rights Era: Now You See It, Now You Don't* (New York: State University of New York Press, 1995), chap. 2.

[10] See bell hooks, *Talking Back: Thinking Feminist, Thinking Black* (New York: Routledge, 2015), 114.

[11] Ronald E. Chennault, "Giving Whiteness a Black Eye: An Interview with Michael Eric Dyson," in *White Reign: Deploying Whiteness in America*, ed. Joe L. Kincheloe et al. (New York: St. Martin's 1998), 301.

[12] Andrew Hacker, *Two Nations: Black and White, Separate, Hostile, Unequal* (New York: Charles Scribners's Sons, 1992), 34.

[13] Derrick Bell, *Faces at the Bottom of the Well* (New York: Basic Books, 1992), 10.

[14] Bell, *Faces at the Bottom of the Well*, 3. Carl Rowan, "Tiger Woods Is Not the Answer," *New York Post* (June 18, 1997), 27.

[15] Touré, "Alicia Keys: The Next Queen of Soul," *Rolling Stone* (November 8, 2001).

Misunderstanding the Founding

For the "racism everywhere" crowd, the United States is rotten at its roots and must be refashioned from the bottom up. Joe R. Feagin believes that our founding documents are so racist that we need to write new ones: "Even a brief critical reflection on the founding political documents of U.S. society and on how they were made can lead one to the view that these undemocratically generated documents are in great need of comprehensive revision, if not complete replacement."[16]

One source of this common view is the prevalent explanation given to the "three-fifths compromise," one of the key events in the course of the framing and ratification of the U.S. Constitution. Benjamin Hooks, former president of the NAACP, claims that our Constitution counted blacks as less than full human beings, describing a provision that reduced a black American to "three-fifths of a person."[17] Distinguished historian John Hope Franklin, who must know better, nonetheless falls into the same pattern of speaking, stating that the founding fathers "degraded the human spirit by equating five black men with three white men."[18] Similarly, scholar Kenneth W. Warren argues that the compromise affirms America's jurisprudential history of viewing black individuals as "at once human and yet something less than fully human."[19]

There is one problem with this common understanding of the famous constitutional compromise, which seemingly everyone in the black community "knows" to be an irrefutable demonstration of America's racist foundation. It is inaccurate.

The constitutional convention met in Philadelphia in 1787 with slavery as a principal issue. Southern states made clear that agreement on a framework for union was impossible without allowing for the practice of slavery. A controversy then arose regarding representation in the House. Southern

---

[16] Joe R. Feagin, *Systemic Racism: A Theory of Oppression* (New York: CRC Press, 2006), 297.

[17] Cited in Robert A. Goldwin, *Why Blacks, Women, and Jews Are Not Mentioned in the Constitution, and Other Unorthodox Views* (Washington, DC: AEI Press, 1990), 10.

[18] Cited in Goldwin, *Why Blacks, Women, and Jews*.

[19] Kenneth W. Warren, "Troubled Black Humanity in the Souls of Black Folk and the Autobiography of an Ex-Colored Man," in *The Cambridge Companion to American Realism and Naturalism*, ed. Donald Pizer (Cambridge: Cambridge University Press, 1995), 270–71.

states, wanting to strengthen their pro-slavery coalition, supported counting the slaves when it came to apportioning congressional seats, and not counting them for purposes of taxation. Northern delegates refused to agree to count the slaves at all for representation in the House, as this would give an enormous advantage to southern states with large slave populations. Why should they be counted at all if southern law considered them property? Besides, counting the slaves would only encourage more slave trade.[20]

Thus, it was *pro-slavery southerners* who wanted to count slaves fully, not because they were ahead-of-their-times champions of black dignity but because they wanted to use slave populations in an instrumental way to bolster the number of congressional representatives from slave states. This would, among other purposes, further the goal of keeping slavery intact in the South. If none of the slaves had been counted, the South would have received only 41 percent of House seats. If all had been counted as full persons, it would have had 50 percent, giving the South much more influence over national policies.

The impasse represented a true dilemma for Northern anti-slavery delegates. Robert A. Goldwin summarizes:

> If on the one hand the continuation of slavery was unavoidable, and on the other hand it was a contradiction of the most fundamental principles of the Constitution the delegates wanted and thought necessary, what could principled antislavery delegates do? One effective and consistent thing they could do was try to make the political base of slavery as weak as possible, to diminish its influence and improve the chances of eradicating it sometime in the future.[21]

To that effect, Congressman James Wilson, an abolitionist from Pennsylvania, offered a compromise. Wilson was a signer of the Declaration who would be among the country's first Supreme Court justices. Instead of counting the entire number of slaves for the purposes of calculating representation in the House, only three-fifths of the slave count was to be added to the rest of the population of a state. The net result of the compromise was to increase the Southern congressional delegation only to 47 percent, thus denying the South dominance.

[20] Edwin Meese III, ed., *The Heritage Guide to the Constitution* (Washington, DC: Regnery, 1995), 55.

[21] Goldwin, *Why Blacks, Women, and Jews*, 11.

It is important to note that the Constitution thus stipulated that the number of free persons *of any race* be counted in full, including thousands of Northern free blacks. The framers of the Constitution thus implicitly recognized the equality of black and white. What they were not willing to do was permit the dominance in national affairs of a region where this equality was viscerally denied by slavery. In sum, the three-fifths compromise was not a signal of consensus that a black man was worth less than a white man. It was instead the result of an effort to limit the influence of southern states, or, more exactly, an expression of *disapproval* of slavery. The racialists of today, therefore, are not only wrong about the three-fifths compromise and what it tells us about the American founding; they have the matter completely backward.

The great black abolitionist Frederick Douglass understood the alternatives involved and supported the compromise as "a downright disability laid upon the slaveholding states" by depriving them of "two-fifths of their natural basis of representation."[22] He understood that, at times, trade-offs are wiser, more effective, and more just than the foolish pursuit of utopian "cosmic justice."

The founders understood that if a unified nation was to be realized, securing the freedom of the slaves at that time was not possible. They managed, nonetheless, to create a document with basic principles of justice that would eventually free the slaves. The document, as enacted, called slaves *persons*, not three-fifths of persons.[23] This is not to say that the document was perfect on the issue of slavery. Two other clauses provided for the return

---

[22] Frederick Douglass, "The American Constitution and the Slave: An Address Delivered in Glasgow, Scotland, on 26 March 1860," in *The Frederick Douglass Papers*, ed. John Blassingame (New Haven: Yale University Press, 1979–1992), 3:352, cited in Dinesh D'Souza, *What's So Great About America* (Washington: Regnery Publishing, 2002), 110.

[23] Again, *the aggregate* of slaves was not going to be counted fully. This cannot be translated to individual self-worth as that was not the issue at hand. The fact that free blacks were counted as everyone else demonstrates that the issue was not individual self-worth. This section of the Constitution states that slaves are persons:

> Representatives and direct Taxes shall be apportioned among the several States which may be included within this Union, according to their respective Numbers, which shall be determined by adding to the whole Number of free Persons, including those bound to Service for a Term of Years, and excluding Indians not taxed, three fifths of all other Persons.

of fugitive slaves and delayed any congressional action against the slave trade for twenty years. But these, too, were unavoidable concessions to slave states and did not represent an affirmation of the fundamental inferiority of black Americans. These compromises were not the expressions of a country inherently racist and fully committed to the institution of slavery. They were evidence of a country that was *struggling* with the scourge of human bondage.

A CONSENSUS OF VICTIMHOOD

Today, racialists portray every public issue related to race as tied to the structure of a country founded on racism. Every misfortune falling on blacks is attributed to the inherent reality of a racist nation. The paucity of public discourse on race offers no space for an honest discussion of the nature of racism. Ours is a nation led by a black president, where scholarships are targeted to blacks, and where blacks are prominent in the media and the arts. Ours is a country with hate crime laws, with a public square where the whisper of any unapproved racial assertion constitutes professional suicide, with institutionalized corporate diversity, with a powerful media aligned with diversity and political correctness, and with an academic realm permeated with the ideas of multiculturalism and all kinds of racialisms. In this land of idolized black athletes and movie stars, where most blacks are not only not poor but constitute one of the wealthiest human groups on earth, we are told that blacks cannot find a place.

In some circles, it is deemed unseemly, if not racist, to challenge the idea that America is a racist country. This was clearly the view of those who judged me unfit to serve in black Catholic ministry. The assertion that America is far ahead in conquering the evil of racial oppression is suppressed by the weapon of indignation. We are told that even after the civil rights movement and the progress steadily experienced by most blacks even before that movement, "blacks now increasingly experience a sense of alarm, a turning back of the clock, a renewed sense of apartness, of being outsiders in a hostile world."[24] A dichotomy between action and rhetoric on race issues provides a useful alibi for leaders who can remind us of their statements about personal responsibility here or there while the entire thrust of their public enterprise remains their fight against "institutional racism."

---

[24] Robert Charles Smith, *We Have No Leaders: African-Americans in the Post-Civil Rights Era* (New York: SUNY Press, 1996), 280.

One theory to explain this dichotomy is that blacks no longer truly believe in the supposed consensus of victimhood and that they are only wearing that mask as a strategic device.[25] It is also possible that victimhood resides mostly at the bottom rung of the community where despair reigns. However, it is arguably the case that victimization exerts its most oppressive influence in the thoughts of the elite. In the alliance between professional victimologists and their "protected communities," the experts in victimology hold the key to a new vision of black progress.

Not even the election and reelection of a president of African descent has moved those who see America as the epitome of racism to question their premises. Confronted with overwhelming data that demonstrate consistent attitudinal changes in the way whites perceive blacks, liberal scholars simply discard the statistics as unreliable due to respondents' purported unwillingness to report racist attitudes on surveys. Robert C. Smith is typical: "This decline is not necessarily a decline in such attitudes, but perhaps a decline in the willingness to express such attitudes in the quasi-public forum that is a sample survey. That is, in the post-civil rights era it has become less socially acceptable to express racist attitudes in public."[26]

Is it not equally possible, or even more likely, that the unwillingness to express racist public opinions is indicative of a decline in racist attitudes? The evidence suggests exactly that. Poll data has been consistently indicating a significant shift in white attitudes toward blacks since the early 1950s, pointing to behavioral changes long before the expression of racist attitudes became "less socially acceptable," but this narrative contrasts with the one that contemporary racialists embrace. The civil rights movement is presented as a revolution that initiated change in our society instead of as the product of a society that was *already* changing.[27]

Because racism is conceived of as being structural and institutional, data showing black achievement cannot alter the deterministic vision that America is racist, whiteness rules, and every problem can be explained in terms of oppression. If blacks open a door, it was because whites allowed it for some hidden motive, and any gain will always be in jeopardy. If a

---

[25] John McWhorter, *Authentically Black: Essays for the Black Silent Majority* (New York: Gotham, 2004), 2.

[26] Smith, *We Have No Leaders*, 38.

[27] For data, see Stephan Thernstrom and Abigail Thernstrom, *America in Black and White: One Nation, Indivisible* (New York: Simon and Schuster, 1999), chap. 4.

door is not opening, whites are preventing progress. If more blacks become successful, still no amount of individual success can mitigate our collective oppression. If whites accept certain black cultural expressions, they are co-opting our culture. If they do not accept that expression, they are openly racist. There is no way out of this vicious circle.

I am reminded of my conversation with a black pastor, shortly after Barack Obama's first presidential election, about the significance of Obama's victory in terms of American racial attitudes. He was unmoved in his view of America as racist to the core: "Racism continues as usual. America has always accepted the black 'superstar,' that's all."

In this distorted vision of race relations, if whites are incapable of anything but racism, the opposite holds true for blacks. Coramae Richey Mann argues that the lack of institutional power makes it "definitionally impossible for blacks to be identified as racist."[28] This kind of reasoning, of necessity, places the basis for an assessment of black reality on external forces affecting blacks. Any component other than racism is subordinated to the forces of evil unleashed upon the community. In addition, "behavioral racism" is said to be connected with the unwillingness of whites to accept liberal policies geared to remedy institutional racism.[29] Whites who oppose collectivist and redistributive policies are, by definition, racist. Blacks who dare to challenge the paradigm of perennial racism and collectivist solutions are even worse: traitors.

The Ghettoization of Black Intellectual Life

One of the effects of the stark division between black and white that racialists promote is the ghettoization of black culture—the deliberate separation of black ways of life from mainstream American experience. At the street level, every aspect of mainstream culture is seen with suspicion and black kids grow up thinking that speaking standard English or liking "the books" is somehow unauthentic. Being black has become synonymous with reeling in defeat.[30]

---

[28] C. Mann, "The Reality of a Racist Criminal Justice System," *Criminal Justice Research Bulletin* 3, no. 5 (1987): 2.

[29] Smith, *Racism in the Post-Civil Rights Era*, 41–42.

[30] See McWhorter, *Losing the Race: Self-Sabotage in Black America* (New York: Harper Prennial, 2001) for an extensive analysis of black attitudes toward education.

Yet, ghettoization extends to academia as well. Tales of discrimination, no matter how absurd or exaggerated, are accepted at face value. White academics are held hostage to this kind of faulty academic work by the threat of being labeled racists if they even dare to pose legitimate questions.[31] As they are invested with power and privilege for being white, they must accept the insider's views of discrimination as a given. The members of oppressed groups possess "epistemic privilege." This supposed privilege offers minorities "more immediate, subtle, and critical knowledge of their oppression" than that which is accessible to white people. They may not be able to articulate their oppression well as they, being victims, have been denied access to education. Therefore, emotions and feelings replace reason as the principal tools in assessing instances of discrimination.[32]

Intellectual debate is absolutely necessary in the arena of academic inquiry. The problem in black academia is that all viewpoints are approached according to strict sociopolitical demarcations.[33] Thoughtful dissenting opinions are treated with hostility if they are not in line with the hypothesis of injustice and oppression, white racism, and the need for state intervention. This corruption of the ideal of a genuine academic setting where true inquiry is fostered has demoralized many within the universities who have felt the oppressive hold of political correctness and ideology.[34]

---

[31] See Mary Lefkowitz, *Not Out of Africa* (New York: Basic Books, 1997), 2–4. Lefkowitz offers a good discussion of cultural history at 48–52.

[32] Beulah Compton and Burt Galaway, *Social Work Processes*, 6th ed. (Pacific Grove, CA: Brooks/Cole, 1999), 244–45.

[33] Many years ago, F. A. Hayek wrote the following regarding these collectivist intellectuals:

> The general intellectual climate which this produces, the spirit of complete cynicism as regards to truth which it engenders, the loss of the sense of even the meaning of truth, the disappearance of the spirit of independent inquiry and of the belief in the power of rational conviction, the way in which differences of opinion in every branch of knowledge become political issues to be decided by authority, are all things which one must personally experience—no short description can convey their extent.

F. A. Hayek, *The Road to Serfdom* (Chicago: University of Chicago Press, 1944), 179.

[34] Elizabeth Fox-Genovese and Elisabeth Lasch-Quinn, *Reconstructing History: The Emergence of a New Historical Society* (New York: Routledge, 1999), 24.

Conventional processes of inquiry are not merely shunned but are frontally attacked.[35] Traditional research is seen as reflecting particular standpoints that are not fitting to interpret the black experience; only true blacks, and a few whites fully in agreement with the liberal consensus, can interpret black reality. Patricia Hill-Collins is typical in her dismissal of the conventional research process as a "Eurocentric masculinist knowledge-validation process."[36] This process is said to be controlled by whites and works to suppress other lines of inquiry (in her case, black feminist thought). Traditional lines of inquiry are seen as detached, positivistic, unemotional, and oppressive. Hill-Collins tells us that "[s]uch criteria ask African-American women to objectify themselves, devalue their emotional life, displace their motivations ... and confront in an adversarial relationship, those who have more social, economic, and professional power than they." Due to the inability of black and feminist scholars to validate their claims through the "white man's process," there is a need to create a new "Afrocentric and feminist epistemology." The new epistemology is to be full of emotions, accounts of "concrete experience," dialogue, "the ethic of caring," and "the ethic of personal accountability."[37]

These researchers apparently believe that instead of trying to become aware of one's biases, cognitive limitations, and blind spots in order to minimize their negative effects, we need to utilize them as constitutive parts

---

[35] Philosopher Samuel Gregg refers to the disturbing subjectivism prevalent in the West: "Truth has been relegated to cultural perspective. There is a multiplicity of truths: my 'truth', your 'truth', black 'truth', white 'truth', women's 'truth', homosexual 'truth' and so on *ad nauseam*." Gregg, *Morality, Law, and Public Policy* (Sydney: St. Tomas More Society, 2001), 81.

[36] See Patricia Hill-Collins, "The Social Construction of Black Feminist Thought" in *Black Women in America: Social Science Perspectives*, ed. Micheline R. Malson et al. (Chicago: University of Chicago Press, 1988), 303. Molefi Kete Assante refers to a similar new relativistic formulation of historical inquiry in his *Kemet, Afrocentricity, and Knowledge* (Trenton, NJ: Africa World Press, 1990), 117.

[37] Hill-Collins, "The Social Construction of Black Feminist Thought," 306–7, 316–20. This "ethic" is a good way to discard any opinions presented by those who are not members of the group. For Hill-Collins only black women can research black women. The process secures the validation of much absurdity in Afrocentric and feminist thought. What is hailed as liberation from Eurocentric pride does not lead to honest and independent research; instead, it straps us into the straitjacket of racial and gender categories.

of research analysis. Liberation theologian Juan Luis Segundo captures the phenomenon in his description of theology as a nonautonomous instrument that must arrive at ideological conclusions. The scholar must study the world to change it in a particular direction; thus, he must immerse himself in "the struggle": "thinking that intends to change the world means thinking from within the struggle, and of course thinking that will tip the scale in favor of the proletariat."[38] This is a Marxist principle: as "the ruling ideas of each age have ever been the ideas of its ruling class," our "bias" becomes our strength against the oppression of ideas.[39]

Cultural correctness, independently of evidence, distinguishes that kind of pseudo-research and acts as a validation criterion, offering bias and partisanship as a legitimate system of inquiry. History is seen as a type of fiction that projects the cultural values of dominant groups. The result is not history "but rather a kind of hybrid between myth and history, a myth about history."[40] As Mary Lefkowitz notes, "The debate has moved away from facts and evidence, to perceived motivations, and the quality of a discussion now depends on whether the participants in the discussion have good or beneficial motivations, as judged by themselves."[41] In other words, inquiry is to serve a cause, not the search for truth; the cause is seen *a priori* as *the* truth. This cognitive revolution sacrifices research and inquiry on the altar of ideology with the justification that, after all, objectivity is never possible.

FREEDOM—A SERIOUS THING

In an insightful analysis, Shelby Steele identifies the refusal to acknowledge the expansion of the margin of choice available to blacks in America with the concept of "integration shock" leading to "race holding."[42] An existential shock occurs when a dramatic shift in the fate of individuals exerts new demands and sends individuals into unfamiliar territory. In his autobiogra-

---

[38] Juan Luis Segundo, *The Liberation of Theology*, trans. John Drury (New York: Orbis, 1975), 14.

[39] Karl Marx, *The German Ideology* (London: Lawrence & Wishart, 1938), chap. 1.

[40] Lefkowitz, *Not Out of Africa*, 49–50, 153.

[41] Lefkowitz, *Not Out of Africa*, 48.

[42] Shelby Steele, *The Content of Our Character: A New Vision of Race in America* (New York: St. Martin's Press, 1990), 23–26.

phy, Booker T. Washington recalls such a shocking moment just after the exuberance and joy of blacks becoming a free people:

> The wild rejoicing on the part of the emancipated colored people lasted but for a brief period, for I noticed that by the time they returned to their cabins there was a change in their feelings. The great responsibility of being free, of having charge of themselves, of having to think and plan for themselves and their children, seemed to take possession of them. It was very much like suddenly turning a youth of ten or twelve years out into the world to provide for himself.... To some it seemed that, now that they were in actual possession of it, freedom was a more serious thing than they had expected to find it.[43]

After the long, dark night of the soul, such an existential sensation was to be expected. That experience, however, only meant that freedom was knocking at the door of their bondage, that they could now live a more autonomous life even as the boundaries of this newly discovered freedom were limited. Fear, conflict, and alienation are the expected reaction of any human being facing the daunting reality of having a margin of choice.

Booker's experience is not surprising then, but the nature of the exertions has changed. Race has become an excuse—the shield protecting us from a fear of inadequacy. Steele explains: "When one lacks the courage to face oneself fully, a fear of hidden vulnerabilities triggers a fright-flight response to integration shock. Instead of admitting that racism has declined, we argue all the harder that it is still alive and more insidious than ever."[44] The shock currently presents a greater spiritual challenge as the margin of choice provides more opportunity and less external constraint. Freedmen did not have much time to reflect on inadequacies; they had to carve out an existence under the cloud of a resentful society averse to offering much support for those who once were their property.

It is true that by virtue of its minority status, its unique experience of being the only racial group brought against its will, and its common past of oppression, the black community was naturally more ideologically homogeneous. However, this commonality, or cultural and political consensus, has been greatly distorted and misunderstood by ideologues proposing

---

[43] Booker T. Washington, "Up from Slavery: An Autobiography," *The Outlook* 66 (November 3, 1900): 566.

[44] Steele, *Content of Our Character*, 24.

static concepts of historical processes. Blacks came to America from a vast continent containing an array of ethnic, linguistic, and cultural differences; they found themselves in bondage there and were brought here in bondage. After the termination of two centuries of slavery, there emerged a new kind of black American who was culturally and biologically different from the Africans whom they left behind. Aspects of the African past merged with aspects of the culture of the enslavers, who were also characterized by diverse cultural identities. Confronted with a newly discovered legal freedom, gained under daring and trying circumstances, blacks experienced a practical need for a moral and cultural consensus, one similar to that forged under the vicissitudes of slavery.

There was in America, however, a common thrust of individualism and personal achievement that could not fail to influence blacks. Deprived of the possibility of asserting their individuality in full, it manifested itself in them as a thirst: a thirst for individual affirmation within the context of communal life. "This special combination of individual drive with a sense of collective responsibility," says Alan Keyes, "is one of the distinguishing marks of black-American character. It represents in the moral and psychological sphere the mixture of group empathy and improvisation we find in jazz, as well as in the interplay between verse leader and congregation that often appears in Negro spirituals and gospel music."[45]

Although a degree of homogeneity of thought was a tool for survival in the past, it was never conformist. The collectivist policies that inaugurated the era of dependency for blacks distorted the sense of community that existed before the age of big government. Circling the wagons around received ideas about life and politics not only can serve as a shield against external oppression but also as a self-imposed prison detaching men from real opportunities and new horizons of intellectual and social discovery.

In other words, commonality of thought and action in the black community was not originally collectivist in nature. Blacks were neither atomized nor amalgamated; they were unique and unrepeatable *persons*. A healthy individualism merged a personal ambition to succeed with a communal interest and solidarity that prevented blacks from thinking of themselves apart from their community. The family and the church nurtured this social individualism while providing the strongest communal arrangements and

---

[45] Alan Keyes, *Masters of the Dream* (New York: Morrow, 1995), 11.

basic social structures; the "I am" was always harmoniously connected with the "we feeling" of collective identity described by sociologist John Ogbu.[46]

STEWARDS OF OUR OWN DESTINY

Blacks began to progress socioeconomically long before the era of increased government intervention. The historical trend of black progress before the late 1960s is not a topic of much discussion by most scholars (who insist that not even *after* the 1960s have blacks had much to cheer about). The rate of black progress after the 1964 Civil Rights Act has been, in certain sectors, slower than before the passing of the Act.[47] Progress before the 1960s was the marvelous achievement of blacks who had the determination to press on toward economic and social success in spite of great obstacles.

The history of that achievement is often forgotten by those who focus on external forces as the most important elements of black reality.[48] Government initiative and government policies enacted through the action of so-called leaders are tenaciously defended while, as Thomas Sowell reminds us, the great achievement of blacks themselves is neglected:

> One of the consequences of that myth is that, **while most blacks lifted themselves out of poverty, the public image is that government programs were responsible**. This has left many whites wondering why blacks can't advance themselves by their own efforts, like other minorities—and left many blacks likewise convinced that without government programs they would be lost.[49]

The number of blacks in white-collar occupations grew exponentially from 1940 to 1970. In 1940, only 5 percent of black men and 6 percent of black women held white-collar jobs. By 1970, however, the numbers had risen to 22 percent of black men and 36 percent of black women.[50] In

---

[46] John U. Ogbu, *Black American Students in an Affluent Suburb: A Study of Academic Disengagement* (Mahwah, NJ: Lawrence Erlbaum Associates, 2003), chap. 9.

[47] Thomas Sowell, *Civil Rights: Rhetoric or Reality* (New York: Quill, 1984), 48–50.

[48] Abigail Thernstrom and Stephan Thernstrom, "The Real Story of Black Progress," *Wall Street Journal*, September 3, 1997.

[49] Thomas Sowell, "American History vs. Affirmative Action Hogwash," *Capitalism Magazine* (July 10, 2002), http://capitalismmagazine.com/2002/07/american-history-vs-affirmative-action-hogwash/.

[50] Thernstrom and Thernstrom, *America in Black and White*, 186.

1940, 60 percent of black women were employed as domestic servants but by 1998 that number had descended drastically to just over 2 percent. By the same year of 1998, 60 percent of black women held white-collar jobs.[51] After providing extensive data regarding the reality of black economic progress antecedent to the era of government intervention, Abigail and Stephan Thernstrom conclude that "there was a substantial black middle class already in existence by the end of the 1960s." In the years since, "it has continued to grow, but *not at a more rapid pace* than in the preceding three decades, despite a common impression to the contrary. Great occupational advances were made by African Americans before preferential policies were introduced in the late 1960s."[52]

Upward mobility was achieved by individuals who pursued their interest *in spite* of oppression. Even Malcolm X, still speaking from the perspective of Black Nationalism, understood clearly how the state could not help our people: "Anytime you are living in the twentieth century and you're walking around here singing 'We Shall Overcome,' the government has failed you.... White liberals who have been posing as our friends have failed us. Once we see that all these other sources to which we have turned have failed, we stop turning to them and turn to ourselves."[53]

"Ourselves" in Malcolm's universe, however, was still the group, not the individual. In his vision, the Nation of Islam was that collective haven where blacks would find collective peace and prosperity. He did not completely escape the distortion regarding commonality that asserts that the causes of our oppression are structural at the highest level, and so the solutions must also be structural at the same level.[54]

---

[51] Abigail Thernstrom and Stephan Thernstrom, "Black Progress: How Far We've Come—and How Far We Have to Go," *Brookings Review* 16 (Spring 1998). In 1940, the gap in high school education between blacks and whites was 29 percentage points, but, by 1970, it had gone down to about only 10 percentage points. See "A House Divided" (October 21, 1970), a transcript of a film by the Hoover Institution, http://www.hoover.org/multimedia/uk/3420831.html.

[52] Thernstrom and Thernstrom, *America in Black and White*, 187; emphasis in the original.

[53] James H. Cone, *Martin & Malcolm & America: A Dream or a Nightmare* (New York: Orbis Books, 1991), 197.

[54] Structural sin exists indeed, but we may confuse its reality. Personal sin makes sinful men accomplices of one another in structures that hurt individuals. These sins are the expression and effect of personal sins. See John Paul II, Apostolic Exhor-

To say that we are, as individuals, masters of our own destiny, does not imply that political and economic structures do not exert influence. It rather emphasizes the priority of the person in any endeavor of life. It rejects, too, Cornel West's portrayal of American society as one where a few blacks are lucky to succeed while the many press forward to no avail:

> Conservative behaviorists talk about values and attitudes as if political and economic structures hardly exist. They rarely, if ever, examine the innumerable cases in which black people do act on the Protestant ethic and still remain at the bottom of the social ladder. Instead, they highlight the few instances in which blacks ascend to the top, as if such success is available to all blacks, regardless of circumstances.[55]

West fails to recognize that the crucial issue is mobility across a socioeconomic spectrum, not a jump to the top. More importantly, he does not see that misrepresenting the nature of the society in which we live as oppressive and static for most blacks depresses the spirit under the weight of victim talk.

Salvation from Above

Contemporary black intellectuals have consistently minimized the growth of the black middle class.[56] There is a definite political agenda behind these omissions. Stephan and Abigail Thernstrom, again, are correct in assessing the reasons for the approach:

> One reason is that the stereotype serves an important political purpose: it nurtures the mix of black anger and white shame and guilt that sustains the race-based social policies implemented since the late 1960s. To call attention to the rapid growth of the black middle class, defenders of the racial status quo fear, would invite public complacency and undercut support for the affirmative action regime.[57]

---

tation *Reconciliation and Penance*, no. 16, http://w2.vatican.va/content/john-paul-ii/en/apost_exhortations/documents/hf_jp-ii_exh_02121984_reconciliatio-et-paenitentia.html.

[55] Cornel West, *Race Matters* (1993; repr., Boston: Beacon Press, 2001), 13.

[56] James A. Geschwender and Rita Carroll Seguin, "Exploding the Myth of African-American Progress," in *Black Women in America: Social Science Perspectives*, ed. Micheline R. Malson et al. (Chicago: University of Chicago Press, 1988), 115–29.

[57] Thernstrom and Thernstrom, *America in Black & White*, 184.

The federalization of the black struggle for social justice, although necessary for certain short-term reasons, created a nefarious trade-off by institutionalizing top-down solutions to the racial problem. Those who were oppressors became patrons, and the legal advances became something borrowed and external. Policies created with the justification of countering oppression (in housing, employment, direct services, entitlements) established bureaucracy as an agent of change—a bureaucracy that did not take into consideration local realities and that made personal choice and morality irrelevant. The political mood shifted from the need to address problems to the need to perpetuate policies and initiatives. In many cases, those who were community leaders became government emissaries responding to government agendas. This reinforced a slave mentality, as the government became a "benevolent plantation" where blacks were asked to make a Faustian bargain: Receive all they need to stay comfortably within the plantation in exchange for conformity (and the vote, of course).[58] The balance of individualism and collective responsibility shifted dramatically toward collectivism.

This reliance on collectivist social engineering, which Thomas Sowell positions under the "unconstrained vision of social causation," is clear in the recent history of blacks in America. It is also a betrayal of their past. The underlying belief of collectivist social engineering is that human beings are inherently good and can create structures that will produce intentional social benefits. Under such a vision of causation, man can "directly feel other people's needs as more important than his own, and therefore is capable of consistently acting impartially, even when his own interest or those of his family were involved."[59] Envisioning social issues as basically engineering problems, bureaucracy is seen as a good method of allocating resources. The experts who direct this method are *the anointed ones* who can better assess the needs of the many.[60] As policies fail, the preferred alternative is not to rethink the policies but to augment the funding or redefine the goals and focus on so-called structural inequities.

---

[58] Keyes, *Masters of the Dream*, 50.

[59] Thomas Sowell, *A Conflict of Visions: Ideological Origins of Political Struggles*, rev. ed. (New York: Basic Books, 2007), 24–27.

[60] Sowell discusses at length the purported moral superiority of the left and their belief in their own power to correct social problems. Thomas Sowell, *The Vision of the Anointed: Self-Congratulation as a Basis for Social Policy* (New York: Basic Books, 1995).

Central to this view of social justice is the notion of *equality of results*. Assuming that we are capable of foreseeing the consequences of our actions and build inherently just structures, it posits a relationship of causality between societal structures and the poor condition of blacks.[61] Therefore, there is a moral responsibility for society to equalize results through structural change focused on the redistribution of wealth to specific groups. If the intended result does not occur, individuals are seen as victims of entrenched social structures.

The second phase of the civil rights movement deviated from the moral focus of the original movement and based most of its efforts on the creation of a corpus of law and the establishment of governmental solutions to problems by way of agencies and initiatives. Bureaucracy was the solution proposed to heal the problems in society and to create positive racial change. The modern liberal idea of providing every conceivable social benefit through government initiative while requiring the least possible effort or commitment to change has been shown to be empty and degrading. Statism replaced subsidiarity. A great evil has resulted from interventionism and its byproduct: *victimhood as identity*.[62]

A principle of equality that makes men equal, independent of their subjectivity, creates in them the habit of guiding their lives by appetites and demands. Hence, it is important to reject the collectivist notion of processes and the relativist understanding of values. Economists talk of human capital in terms of employable skills—and in terms of the need to invest in providing them. Yet, we need to move one-step earlier, a step toward culture and morality, to discover foundational reasons for economic reality.

To acquire employable skills or engage in meaningful activity, the human must be rightly disposed. Both culture and morality play crucial roles in the formation of character and the movement of the will. In my ministry work, I have invested resources in many individuals like Antwan (chapter

---

[61] Robert H. Bork is right in his criticism of structuralism:

> Structural theories are simply an admission that actual discrimination cannot be shown, coupled with an unsupported assertion that it must nevertheless be pervasive. Only modern liberals and people with a vested interest in discovering racism would advance such an empty theory.

Robert Bork, *Slouching Towards Gomorrah: Modern Liberalism and American Decline* (New York: ReganBooks, 1997), 237.

[62] For an excellent discussion of these problems, see McWhorter, *Losing the Race*.

4) who are willing and eager to learn. They were ready to sacrifice and commit to whatever it took to succeed. Hiring and training them was not a difficult decision for employers. In short, they became good stewards of their gifts. At times, however, others who came from a better economic situation responded in less productive ways to the offering of similar resources. The decisive factor was not the availability of resources; it was human choice.

Any initiative built on erroneous anthropology is destined to fail no matter how compassionate or scholarly it seems to be. Providing education and training in employable skills will always be an incomplete effort if we ignore culture and human subjectivity. Those who are successful in assisting others understand, as Abigail Thernstrom tells us, "[t]hat culture affects academic learning and the acquisition of skills and knowledge that will lead to good jobs in life." "Successful schools," she explains,

> insist that their students learn how to speak Standard English, show up on time properly dressed, sit up straight in their desks, chairs pulled in, workbooks organized.... They walk down halls quickly and quietly, they always finish their homework, they look at people when they are talking to them, they listen to teachers politely and follow their directions precisely. They treat their classmates with equal respect.

In these schools, "Even minor infractions of the rules ... have immediate consequences." Importantly, Thernstrom notes, "The effort to put disadvantaged youth on the traditional ladder of social mobility has another related component, which is never explicitly articulated. The best inner-city schools and students define themselves as individuals."[63]

We Must Remember

Memories can either chain or liberate. In the second chapter, we saw how God imprinted a hidden memory of a past without shame into our beings and that to remember, and remember in line with right reason, is our salvation. The Platonic concept of *anamnesis* (recalling to memory; recollection) serves to clarify the meaning of memory. It reminds us that conscience is not an external imposition but a natural inclination to recognize truth. Saint Paul referred to this inclination when he spoke of a law "written on [our]

---

[63] Abigail Thernstrom, quoted in "Moving Men into the Mainstream: The Next Steps in Urban Reform" [transcript of Manhattan Institute conference], *Civic Bulletin* no. 44 (October 2006).

hearts" (Rom. 2:15). The same thought is present in Augustine: "We could never judge that one thing is better than another if a basic understanding of the good had not already been instilled in us."[64] This anamnesis is not like the storage of information readily available, but, as Joseph Cardinal Ratzinger eloquently explains, "It is so to speak an inner sense, a capacity to recall, so that the one whom it addresses, if he is not turned in on himself, hears its echo from within."[65]

This truth applies to black history. There is a need for the healing of memory and for developing our conscience to exorcise the idea of victimhood from the psyche. When that memory is healed, we will begin to see that the truth of history and the truth of salvation lies in every human person, in every beautiful black soul who, without rejecting the "we" feeling, never forgets the "I" of human uniqueness and unrepeatability. The healing will not be accomplished through the politics of anger and victimhood. It has nothing to do with whites or with a collective label of blackness. It has everything to do with each person's affirming his individual dignity.

The truth about black identity is not a never-ending double consciousness but a unique realization of our subjectivity in the individual realm and a personal affirmation of our American identity in the communal realm. The truth about the black family is not found in the forced separations, the rapes, and the poverty but in modeling ourselves after those who left it all in search of loved ones and those who raised their children and kept their families intact when there seemed no good reason to do so.

The deepest truth needed to heal our memory is not to be found in some mythical African paradise or in the federal government's rescuing blacks through schemes that supposedly ameliorate the oppressive effects of structural racism. The truth is in the lives of those who struggled, fell, and stood up again to fight and even die for freedom and dignity. The truth about the civil rights movement is not to be found in the triumph of anger and revenge and in the emotional releases of "black power" but in faith and adherence to the values embedded in the Declaration of Independence: that *all* men are created equal and are endowed by our Creator with certain

---

[64] Cited in Joseph Cardinal Ratzinger, *On Conscience: Two Essays* (San Francisco: Ignatius Press, 2007), 32.

[65] Joseph Cardinal Ratzinger, "Conscience and Truth" (paper presented at the 10th Workshop for Bishops, Dallas, Texas, February 1991), http://www.ewtn.com/library/CURIA/RATZCONS.HTM.

8

SEPARATISM AND THE POLITICS
OF DESPAIR

---

*Black people will never gain full equality
in this country.*

—Derrick Bell,
Faces at the Bottom of the Well

While working as a high school teacher years ago, I was asked by a
coworker to help a friend of hers study for a certification exam. The
young black man, whom I will call Jerry, had a bachelor's degree in political science but could not pass the political science test toward certification.
After failing several times, Jerry was desperate. The test was not difficult,
but it did presume a basic knowledge of the subject. I was doubtful that I
could reteach four years of college in one afternoon, but I decided to try.

We met at the library of a local community college. I gave him some
testing tips and offered some of my political science books for his perusal.
He seemed uninterested and nervous. Our meeting lasted about an hour,
and I encouraged him to relax, do some reading, and try the test again. Jerry
kept telling me that this was his last opportunity and that, if he failed, his
employment would be terminated. After I offered my continued assistance,
if needed, we parted ways.

Later that night, Jerry called me. After some small talk, he revealed his
true intentions, which he was obviously afraid to state in person. He wanted
me to take the test for him! In effect, he had a plan already worked out to

produce a fake identification card, provide me with transportation, and pay me in exchange for the favor.

His deportment was at first respectful, even obeisant, as he implored me to help a brother. When I refused, he became combative, implying that I would bear the blame if he lost his job. I abruptly ended the conversation.

A few hours later, Jerry called again. Apologizing profusely for his earlier attitude, he began to cry. Tearfully, he told me that his wife was pregnant and if he were to lose his job, she would leave him. I still refused. Newly married myself and with a small child, I felt terrible for him, but I was also angered that he would put me in such a predicament. This time he was the one who ended the call abruptly. I did not hear from him again.

A couple of years later, I attended a teacher workshop and, to my surprise, Jerry was there, fully certified. He had obviously found a way to pass the test, ethically or not. The gathering was awkward as he avoided me the whole afternoon. One of the workshop exercises involved was presenting to the group ideas for bettering education. I was stunned when he stood up in front of the crowd and declared that the most important ingredient of a good school is diversity!

It is of course impossible to generalize from this single incident and claim that Jerry's difficulty was a function of the racial politics of the last fifty years. Without knowing his individual circumstances, we cannot make any conclusion about the decisive factors that formed his character. Moreover, there are obviously people of every race who display the same willingness to cheat and manipulate in order to overcome their own real or perceived shortcomings.

Be that as it may, systems focused on victimization facilitate the use of excuses and slogans such as "diversity" that detract from the personal effort and responsibility needed for work in civil society.

"VICTIMS 'R' US" AND THE POLITICS OF DESPAIR

Those who advocate liberation theology, dependency theory, and racialism tend to see themselves as oppressed victims. They are on the periphery of society, marginalized by those at the center who exert dominance. Everything else depends on this basic myth. The most important consequence of this assertion is that, in a self-fulfilling prophecy, it shifts power and responsibility to others. Because I am not responsible for my condition and an evil oppressor is, my principal duty and meaning in life is reactionary: I must resist, I must fight.

The story of our condition, in this view, is dialectical wherein my life is constituted by the fundamental interpretive keys to my existence: antagonism, division, and struggle. We can apply Michael Novak's characterization of liberation theology by substituting class with race: "History is combat, of one [race] against another. History is [race] struggle. The basic ethical question is: Whose side are you on, oppressor or oppressed? Taking sides becomes the first ethical choice."[1] That is why individuality is a threat—or better, a sin. The plant that grows from such anthropological seeds is despair. You cannot sow antagonism in the hope of later reaping justice and peace.

In the Marxist analysis of black liberation theology and racialism, the dialectic moves inexorably from one oppression to the other. If we are victims of whites, then whites must disappear if we are going to end the dialectic and bring about the synthesis that emerges from struggle. The evil of victimization is connected to the structural explanation of oppression in the black community. If poverty and discrimination are the structural evils of a capitalist system and integral to what Western society is, then nearly all of us are victims. All explanations of present situations and all interpretations of history are viewed through the prism of grievances.

Thus, reconciliation with whites is not an option. The only option is their elimination. It is on this first anthropological error that the entire edifice of racialism rests—and eventually crumbles. Oppression and victimization may be the environment within which a seed is planted, but that seed must be one of love, justice, and freedom. Only then can we hope for a flowering of reconciliation and peace. As Michael Novak explains,

> The first step of Christian self-identification, therefore, is not solely "I am oppressed," but rather, "I am also essentially (never completely) free and in love with justice." Inherently free and in love with justice, I need bend my knee to no one, may stand erect and proud. I am not merely a victim. I am not merely oppressed.[2]

Such a vision may be attained precisely by adhering to the values that are fundamental to the American experience. If the fundamental reality of black existence in America is oppression and victimhood, however, only further oppression awaits. This is the logical deduction from the Marxist

---

[1] Michael Novak, *Will It Liberate? Questions About Liberation Theology* (New York: Paulist Press, 1986), 108–9.

[2] Novak, *Will It Liberate?*, 110.

analysis of liberation theology. In effect, racialist theories of oppression are invested in continued dependency on whites. Mental habits of dependency nurture the theories of the most rabid activists and theoreticians. We implicitly accept that whites remain in control of our lives. Even in their activism, racialists remain passive.

Today, we are experiencing an ominous *politics of despair.*[3] The modern black liberal outlook is based on resentment, hopelessness, and the negation of reality. The reality of the opening and expansion of real possibilities for blacks is constantly denied or, at least, minimized. America is portrayed as unrepentant and racism as ever transforming and never receding—our very existence depends on accepting our victim status. Black liberation theologian J. Deotis Robertson says it well, "Black liberation theology is about life, for we are not free. The black man is victimized almost daily in some way to remind him that he is not free."[4]

This notion has a negative impact in the minds of young blacks trying to advance in life. Confronted with the perception of impotence, hopelessness, and alienation in a land perceived as foreign, they are often asked to project their hopes into the idea of being uplifted as a group by government action. Desperation sends us in pursuit of the illusion of deliverance from above. The more alienated the individual becomes, the more he projects his hopes and aspirations onto what he perceives as his salvation: government initiative. Government becomes a totem; the new master. By assigning such value to a system, we defraud ourselves. In a single act embedded with meaning and value, we transfer to a foreign entity the power to transform and rule the destiny of our lives.

However, salvation never comes; the meager benefits forcibly extracted from the machine of government are always in peril, always receding under

---

[3] My understanding of the politics of despair comes from an analysis of theologian Henri de Lubac's writings. In *The Drama of Atheist Humanity*, de Lubac analyzes Ludwig Feuerbach's theogony (the genealogy of a group or system of gods). Utilizing the Hegelian concept of "alienation," Feuerbach spoke of man as finding himself "dispossessed of something essentially belonging to him for the benefit of an elusive reality." Feuerbach believed that man projects onto the idea of God what is in reality his—with God becoming the object of praise and the sum of all that is truly valuable. What we value will determine our action and what we perceive as the material foundation of our condition influences the value we assign to certain goods.

[4] J. Deotis Roberts, *A Black Political Theory* (Louisville: Westminster John Knox Press, 1974), 151.

the heavy influence of external factors and antagonistic agents coming from "The System" itself. The new master is then transformed into an evil god that cannot deliver man from his condition. In tragic despair, and not cognizant of his value, man conceives of himself as a helpless victim of a government structure he hates but still worships. Many turn to apathy, criminality, and vice as their families and communities crumble. This helplessness becomes a powerful political tool used to extract concessions from government by appealing to both white guilt and the threat of despair that generates violence and chaos. By appealing to external forces to define their being and project their hopes, self-declared victims experience an impoverishment that fills the perceived emptiness with a hope of foreign deliverance.

In Hegelian fashion, the dialectic moves inexorably. The same objectified totem of the state becomes the salvation of our race. A radical transformation of the system is the necessary step toward a new synthesis in which we will regain essence. Man's essence is recoverable only by losing individual identity in favor of the amalgamation of blackness. Despair, alienation, and even suffering are seen as necessary stages in losing ourselves, regaining consciousness, and recovering ourselves in the safety net of group identity. The turning point of black history will be that day when we recognize and accept the absolute priority of our individuality as persons made for our own sake.

These are the currents of thought that informed my intellectual upbringing in Puerto Rico. For Gustavo Gutierrez (one of the key figures in the development of liberation theology), utopia refers to a "historical plan for a qualitatively different society" and expresses an "aspiration to establish new social relations among human beings."[5] The ideas of Latin American liberationists and black American racialists have cross-pollinated. Cornel West calls for Marxist and black theologians to collaborate in a "mutually arrived-at political action."[6] In this utopian concept, the politics of despair is the essential tool for a denunciation of the oppressive order and the emergence of a new consciousness. In black liberation theology, the oppressed masses obtain salvation by the rejection of individuality and the subordi-

---

[5] Gustavo Gutierrez, *A Theology of Liberation* (New York: Orbis Books, 1973), 135. See also, Neil Ormerod, *Introducing Contemporary Theologies: The What and the Who of Theology Today* (New York: Orbis Books, 1997), chap. 13.

[6] Cornell West, "Black Theology in Marxist Thought," in *Black Theology: A Documentary History*, vol. 1, ed. James H. Cone and Gayraud S. Wilmore (New York: Orbis Books, 1993), 409.

nation of self under the label of race. The new synthesis will be achieved by way of collectivist politics transforming the totem of the state into the instrument for bringing about the heaven on earth of socialism and losing the self in the inexhaustible and irreducible construct of race.

This way of thinking provides a rationale for the many who today whistle past the graveyard of inner-city life. Instead of locating causes—and solutions—within black communities and individuals, the difficulties observed in our cities are reduced to a function of white oppression. The causality here is linear and simple: oppression causes poverty, and poverty causes all other evils.

There is tremendous pressure to jump on the bandwagon of linear analysis that always ends in blaming "whitey." This mode of thought becomes the interpretive lens, the normal science defining the socialization process in a community. It transfers certain implicit rules to the young concerning what it means to belong to the kinship group. As such basic communities are tied by customs and beliefs regarding appropriate behavior, responsibility toward each other, and attitudes about society as a whole, that which is infused as a vision within the group has radical consequences.

This denial of reality concerning the causes of black failure is negative in terms of what it repudiates (denying the beneficial historical changes in society) and positive in terms of what it affirms about racial identity. The purpose of this binary denial is first to maintain an "acceptable social façade" where we are aware of the family's "dirty laundry" but agree not to disclose it to those who do not already know.[7] Second, it is to promote a willful blindness on the part of those benefiting from the status quo in the community; those who are heavily invested in the vision of causality that serves as the system's foundational story.

Peeking behind the façade to see and tell must be avoided at all costs by appeals to commonality and relevance. It is important to note here that the "complex simplification" vision did not just appear out of thin air. It developed as a response to real and imaginary common needs. The task of separating the unarticulated rules of the system from the real or imaginary

---

[7] As psychiatrist Antonio Ferreira states, "The individual family member may know, and often does, that much of the [family] image is false and represents no more than a sort of official party line." Antonio J. Ferreira, "Family Myths and Homeostasis," *Archives of General Psychiatry* 9 (1963): 458, cited in Waltzlawick et al., *Change: Principles of Problem Formation and Problem Resolution* (New York: Norton, 1974), 42–43.

needs that caused their initial appearance is remarkably difficult. Because the paradigm is reactionary, as all paradigms of normal science are, we must expect turmoil in trying to shake the system.

The need, we will also be told, is to fix the macrosystem that causes our problems, and time is of the essence. There are environmental factors at play that affect "our" people, and those who blame the victim are wasting our precious time. We are back again at the simplification problem of unidirectional understandings of causality. "Because these matters are urgent," says political scientist Heinz Eulau, "they require immediate solutions; immediate solutions do not permit complicated analysis; complicated analysis is only a pretence for doing nothing."[8] This methodology becomes what Silvio Funtowicz and Jerome Ravetz call *postnormal science*, where decisions are made with urgency in times of real or perceived crisis, even when all factors cannot be accounted for and where it is acknowledged that mistakes can be devastating.[9] In the realm of race as well as of science, such methodology seems more like a ploy to stifle opposing views by accusing them of hidden biases or of inaction. It ignores contrary positions at the service of political goals.

Eventually, however, the linear thesis loses its explanatory power and sends the entire system into a crisis—a crisis experienced during scientific revolutions as well as during cultural ones. With respect to the dysfunctions of much of black American life, we have been in such a crisis for a while.

THE LIBERAL VISION

Black America's crisis has remained intractable due to the flawed *externalist* approach to its causes taken by most black leaders and scholars. This pattern is similar to the one used by African leaders to explain the present problems in Africa. Professor George B. N. Ayittey explains:

---

[8] Heinz Eulau, "Reason and Relevance: Reflections on a Madness of our Time," *Student Lawyer* 1 (1972): 16, cited in Waltzlawick et al., *Change*, 45.

[9] J. R. Ravetz, "Usable Knowledge, Usable Ignorance: Incomplete Science with Policy Implications," in *Sustainable Development of the Biosphere*, ed. W. C. Clark and R. C. Munn (New York: Cambridge University Press, 1986), 415–32; Silvio Funtowicz and Jerome R. Ravetz, "A New Scientific Methodology for Global Environmental Issues," in *Ecological Economics: The Science and Management of Sustainability*, ed. Robert Costanza (New York: Columbia University Press, 1991), 137–52.

The externalists believe that Africa's woes are due to external factors. Disciples of the externalist school include most African leaders, scholars, and intellectual radicals. For decades the externalist position held sway, attributing the causes of almost every African problem to such external factors as Western colonialism and imperialism, the pernicious effects of the slave trade, racist conspiracy plots, exploitation by avaricious multinational corporations, an unjust international economic system, inadequate flows of foreign aid, and deteriorating trends of trade.[10]

A confusion of correlation with causation is at play here. Due to the fact that crime and low educational attainment are often found alongside want, poverty is assumed to be the cause of these evils. Poverty in turn is explained as a result of victimization. In reality, there is ample evidence coming from the experiences of varied ethnic groups that there is no causative relationship between poverty and other evils often associated with it.[11]

By way of illustration, during the late twentieth century, nonblack students from very poor families (under $10,000 yearly income) scored an average of 44 points higher than black students.[12] Asian American students from families making a mere $6,000 a year scored higher on SAT tests than black students coming from families making at least $50,000 a year.[13] Chinese in other nations of Southeast Asia, although suffering great discrimination, are the greatest producers of wealth and possess higher standards of living than majority populations.[14]

It is difficult to explain away the four-year racial gap in learning between Latino and black students on one side and white and Asian students on the other. As Abigail and Stephan Thernstrom wrote in 2003, "[t]he NAEP [National Assessment of Educational Progress] results consistently show a frightening gap between the basic academic skills of the average African

---

[10] George B. N. Ayittey, *Africa in Chaos* (New York: St. Martin's Press, 1998), 37–38.

[11] For extensive research, see Thomas Sowell, *Race and Culture: A World View* (New York: Basic Books, 1994). See also John Perazzo, *The Myths That Divide Us* (New York: World Studies Books, 1999) chap. 9. For a good discussion of causation versus correlation, see Thomas Sowell, *The Vision of the Anointed: Self-Congratulation as a Basis for Social Policy* (New York: Basic Books, 1995), 55–57.

[12] Dinesh D'Souza, *Illiberal Education* (New York: The Free Press, 1991), 265.

[13] Thomas Sowell, *The Economics and Politics of Race* (New York: William Morrow & Co., 1985), 140.

[14] Walter E. Williams, *The State Against Blacks* (New York: McGraw-Hill, 1982), 4–5.

American and Latino student and those of the typical white and Asian American."[15] By 2005, in reading, 52 percent of black eighth graders scored at or above basic proficiency (signifying partial mastery of skills) compared to 82 percent of whites. Thirty-nine percent of whites scored at or above proficiency (demonstrating solid academic performance) while 12 percent of blacks did. Similar differences appeared in math proficiency. Although the gap has narrowed somewhat, the change is not statistically significant.[16]

Poverty cannot explain these persistent differences. We can talk at length about the deleterious effects of poverty and its ultimate causes, but the fact remains that poverty cannot be readily established as a causal factor for problems such as poor educational attainment or crime.[17] The success of other marginalized ethnic groups tells us that these external influences cannot account in great measure for the present socioeconomic realities of black America.[18]

In the face of these data, many cling to the position that external factors are the source of social pathologies. Once the culprit for our problems is identified as "the system," there is an immediate appeal to "fix" it. This approach, consistent with an unconstrained vision of social processes, has created a crisis where psychological separatism is one component. A people who survived, struggled, and began to progress considerably before the era of big government were led astray by a leadership focused on government relief as the tool for uplifting the race. A people who even under truly victimizing conditions refused the demeaning label of victim became convinced of their perpetual victimization. Victimhood has become an explanation that serves well the pursuit of an extremely pliable concept of social justice based on despair as a political tool.

Psychological separatism springs from this blighted soil. Victimized by a white power machine, blacks feel alienated from a system perceived as foreign and oppressive. Paradoxically, it is to this "white" system that blacks continually run for solutions. The contradictory double consciousness of

---

[15] Abigal Thernstrom and Stephan Thernstrom, *No Excuses: Closing the Racial Gap in Learning* (New York: Simon & Schuster, 2004), 12.

[16] National Center for Education Statistics, *The Nation's Report Card: Reading 2005*; National Center for Education Statistics, *The Nation's Report Card: Math 2005*.

[17] Thernstrom and Thernstrom, *No Excuses*, 121.

[18] See Thomas Sowell, *The Economics and Politics of Race: An International Perspective* (New York: Quill, 1983); Sowell, *Race and Culture*.

dependency and separatism is devastating to the psyche of individuals and demoralizing for those who find themselves in that predicament. It has created a moral vacuum in the black community and a leadership often insistent on a public stance of anger and denunciation while in private some of these very leaders are heavily involved with the system. Louis Farrakhan, one of the most vitriolic opponents of the American system and considered by many to be a strong leader for black independence, is one of the government's greatest beneficiaries. The federal government in the past has awarded the Nation of Islam over $30 million worth of security contracts per year. Farrakhan established a multimillion-dollar empire, "dependent in large measure, on public funds."[19]

We should not be surprised, as collectivist separatism ends up condemning people to deeper dependency on the very system they hate. By insisting on increased government intervention, black liberals invest in a system that rewards need. Collectivist separatism interferes with the delicate human reality of incentives. Greater government intervention makes it attractive to remain attached to the system rather than lose the "benefit." Resentment is inevitable. Those who resist the vicious cycle of dependency on government are accused of rejecting the other side of the same coin of victimhood: separation from the system. Ironically, rejecting dependency is seen as letting "the community" down and siding with the oppressor.

Separatism then is an incubator of pathological behavior that creates deep insecurities in a group of people imprisoned in an existential predicament. Many black academics can see only meaningless progress. A prime example is Derrick Bell, who argues that the attitudes that enabled slavery have never really disappeared. "Indeed," he writes, "the racism that made slavery feasible is far from dead in the last decade of ... twentieth-century America; and the civil rights gains, so hard won, are being steadily eroded. Despite undeniable progress for many, no African Americans are insulated from incidents of racial discrimination."[20]

Derrick Bell's opinion bears the mark of the dichotomy of dependence–independence that a collectivistic mind-set has created in the black com-

---

[19] James Popkin, "Propagandists or Saviors?" *U.S. News & World Report* (September 12, 1994), 40–43; Steven A. Holmes, "As Farrakhan Groups Land Jobs from Government; Debate Grows," *The New York Times*, March 4, 1994; Amy Alexander, *The Farrakhan Factor: African-American Writers on Leadership, Nationhood, and Minister Louis Farrakhan* (New York: Grove Press, 1998), 75.

[20] Derrick Bell, *Faces at the Bottom of the Well* (New York: Basic Books, 1992), 3.

munity. The "so hard won" civil rights are the result of a fight against white racism while the "undeniable progress for many" is peripheral and secondary. Under this vision, the progress of many is *individual*, hence making it secondary. The threats are *collective* and are thus meaningful. Personal success is seen as a betrayal if the beneficiary does not publicly denounce the very society that made success possible.

Treading the path of introspective analysis is perilous because the ugly truths awaiting us cannot be spoken openly without inciting accusations of inauthenticity or historical ignorance. But the truth must be told. Separatism is the most effective form of myopic social assessment as it promises falsely that if we just separate in some form, the problems disappear. When internal problems are discussed, we get what Keith Richburg got from Africans talking about Africa's problems: "defensiveness, followed by anger, and then accusations that I did not understand the history. And then I got a long list of excuses."[21]

We are confronted again with the paradox of separatism when Bell laments the erosion of civil rights victories that he still considers insufficient and ultimately meaningless: "Black people will never gain full equality in this country," he predicts. "Even those Herculean efforts we hail as successful will produce no more than temporary 'peaks of progress,' short-lived victories that slide into irrelevance as racial patterns adapt in ways that maintain white dominance."[22]

This understanding of social struggle is pessimistic and contrary to the history of black Americans who steadfastly resisted oppression while affirming their Americanism. It is not by forging a separate and unequal identity based on the surrender of individuality in a sea of sameness that we will find ourselves. The history of the survival of our people gives us the answer: steadfastness and defiant endurance based on faith that will turn the former

---

[21] Keith B. Richburg, *Out of America: A Black Man Confronts Africa* (San Diego: Harcourt, 1998), 172.

[22] Bell, *Faces at the Bottom of the Well*, 6. There is a raft of books dedicated to presenting a grim picture of black life in America. See Chester Hartman, ed., *Double Exposure: Poverty and Race in America* (New York: M. E. Sharpe, 1996); Ulwyn L. Pierre, *The Myth of Black Corporate Mobility* (New York: Garland Publishing, 1998); Paul Louis Street, *Racial Oppression in the Global Metropolis: A Living Black Chicago History* (Lanham, MD: Rowman & Littlefield, 2007); Alphonso Pinkney, *The Myth of Black Progress* (New York: Cambridge University Press, 1986).

enemy into a friend, even a brother, and the once-foreign land of captivity into our true home.[23]

Separatism is fed by the guilt of white liberals. By never challenging distorted theories of racism as an ever-present reality, they encourage blacks' rejection of white society. It is common for black liberal elites to become outraged and offended if a white person dares to challenge their assumptions. Many white liberals seem not to realize how condescending their attitude toward blacks is when they refuse to disagree. In their dutiful acceptance of every accusation of guilt, whites support the litany of excuses used to explain every manifestation of black militancy and underperformance. It is telling that it was during Lyndon Johnson's presidency—no president gave the black civil rights establishment more—that the black revolution had its most violent eruptions.[24]

The dance of black rage and white retreat keeps us in a cycle of hopelessness. The more concessions white liberals make, the more demands blacks will present. In spite of obvious progress, voices in the black community continue their attack on the mainstream. The more virulent the attack on white society is, the greater the insecurity of the attacker. In the early 1990s, for example, one-time NAACP executive director Benjamin Chavis claimed, incredibly, that racism "is worse today than it was in the '60s."[25]

---

[23] Alan Keyes expresses it this way:

> The black church is the spiritual storehouse of the black multitudes, and when the moment came, they were ready for it. Academics attacked black Christianity for fostering submissiveness. Communist and other leftist intellectuals criticized the black church for its lack of commitment to social change. Yet slavery is dead. Communism is dying. Legally enforced segregation and discrimination are things of the past, but the black church endures, and has once already led the way to genuine success in the struggle for justice.... The Civil Rights movement of the 1960s owed its success to the deep, enduring character of black Americans. Far more than the cultural expressions of the intellectual elite that have more or less openly despised it, the church-embodied faith of black Americans gave that character its winning strength.

Alan Keyes, *Masters of the Dream* (New York: Morrow, 1995), 65.

[24] See Alonzo L. Hamby, *Liberalism and Its Challengers: From F.D.R. to Bush* (Oxford, U.K.: Oxford University Press, 1985), 262–65.

[25] Benjamin Chavis, "Fighting Racism," *USA Today*, 21 January 1991. Quoted in Abigail and Stephan Thernstrom, *America in Black and White: One Nation, Indivisible*

The pessimism and pain in black America lies primarily in the hands of black writers and leaders who have abandoned the values of our ancestors and have made whining the black public voice. The hate and anger of books such as *Makes Me Wanna Holler* or *The Rage of a Privileged Class* are a disservice to young blacks. We need to tell them the truth about a future full of possibilities in a country that is theirs. If we fail to tell the truth, we are guilty of a crime against hope. This hope is not a political slogan to push for increased government intervention but a genuine hope that affirms the inescapable burden of personhood calling us to be responsible beings. Shelby Steele lays out the need in no uncertain terms:

> Our leaders must take a risk. They must tell us the truth, tell us of the freedom and opportunity they have discovered in their own lives. They must tell us what they tell their own children when they go home at night: to study hard, pursue their dreams with discipline and effort, to be responsible for them, to have concern for others, to cherish their race and at the same time make their own lives as Americans.[26]

If black advancement is connected to the expansion of government power, frustration is inevitable. The expectation today is that government initiatives will lift blacks up as a group instead of individual blacks creating a culture of success, which will in turn trigger internal change. Instead of a measured optimism directed toward personal initiative, we are offered another reason to resent the world around us—*poverty can be eliminated entirely by concerted initiative, but America refuses.*

It is unfortunate that such a vision of categorical solutions is prevalent in national, global, and even Christian initiatives. In a proposal to the National Council of Churches of Christ, U.S.A., the National Jobs for All Coalition asks us to

> Imagine a society without poverty. Imagine a society in which all people who want and need to work have jobs that enable them to earn a living adequate for health and well-being. Imagine a society in which recession and periodic loss of job and income no longer threaten. Imagine

---

(New York: Touchstone, 1997), 494.

[26] Shelby Steele, *The Content of Our Character: A New Vision of Race in America* (New York: St. Martin's Press, 1990), 173–74.

a society in which all people can sit under their own vine and fig tree and none is afraid! Such a society could be ours.[27]

In 2006, thirty-five churches in Minnesota united to form A Minnesota Without Poverty coalition. The movement's purpose is to "build, organize, and mobilize a state-wide, interfaith movement to end poverty in Minnesota by 2020."[28] The End Poverty Millennium Campaign signed by world leaders in 2000 set the goal of ending worldwide poverty by 2015.[29] The editors and writers of *Eradicating Global Poverty* put together by the National Council of Churches agree.[30]

A common thread in all of these initiatives is the assertion of endless possibilities available to us and confirmed for us by the "experts." We can bring heaven to earth. For black America, and for many poor communities, the fusion of radical pessimism about America and utopian optimism about our possibilities if we only change the system creates increased antagonisms, continuous cries for government intervention, and a thrust toward separatism and despair.

What we need instead is honesty about our limited human possibilities. A concerted effort to return most charity work and initiative to the private sector through major incentives toward giving is essential in building true coalitions of compassion. We must avoid the pompous rhetoric of grandiose schemes for a new and perfect world where poverty disappears. It is not going to happen, even in a nation full of possibilities. By grounding our action in a reasoned optimism about American society and a realistic acceptance of the dynamism of authentic human freedom, we can find our way toward a better life for most people. "The issue is not how to create a perfect world without poverty," says Father Robert Sirico,

---

[27] "Five Years Closer to Economic Justice: A Proposal to the National Council of Churches of Christ, U.S.A." (National Jobs Coalition, 2000). See document at http://www.njfac.org/NCC-FiveYrsCloser.htm. Similarly, the Catholic Campaign for Human Development states: "It's time to end poverty in America once and for all. The Catholic Campaign for Human Development (CCHD) invests in community-based solutions—that know no racial or religious boundaries."

[28] See http://www.mnwithoutpoverty.org/.

[29] See http://www.endpoverty2015.org/.

[30] National Council of Churches, *Eradicating Poverty: A Christian Study Guide on the Millennium Development Goals* (Cincinnati, OH: Friendship Press, 2006).

but how we can create a system that is most adept at finding those who need our help, meeting their needs, and when possible, helping those people toward a life of independence.... Authentic charity cannot be centrally planned any more than an economy can be. The spontaneous efforts of private individuals, houses of worship and charities will work, however imperfectly.[31]

CLUSTERS OF INFERIORITY

Victims must be grouped, a task that inevitably underlies and highlights tacit assumptions of inferiority. The argument that, because minorities are just that, minorities, they will always be in a disadvantaged position, tells us that the intention is for affirmative action to never end.[32] To account for the cosmic injustice of demography, diversity must be imposed by law. As people tend to promote those who share attributes with them, we are told, even "nonracist" whites will still promote whites. Therefore, we must introduce minorities into the mix to reflect their proportional representation in the *general* population.

But blacks, too, will promote those who look like them. Therefore, the 14 percent of slots reserved for blacks must be both a floor and a ceiling. We must have that many blacks, regardless of whether or not there are precisely that many blacks—no fewer, no more—who meet the standards for a given position. Although affirmative action began as a policy to undermine the use of race, color, gender, or national origin, it is now those traits that justify the policy.

The conundrum lies in the fact that such a political outlook creates stakes for the perpetuation of benefit. What happens after a benefit runs its course? The leadership invested in the preservation of power must create other needs and demand further action or the fate of the group is said to be in jeopardy. Solutions for ethnic or gender problems, real or perceived, depend on an analysis that perpetuates the need for individuals to *remain* in clusters of inferiority. The value of solidarity, in itself a basic social good, comes at the price of asserting victimhood and inferiority. Moreover, solidarity is

[31] Robert A. Sirico, "The U.S. After the Welfare State," Acton Institute, March 1995, http://www.acton.org/public-policy/effective-compassion/accountability/us-after-welfare-state.

[32] Orlando Patterson, *The Ordeal of Integration: Progress and Resentment in America's "Racial" Crisis* (New York: Basic Civitas Books, 1997), 161–63.

not what we get; we get tolerance—in itself not a virtue. I put up with you and resign myself to have a few who look like you around as tokens of a race and a security blanket against lawsuits or bad publicity. The minority specimen intensifies his distrust of the mainstream and reinforces his belief in the need to remain clustered. Why would a minority person make any effort to assimilate the mores of a mainstream he distrusts?

Inevitably, those pretending to establish policy create a false dichotomy: either members of a group are inferior, *or* they are victims of society. In this class/race-struggle system, they find their victims (any group they choose), their heroes (themselves), and their villains (capitalism, the West, religious people, and anyone daring to offer alternative paradigms). In both extremes, men are seen as determined by externalities and incapable of transcending the mark of their genes, race, ethnicity, or sex.

Barbara B. Solomon, for example, asserts that in working with black individuals in distress the greatest concern ought to be not the individual person but structures of oppression acting against that individual. Social workers, then, ought to understand that "[p]owerlessness is a more virulent stressor than anxiety. Consequently, empowerment becomes a more important treatment goal than reduction of anxiety."[33] In a sea of misguided compassion coming from elites' writing policy under false assumptions and from those actively working with the poor and minorities, the human person as an agent of choice is lost—all that is left is the preferred label.

Sociologist Peter Berger has identified an ideological shift among those working with people within such clusters of inferiority. Prey to the 1960s' Cultural Revolution, the social sciences became "an instrument of ideological advocacy."[34] As members of an advocacy group, social scientists became defenders of leftist social analysis. In their hands, research instruments are simply useful tools to advance their ideological goals.

For example, the Quick Discrimination Index (QDI) is a thirty-item, Likert-type self-report inventory. The index has been widely regarded by counselors as a standard tool for the systematic study of prejudice and tolerance toward minority groups and women. Disagreement with the following items indicates a higher receptivity and awareness of diversity and gender equality:

---

[33] Cited in James W. Green, *Cultural Awareness in the Human Services* (Boston: Allyn & Bacon, 1999), 200.

[34] Peter Berger, "Whatever Happened to Sociology?" *First Things* (October 2002).

"I really think affirmative-action programs on college campuses constitute reverse discrimination."

"I am against affirmative-action programs in business."

"In the past few years, too much attention has been directed toward multicultural or minority issues in education."

"Most of my close friends are from my own racial group."

"In the past few years, too much attention has been directed toward multicultural or minority issues in business."

"I think the school system, from elementary school through college, should encourage minority and immigrant children to learn and fully adopt traditional American values."

Agreement with the following statement, among others, reflects a nonracist attitude: "It upsets (angers) me that a racial minority person has never been president of the United States."[35]

From the perspective of the ideology at play here, the "wrong" position on a policy question (affirmative action) constitutes evidence of racism, whether one's position has anything to do with an attitude of racial superiority or not. Even an accidental circumstance (the racial identity of one's friends) is evidence of racism. Too bad for the farmer in a small North Dakota town where no African-Americans reside—he cannot escape being racist!

Condemned to the eternal label of victim, minorities become objects of analysis rather than protagonists of their own success. Those imprisoned by this label depend on so-called government helpers—bureaucrats who tirelessly tinker with the poor but who are at the same time invested in maintaining them in clusters of inferiority.

[35] Marianne Schneider Corey and Gerald Corey, *Becoming a Helper*, 4th ed. (Pacific Grove, CA: Brooks/Cole, 2003), 194–95. The QDI is online at http://drkdrcounselingcourses.weebly.com/uploads/4/9/6/6/4966511/quick_discrimination_index_instrument.pdf.

9

ACCOMMODATION AND
HISTORICAL SURVIVAL

---

*If we allow men freedom because we presume
them to be reasonable beings, we also must
make it worth their while to act as reasonable
beings by letting them bear the consequences
of their decisions.*

—F. A. Hayek,
The Constitution of Liberty

It was about ten o'clock at night. My wife, Crystal, and I heard someone
pounding on the front door of our home. Peeking through the window,
I recognized "Charlene," a girl from my church youth group. She was
leaning against our door and crying. Crystal helped her inside. Charlene
looked exhausted and desperate. "I can't take it anymore," she moaned.
"I just can't!"

While my wife struggled to console Charlene, we both wondered what
could have brought on this scene. We did not know enough about the girl's
home life to understand what might be the cause of her breakdown. When
Charlene had calmed enough to explain, we learned the truth. For several
months, the fifteen-year-old girl had been taking care of her siblings while
her mother was out abusing drugs for days on end. No one in the family
knew where the mother went. From time to time, she would reappear for
a few hours only to vanish again into the shadows of the drug underworld.

During all this time, Charlene had been trying her best to go to school and support herself and her siblings. The burden becoming too heavy, Charlene fled, leaving management of the household to the next in line. She ended up on our doorstep.

As I drove to a local pharmacy to buy her some toiletries, my emotions were a mixture of anger and fear. I was angry with Charlene's mother and with the society that permitted this tragedy to happen. I was scared for Charlene's future and what lay ahead for her brothers and sisters.

My mind filled with questions regarding the human condition. What could possibly drive individuals to make such disastrous decisions? What could motivate a mother to throw away her life and send her children into a lonely and desperate existence? Were her decisions free choices or the expected behavior of a prisoner of desire? How could anyone remedy such a situation?

My immediate temptation was to involve government. "They should come in and fix this!" I thought. My initial reaction was soon tempered by doubts about how "they" could really solve anything. What could strangers from government bureaucracies of compassion do?

After a short stay with us, Charlene decided to go back home and continue to take care of her siblings, facing again the domestic drudgery and loneliness. We were reluctant to let her go, but she seemed determined, and her grandmother was by then trying to help. Some time after the incident, the mother returned home, apparently determined to find a way out of her addiction. It has now been several years since the mother's return. She remains with her children and continues to recover. As if from the ashes of a broken existence, there sprouted in Charlene's mother the courage to choose to escape her misery. Just a couple of years ago Charlene became a nurse and, fueled by a desire to help others, joined my ministry's board of advisors.

Through this incident, I realized that the way I responded to the social pathology in the lives of the people I worked with was dependent on the vision of the human person I decided to adopt. That vision would determine whether I viewed people as blind victims or as subjects imbued with meaning. Either a predetermined genetic makeup built by the evolutionary process was destiny, or they possessed the power to actualize their dignity even amidst challenging internal and external forces. Before my very eyes, the drama of the meaning of the human condition unfolded, and I found myself confronted by it and impelled to find an answer to it.

Is the human person the ontological and epistemological starting point for our assessment of human suffering and black reality?[1] Our understanding of the human person not only provides a sense of man's proximate condition as well as his potential and limitations but also a vision of his ultimate ends. The anthropology described in chapter 2 is the only adequate explanation for the historical realities of both terrible oppression and amazing progress.

And Now What?

The horror of slavery is part of the identity of every person of African descent. That history naturally produces feelings of anger and pain. "If ever there was a victim," asserts Orlando Patterson, "the American slave, like slaves elsewhere in the Americas and the world, was most certainly one. Slavery and the post-juridical serfdom of Jim Crow are what make the Afro-American experience unique in America."[2]

It was inevitable that the experience of oppression would have a negative impact on a group of people whose history was infused with such evils. There is, however, a factor consistently missing, or at least greatly understated, in most depictions of blacks' history: their survival. African Americans survived and even prospered in spite of their troubles.[3] No one has expressed better than Booker T. Washington the paradox of a people who paid in bondage the price of freedom:

> Think about it: we went into slavery pagans; we came out Christians. We went into slavery pieces of property; we came out American citizens. We went into slavery with chains clanking about our wrists; we came out with the American ballot in our hands.... Notwithstanding the cruelty and moral wrong of slavery, we are in a stronger and more hopeful

---

[1] Anthony J. Santelli et al., *The Free Person and the Free Economy: A Personalist View of Market Economics* (Lanham, MD: Lexington Books, 2002), 7.

[2] Orlando Patterson, *The Ordeal of Integration: Progress and Resentment in America's "Racial" Crisis* (New York: Basic Civitas Books, 1997), 78.

[3] "Our common identity owes much to our shared experience of oppression, but it owes much more to the moral and spiritual resources that made it possible to survive in spite of it." Alan Keyes, *Masters of the Dream: The Strength and Betrayal of Black America* (New York: Harper Perennial, 1996), 6.

position, materially, intellectually, morally, and religiously, than is true of an equal number of black people in any other portion of the globe.[4]

Today, African Americans are the most successful and thriving sizeable black group in the world.

The history of their success ought to be the central subject of inquiry, for discovering the values that enable people to survive will help us to meet our present challenges. Black resilience is readily observable in their history of coping with bondage and racism. Blacks exhibited moral integrity in spite of the perennial degradations of the slaves. They resisted by appealing to their faith and holding tight to their families, friends, and church congregations. They developed coping mechanisms centered on faith celebrations and on bonds of mutual support, helping them to move ahead even when many whites doubted slaves' capacity to endure such suffering for very long. Blacks relied on self-help and accommodation as tools of defiance and survival.[5] By declaring a "moral rebellion" against the dehumanizing effects of slavery, they were able to appropriate aspects of the oppressor's culture and lifestyle and transform themselves into exemplars of American ideals. Cultural accommodation is not betrayal; it is indeed the exercise of courage and prudence in the real life of trade-offs and noncategorical alternatives.[6]

This history of resistance, however, is a legacy obscured by later emphasis on grievances. Many black leaders and intellectuals fail to emphasize that strength as they place inordinate attention on what whites did wrong and on blacks' resistance through violent revolt.[7] They fail to see that it was not

---

[4] E. Davidson Washington, ed., *Selected Speeches of Booker T. Washington* (Garden City, NY: Doubleday, 1932), 37.

[5] The spirituals are the greatest testimony of our people's patience and steadfastness under the yoke of slavery. Although some did physically rebel, for the most part our people resisted by appealing to their faith. The religious ceremonies of slaves were full of coded messages and emotional outbursts that reflected both their sorrow and their hope.

[6] See Orlando Patterson, *The Ordeal*, 102–4.

[7] See Ralph Wiley, *What Black People Should Do Now* (New York: Ballantine Books, 1993); Cornell West, *Race Matters* (New York: Vintage Books, 1993); Ellis Cose, *The Rage of a Privileged Class* (New York: HarperCollins, 1993); Toni Morrison, *Playing in the Dark: Whiteness and the Literary Imagination* (Cambridge: Harvard University Press, 1982); Derrick Bell, *Faces at the Bottom of the Well* (New York: Basic Books, 1992);

upheaval that predominantly characterized black resistance but, instead, quiet perseverance.

These leaders also ignore the detour from the values that sustained blacks evident in our most recent history. Many have abandoned the path of honest research in search of the shadows of past misdeeds without a sense of historical perspective. While economic success is viewed with suspicion; defeatism, broken families, and violence are described as "our people adjusting to racism"—a sign of authenticity. Viewpoints that do not square with the hypothesis of racism as the root of all black problems are considered out of bounds.[8] For example, in *The Great Wells of Democracy*, Manning Marable portrays a grotesque existence for blacks in a country where "the segregationist signs have been taken down, but the ugly patterns of racialized inequality and white privilege persist in most respects."[9] Doris Y. Wilkinson states that "race is the foundation of inequality for African Americans in all phases of life. White men and women in any social stratum, regardless of education, skills, ideological convictions, ethnic affiliation, gender, or sexual orientation, are aware that American society favors them over all African Americans."[10]

Is that truly the case? What was the outlet for blacks during the most trying times of slavery? Why did they not degenerate into a morbid and violent mob? What kind of future and opportunity did they have during the depression years in the 1930s? How can anyone appreciate the incredible difference in quality of life between that past and today's situation and still disavow America's profound societal change?

Adhering to an outdated view of American reality is not going to help our people. The fate of young people lies in opening opportunities for engagement in society. Radicalism is not a good answer. It demeans black

---

Nathan McCall, *Makes Me Wanna Holler: A Young Black Man in America* (New York: Random House, 1994).

[8] For several examples of the use of racism as an easy explanation for our problems, see John Perazzo, *The Myths that Divide Us: How Lies Have Poisoned American Race Relations* (New York: World Studies Books, 1999), chap. 2.

[9] Manning Marable, *The Great Wells of Democracy: The Meaning of Race in American Life* (New York: Basic Civitas Books, 2003), 6.

[10] Doris Y. Wilkinson, "Systemic Racism Underlies All Inequality in the United States" in *Inequality: Opposing Views in Social Problems*, ed. Lori Shein (San Diego: Greenhaven Press, 1998), 45.

achievement by confining it to chance or fate, concessions or cronyism. To appeal to categorical phrases such as "white privilege" to explain every conceivable disparity is facile and alienating.

Thus "conservative" has become an epithet among African Americans, and anyone with a different viewpoint will be called one—whether they are or not. The brilliant insights of men such as John McWhorter or Orlando Patterson are regarded as simplistic, uncaring, or dismissive of any external-ist factor affecting groups or individuals. "Thus," Thomas Sowell observes, "anyone who concludes that racial discrimination, for example, explains less of the intergroup differences in income among racial or ethnic groups than is commonly supposed will be said to have 'dismissed' discrimination as a factor, no matter how extensive the data or history examined before reaching that conclusion."[11]

Many liberals have bought so much into the assumption of unredeem-able structural oppression that they continually self-flagellate in the hopes of being forgiven. The antiracism enterprise tells whites that because they benefit from privilege and cannot help but benefit they need to be ashamed of their whiteness.[12] Some organizations work toward total eradication of white privilege within their ranks for a period of years. Organizations form "Antiracism Training Teams" or even create a caucus system where racially divided caucuses meet separately: the "People of Color Caucus" working on internalized racist oppression, and the "White Caucus" working with issues of internalized superiority. Later, both teams meet to work together to try to understand each other better.[13] To "understand each other" means that whites will genuflect and confess their guilt and blacks will profess their victimhood and (maybe) absolve whites.

---

[11] Thomas Sowell, *The Vision of the Anointed: Self-Congratulation as a Basis for Social Policy* (New York: Basic Books, 1995), 213.

[12] White privilege has been described as "an invisible package of unearned assets which I can count on cashing in each day, but about which I was 'meant' to remain oblivious. White privilege is like an invisible weightless knapsack of special provisions, maps, passports, codebooks, visas, clothes, tools and blank checks." Peggy McIntosh, "White Privilege: Unpacking the Invisible Knapsack," excerpted from "White Privilege and Male Privilege: A Personal Account of Coming to See Correspondences Through Work in Women's Studies," Working Paper no. 189, Wellesley Centers for Women, 1988, http://amptoons.com/blog/files/mcintosh.html.

[13] Information on the caucus system appeared on the web site of the Sinsinawa Dominicans (www.sinsinawa.org). The relevant links are no longer accessible.

Yet, individual penance is not enough for the racialists. No, a true antiracist believer must side with the motto of the magazine *Race Traitor*: "Treason to whiteness is loyalty to humanity." The idea is that racism has so tainted our country that our polity is now a sham—a reality that must be destroyed and replaced with another.[14] Love for America is betrayal of blackness.

IS ACCOMMODATION BETRAYAL?

The strategy of accommodation has been extremely successful for blacks, but those gains are normally downplayed in the literature of race.[15] The tool of accommodation is often erroneously associated with middle class black elites who dare not confront the system and are supposedly ashamed of their heritage.[16] However, middle-class values are similar to the values of the slaves and of poor blacks for many generations. The assumption is that if some privileged blacks are raised in a somewhat sheltered environment, they will naturally tend to accommodate or adjust to the said values, while if they are raised in misery they will naturally rebel. Nonetheless, the fact remains that slaves, for the most part, accommodated to their circumstances without losing their pride, their hopes, or their defiance in the face of injustice. The so-called middle-class values helped them survive and begin to slowly progress in the midst of an oppressive society.

What are these values? Education, faith, church attendance, a work ethic, a desire for economic progress, a desire to form a loving and stable family, a quest for security through savings and investing, a desire to acquire and consume, and respectability. These values are not black or white, but universal, and they have served blacks well—as they do any other group that practices them.

The strategy of accommodation created the greatest benefits for blacks in America. In accommodation, the slaves decided not to make whites the primary focus of their concerns and identity. Slaves used the system the

---

[14] See John McWhorter, *Winning the Race: Beyond the Crisis in Black America* (New York: Gotham Books, 2006), 366–68.

[15] Abigail and Stephan Thernstrom, *America in Black and White: One Nation, Indivisible* (New York: Touchstone, 1997), chap. 9; George Wilder, "The Roots of Black Poverty," *The Wall Street Journal*, Oct. 30, 1995.

[16] James H. Cone, *Martin & Malcolm & America: A Dream or a Nightmare* (New York: Orbis, 1991), 21.

best they could to transcend their relationship with whites by focusing on building their moral beings with faith as an anchor. Valued only as property, they denied determinism by affirming their humanity and holding to their faith in God even when the constraints of slavery prevented them from establishing organized churches and institutions.[17] Cultural appropriation is an act of the will, built on practical reason: a will to survive, a will to live. In that sense, I believe that such appropriation has occurred across the spectrum of black America but less among the "outspoken top tenth" and those on the bottom rung. The top and the bottom strata remain the least self-determined.[18]

The answer for those still at the bottom is not to reject "whiteness"; this approach keeps us dependent on white opinion and action. Antiracist campaigns led by radicals remain stuck within the victim-victimizer deterministic paradigm, with blacks moving from passive to engaged victims and whites from being privileged to being ashamed but still privileged. The answer is to invest in young people to help them become successful and engaged citizens. Engaged citizens invest their talent, treasure, and time in actively helping the marginalized. They "devote endless and heroic amounts of effort to changing what they saw wrong, insufficient and unjust, often having grown up knowing just what their current charges are suffering from."[19]

Today's black liberal elite has failed to connect with this history of cultural appropriation. As Alan Keyes masterfully summarizes: "By accepting racism as the epitome of the black problem, liberals made race the defining term of the black identity."[20] The reality of the history of our people is different. Racial oppression is not the *content* of our experience as a people but the *background* against which the content of our character was built. This

---

[17] Keyes, *Masters of the Dream*, 16–17, and chap. 3.

[18] Here I disagree somewhat with Patterson's assessment that cultural appropriation is more common among the most intellectually curious. As I believe that it is a matter of the will as it is moved by reason, the great cultural appropriation has not occurred in general among those on the bottom rung where the will has been so corrupted and reason has been clouded by the exertion of uncontrolled appetites nor among the elites who have sided with countercultural ideologies, thus betraying the foundational values of America. It has occurred by the hard work of middle- and working-class blacks who have accepted as theirs the basic assumptions of American values and American democracy.

[19] McWhorter, *Winning the Race*, 372.

[20] Keyes, *Masters of the Dream*, 86.

concept has deep anthropological implications. By robbing individuals of their reality as subjects, we make impossible their self-realization and self-determination as responsible persons.

The deficient anthropology under which black reality in America has been depicted has unfortunate consequences. Whites define our existence and we never leave the reality of the slavery system. Blacks become not protagonists of a history of strength forged in the midst of incredible obstacles but pawns in the drama of white oppression. Derrick Bell is right when he says that "the fact of slavery refuses to fade" but mistakes its present locus. It is present today in the emphasis of academics and leaders on racism as the main object of their inquiry. Alan Keyes explains the implications of such an outlook: "In this view, blacks appear as passive victims, as objects of action rather than as actors in their own right. In principle, though, this means that if the history has a positive outcome, if we vanquish racism, there will no longer be a role in the American drama for black Americans as such."[21]

Moral life, according to Karol Wojtyła, is impossible without freedom, "which forms a real and inherent component of the structure, indeed a component that is decisive for the entire structure of moral becoming. Freedom constitutes the root factor of man's becoming good or bad by his actions; it is the root factor of the becoming as such of human morality."[22]

The vision of blacks as objects moved by forces denies their capacity for integral human fulfillment. This deterministic system creates self-erosion, which denies persons their ontological freedom.

WHITE AND BLACK GOLD

We have already seen how slavery should be treated: admitting its wide-ranging and pernicious effects yet denying it a decisive role in present black reality. This view gains perspective by recognizing that the injustice of slavery is not unique to the black experience in America. Likewise, the desire to enslave a class of people did not originate with racial ideology nor was it an exclusively European phenomenon. Slavery is older than Islam,

---

[21] Keyes, *Masters of the Dream*, 83.

[22] Karol Wojtyła, *The Acting Person*, trans. Andrzej Potocki, *Analecta Husserliana: The Yearbook of Phenomenological Research*, vol. 10 (Dordecht, Netherlands: D. Reidel, 1979), 99.

Buddhism, and Christianity and was universally accepted as a way of life throughout most of human history. In fact, the very word comes from a nonblack ethnic group, the Slavs, who suffered bondage on a grand scale both in Europe and in the Ottoman Empire. Russians, Slavs, and other Europeans were often enslaved by pirates and others who sold them at slave markets in North Africa and in the Ottoman Empire.[23]

It is thus ironic that many Afrocentrists are in fact so Eurocentric in their view of world history. The cultural dependency features of Afrocentrism are tied to the greatness of Western culture. Western civilization remains the epitome of cultural success, and the cultures of Africa remain unexplored and assessed only secondarily through theories of victimization that focus on the marvels of Western culture.[24] In the Afrocentric myth, Mother Africa, the great Valhalla, was victimized by the Greeks, who seized all her knowledge and presented it as their own. The problem with this analysis is that the Africa described as the mother of all knowledge is a myth. Some even attempt to trace the beginnings of the black church to the mystery system in ancient Egypt.[25] Afrocentric pseudo-history is a collection of bogus claims and misreadings of classical texts that cannot be substantiated by time-tested methods of intellectual inquiry.[26]

Not only do Afrocentrists attribute every possible Western accomplishment to an African origin (implying that blacks gain by appropriating

---

[23] Thomas Sowell, *Race and Culture: A World View* (New York: Basic Books, 1994), 186–87; Patrick Manning, *Slavery in African Life: Occidental, Oriental, and African Slave Trades* (New York: Cambridge University Press, 1990), 27–29.

[24] As classicist Guy McLean Rogers states about one of the major Afrocentric texts, *Black Athena* by Afrocentrist Martin Bernal, "The cultures which Bernal argues laid the foundation of Western civilization are valued primarily for laying the foundations of the West. They are not studied on their own terms, or for their own cultural achievements.... As others also have noticed, *Black Athena* therefore remains inescapably Eurocentric in its approach and method." Guy McLean Rogers, "Multiculturalism and the Foundations of Western Civilization," in *Black Athena Revisited*, ed. Mary Lefkowitz and Guy McLean Rogers (Chapel Hill, NC: University of North Carolina Press, 1996), 442.

[25] Elijah Mickel, "Self-Help in African American Communities: A Historical Review," in *Social Work Processes*, ed. Beulah Compton and Burt Galaway (Pacific Grove, CA: Brooks/Cole, 1999), 410.

[26] See Mary Lefkowitz, *Not Out of Africa: How Afrocentrism Became an Excuse to Teach Myth as History* (New York: Basic Books, 1996).

European excellence), but they also attribute every possible social evil to Western civilization. Habitually accustomed to attribute slavery only to the West, they mostly ignore the abundant evidence of non-Western slavery. Islamic and North African slave systems receive passing reviews. The study of slavery in India, China, the Ottoman Empire, and the extensive intra-African slavery network is viewed as a curiosity engaged only by eccentric academics.[27] The Islamic slave system in Africa was extensive and involved more people than the transatlantic slave trade, yet it remains relatively unknown. This system consisted of the enslavement of European Christians in North Africa and black slaves in the sub-Saharan regions of the continent. Islamic slavery was brutal and degrading. In Zanzibar, "rows of girls from the age of twelve and upwards [were] ... exposed to the examination of throngs of Arab slave-dealers and subjected to inexpressible indignities by the brutal dealers."[28] Arab slave raids were a dreadful experience and treatment was horrendous:

> Families were divided, and because there was a greater demand for women and children, men were often executed....
>
> For those who were enslaved, the dangers involved forced marches, inadequate food, sexual abuse, and death on the road.... Still other captives, the prime boys, faced castration because the price for eunuchs

[27] Thomas Sowell, *Black Rednecks and White Liberals* (Jackson, TN: Encounter Books, 2006), 111–13. On European slavery in Northern Africa, see Milton Giles, *White Gold: The Extraordinary Story of Thomas Pellow and Islam's One Million White Slaves* (London: Hodder & Stoughton, 2004); on India, see Utsa Patnaik, Manjari Dingwaney Tulsa Patnaik, and Manjari Dingwaney, *Chains of Servitude: Bondage and Slavery in India* (Reno: University of Nevada Press, 1985); on China, see Henry W. Bunn, "Girl Slavery in China," *The New York Times*, October 31, 1920; on the Ottoman Empire and Africa, see John Perazzo, *The Myths That Divide Us*, 353–57; Robert Hughes, *Culture of Complaint: The Fraying of America* (New York: Oxford University Press, 1993), 142; John Reader, *Africa* (New York: Alfred A. Knof, 1997), 291; R. W. Beachey *The Slave Trade of Eastern Africa* (London: Rex Collins, 1976), 182; Thomas Sowell, *The Economics and Politics of Race* (New York: William Morrow & Co., 1985), 228; and Basil Davidson, *The African Slave Trade: Precolonial History, 1450–1850* (Boston: Little, Brown Publishers, 1980), 42.

[28] Ehud R. Toledano, *The Ottoman Slave Trade and Its Suppression: 1840–1890* (Princeton: Princeton University Press, 1982), 51–53, quoted in Perazzo, *Myths That Divide Us*, 356.

was always very high—and no wonder the price was high, given that as many as nine out of ten died from unsuccessful operations.[29]

The idea that blacks lived in basic freedom and peace in the African continent and suddenly found themselves deprived by the mighty hand of the Northern white oppressor is simply a myth. The African populations coming to American shores had already suffered terribly from the negative effects of bondage in their native lands. As Zora Neal Hurston aptly observed:

> The white people held my people in slavery in America. They had bought us, it is true, and exploited us. But the inescapable fact that stuck in my craw was: my people had sold me.... My own people had exterminated whole nations and torn families apart for a profit before the strangers got their chance at a cut. It was a sobering thought. It impressed upon me the universal nature of greed and glory.[30]

Not only were Africans sold to Westerners by other Africans: Intra-African slavery existed before the first white man set foot on the continent, and it grew exponentially after both Western and Oriental traders ceased buying slaves. After 1850, the price of slaves dropped and the purchase of African slaves by other Africans skyrocketed. The latter part of the nineteenth century saw the greatest expansion of African slavery, to the extent that entire societies in both western and eastern African countries became organized around slavery.[31] Highly specialized intra-African states such as Asante, Dahomey, and Futa Jallon created networks of trade by utilizing tributary and client networks consisting of minor tribes that supplied them with slaves by preying on marginalized communities.[32] In other words, the enslavement of black people is a practice neither exclusive to nor dependent on white Europeans or Americans.

Slave rebellions and violent uprisings against bondage were not a unique American phenomenon; they also occurred in African countries between the 1850s and the 1900s. African slave-owners, like masters anywhere else

---

[29] Paul E. Lovejoy, *Transformations in Slavery: A History of Slavery in Africa*, 3rd ed. (Cambridge, UK: Cambridge University Press, 2012), 35.

[30] Zora Neale Hurston, *Dust Tracks on a Road* (New York: Harper Perennial, 1991), 154; quoted in Perazzo, *Myths that Divide Us*, 359.

[31] Manning, *Slavery and African* Life, 140–42.

[32] Martin A. Klein, *Slavery and Colonial Rule in French West Africa* (New York: Cambridge University Press, 1998), 39.

in the world, held the power of life and death over their slaves. The civil authorities of different kingdoms severely countered slave uprisings, such as the Yoruba rebellion in Dahomey (now the Republic of Benin) and rebellions in the Niger Delta region and Zanzibar (Tanzania).[33]

Even worse, present African slavery in countries such as Sudan, Benin, and Mauritania receive less attention than the continual recounting of the experience of slavery inflicted by and on people who have long since disappeared from the earth. As recently as 2004, there were an estimated 43,000 slaves in Niger.[34] Although the practice was outlawed in Mauritania in 1981, slavery remains common, practiced by the most powerful group, the white Moors, over the Haratins and blacks.[35] Jok Madut Jok details the long horror of slavery in that country, a product not of modern civil war but of thousands of years of tradition and the historic hostilities between the Islamic north and the black and Christian south.[36] According to a 2004 United Nations Children's Fund (UNICEF) report, "the trafficking of human beings is a problem in every African country."[37]

Slavery exists where the strong exercise raw power over the weak. Vulnerability, not racial antagonism, has been the key factor in human bondage everywhere around the globe. Prejudice and racism against those enslaved in America developed to rationalize the slavery enterprise; they were the result, not the cause, of enslavement.

The real Africa remains concealed when in reality it does not need to be connected to the West to appreciate its contributions and accept its defects. The real Africa was a place where imperfect human beings lived and achieved much in varied aspects of culture. Africa was also a place where cruelty, oppression, and slavery abounded, as much as anywhere else, hundreds of years before any contact with whites. To create a mythical and deeply Eurocentric Africa and present it as a sort of paradise where black men could live in true dignity until the white man came and disturbed the existential bliss is a disservice to history, to America, and to Africa itself.

---

[33] Klein, *Slavery and Colonial* Rule, 102, 144.

[34] "Testimony: Former Niger Slave," *BBC News* (Wednesday, 3 November, 2004).

[35] "Mauritania Still Practicing Slavery," *BBC News* (Thursday, 7 November, 2002).

[36] Jok Madut Jok, *War and Slavery in Sudan* (Philadelphia: University of Pennsylvania Press, 2001).

[37] See "Trafficking in Human Beings: Especially Women and Children in Africa," UNICEF Innocenti Research Centre (Florence, Italy, 2004).

In his brave book *Out of America: A Black Man Confronts Africa*, journalist Keith B. Richburg provides a vivid and gripping memoir of his African experiences. Having observed the horrors of mass murder, brutality, and constant warfare, Richburg identifies the most basic problem: tribalism. "Tribalism remains the single most corrosive, debilitating influence plaguing modern Africa in its quest for democracy and development," he concludes. "To blame Africa's ills on tribalism is a cliché, to be sure. But like many clichés, this one has a basis in truth."[38] Coming back to America, Richburg experienced the same attitude of radical separatism fed by Afrocentric propaganda. It is the same insidious tribalism, absent the piles of corpses. The desire to create quasi-religious celebrations, such as Kwanzaa, and to attribute a distinct black dialect to supposed African roots, as with so-called Ebonics or black English, is a manifestation of the search for a separatist identity.

HISTORICAL SURVIVAL AND THE DIALECTICS OF HISTORY

The success stories of varied ethnic groups around the world reveal that people can rise above the evils inflicted on the group by focusing on the values and strategies used to defy such evil.[39] In the case of blacks in America, that is exactly what they did *before* the advent of "Great Society" liberalism and the co-opting of the civil rights movement. The crippling mindset of the politics of modern liberalism had a demoralizing and demeaning effect on blacks. It was based on the error that preferential treatment holds the key to upward mobility and social progress and that government is the instrument to achieve such goals.

---

[38] Keith B. Richburg, *Out of America: A Black Man Confronts Africa* (San Diego: Harcourt Brace, 1998), 240.

[39] See Thomas Sowell, *Preferential Policies* (New York: William Morrow & Company, 1990); and Sowell, *Race and Culture*. Some argue that comparisons between different ethnic groups concerning their response to oppression cannot be made because circumstances vary. The point being made, however, is that the fact of oppression has been confronted by blacks in America differently at different times. It seems to me that the strategies that have been proven successful to others have also been proven successful for blacks in America. The problem seems to reside in the abandonment of these strategies and the pursuit of other strategies.

The use of historic wrongs to identify the group and relieve persons from responsibility prevents them from ever being fully free.[40] At the most basic level of freedom, we can confidently state that the range of choice available to blacks has increased exponentially.[41] Even so, as F. A. Hayek asserts, "the range of physical possibilities from which a person can choose at a given moment has no direct relevance to freedom." It is our capacity to assume responsibility for our actions in light of the opening of possibilities that determines whether we are free: "If we allow men freedom because we presume them to be reasonable beings, we also must make it worth their while to act as reasonable beings by letting them bear the consequences of their decisions."[42]

By overlooking the margin of choice available today, we close the possibility of assuming full responsibility for our lives. Preferential treatment reduces us to the position of perceived inferiority, as if the people being protected lack the capacity for moral self-realization. It produces self-doubt and creates disincentives to hard work and personal improvement. It is con-

---

[40] Sowell eloquently analyzes how historic wrongs cannot necessarily be used to understand later developments:

> Tempting as it is to imagine that the contemporary troubles of historically wronged groups are due to those wrongs; this is confusing causation with morality. The contemporary socioeconomic position of groups in a given society often bears no relationship to the historic wrongs they have suffered. Both in Canada and in the United States, people of Japanese descent have significantly higher incomes than whites, who nonetheless display a long record of discrimination against Japanese. The same story could be told of the Chinese in Malaysia, Indonesia, and many other countries around the world, of the Jews in countries with virulent anti-Semitism, and a wide variety of other groups in a wide variety of other countries. Among poorer groups as well, the level of poverty often has little correlation with the degree of oppression. No one would claim that the historic wrongs suffered by Puerto Ricans in the United States exceed those suffered by blacks, but the average Puerto Rican income is lower than the average income of blacks.

Sowell, *Preferential Policies*, 149.

[41] See Thernstrom and Thernstrom, *America in Black and White*, chap. 3.

[42] F. A. Hayek, *The Constitution of Liberty* (Chicago: University of Chicago Press, 1960), 12, 76.

trary to the history of a people who in the past refused the label of victim under truly victimizing conditions.

In *Reinventing the Melting Pot*, Tamar Jacoby presents well the two views common among minorities regarding the adoption of an American identity: It is impossible or it is to be feared. The first view posits that assimilation is no longer possible. Immigrants are simply too different in ethnicity, class, and education to Westernize. Thus, although desirable in theory, assimilation remains a chimera. Both anti-immigration activists and multicultural advocates hold this position.

Those who embrace the second option believe that assimilating is a betrayal of who they are. It is an unjust requirement demanding a loss of self in conforming to a foreign identity. The melting pot is a tool of oppression. This group is composed mostly of new immigrants, black and Latino elites, and young people.[43]

Although formulated in reference to the integration of new immigrants into the American mainstream, I believe that this binary continues to apply to black Americans in a unique sense. In fact, there is among blacks a merger of both poles into one single rejection of integration. On the one hand, there are those who accept a very strong racial identity and believe integration is indeed "cultural genocide." Many in the same group fear that integration is more about the acknowledgment of a political stance unacceptable to those who defend "true blackness." They may or may not see integration as a theoretical possibility, but they definitely fear its political implications. In fact, they hold that race as a social construct is about ideology and class struggle as much as it is about skin color.

Consequently, they fear that assimilation into white middle-class values signifies the loss of black identity because black identity *is* the rejection of those values. In the process, blackness is reduced to class consciousness. If integration is possible, whites must change, meaning that the whole structure of a capitalist and bourgeoisie society must radically change. After all, the most fundamental truth about black reality in America, in this view, is founded on the theoretical understanding of human consciousness developed by Karl Marx. In *A Contribution to the Critique of Political Economy*, Marx lays down the deterministic view of consciousness: "The mode of production in material life determines the general character of the social, political and spiritual processes of life. It is not the consciousness of men that determines

---

[43] Tamar Jacoby, *Reinventing the Melting Pot* (New York: Basic Books, 2004).

their existence, but, on the contrary, their social existence determines their consciousness."[44]

The German Marxist poet Bertolt Brecht once wrote "Art is a hammer with which to shape reality." Art, then, has only blunt instrumental value. As a result, it cannot be spoken of as an expression of a basic human good. For many black intellectuals, race is, in similar fashion, a forum for political battles. In a class society, all aspects of culture are partisan and instrumental because they bear the indelible mark of class struggle. Similarly, race and ethnicity become hammers with which we shape reality (or destroy it). They are means toward the ultimate end of a classless society, the only true end. Simply put, race is a weapon of class struggle. Those who believe in the irreducibility of race are welcomed in the struggle as useful idiots.

Similarly, Gus Hall, former head of the Communist Party USA, held that culture must be utilized for ideological purposes: "This is an integral part of the ideological struggle—to influence thought patterns.... The ideological struggle in the field of culture is very sharp. It takes place on the stage, the screen, in music, art and poetry. It pervades fiction and non-fiction, *especially* history."[45] The use of ideology to shape historiography is evident in the rejection of assimilation embraced by a black leadership immersed in the politics of the left and the cultural transformations affecting America during the great disruption of the 1960s. This rejection occurred with a buffer of only a few years after the height of Jim Crow segregation.

In typical dialectical thought, the opening of opportunities for progress and integration is seen as just another skirmish in the war of class struggle. The civil rights movement, unfortunately, was co-opted by Marxist scholars and activists trying to reshape it along the lines of Marxist struggle dialectics. As the conferral of formal rights did not immediately produce the expected rise in black achievement, the dialectic was confirmed: the structures of a capitalist system are designed for oppression alone and integration must be rejected. Now they could confidently preach how structural racism is embedded in the fabric of the very culture we are supposedly invited to

---

[44] Karl Marx, *Selected Writings in Sociology and Social Philosophy*, Eng. trans. (Chicago: Charles Kerr & Co., 1913), 11–12.

[45] Gus Hall, *Power of Ideology* (New York: New Outlook Publishers, 1989) [emphasis mine]. See also http://gushallactionclub.blogspot.com/2008/08/brothers-and-sisters-i-warmly-point-out.html.

join. The only valid responses to such a shift in the dialectic are separatism, black cultural essentialism, and radical structural change.

Is historical survival tied to the reconstruction of an African past, a golden age suppressed by the vanquishing West, or is it part of a larger struggle embedded in the very nature of history? Confronted by a kaleidoscope of diverse and even contradictory cultures, perhaps identity can be grasped by voluntarily segregating ourselves within the salad bowl of ideological multiculturalism. Alternatively, our identity could be redefined according to the dynamics of the dialectics of history, pointing toward its disappearance in the sea of a classless society.

I reject both alternatives. There is a better way.

10

The Inner City and the Inner Man

This is revolution carried to the very marrow of human nature. The new political man!

—Robert Nisbet[1]

A nthony was a lanky and rambunctious kid who seemed always to be in trouble. I remember in bemusement the distinctive three-piece suit he wore to church and the day I had to remove him from the church bus for starting a fire. Though his mother is black, his light complexion set him apart in the Sward Village housing projects in Fort Myers. He had to endure daily name-calling: "white boy" and "cracker." He lived with his mother and grandmother. There was never any father in the picture. Anthony's mom had had a one-night stand with a white man whose identity she no longer remembered.

Fighting and drug dealing were common at Sward Village. Turmoil and death surrounded the many good people who lived in constant terror. Anthony lost many childhood friends, one after the other: destroyed by drugs, fallen in fights over girls, or gone to serve life prison sentences for some stupid crime. Always teased due to his color, Anthony learned to cope and survive by continually acting out and fighting. With no one there to lead him, Anthony slid well down the slippery slope that leads to misery.

---

[1] Robert Nisbet, *The Present Age: Progress and Anarchy in Modern America* (Indianapolis: Liberty Fund, 1988), 119.

At thirteen, he first got in trouble with the law and was forced to leave the somewhat stable environment of his grandmother's home at the projects to move into a nearby house with an uncle, a school bus driver who tried his best to take care of him. Less supervised then, he continued to get in trouble. After recovering from an illness that left him paralyzed from the waist down, Anthony's life went further downhill. He was sent to an alternative learning school for "the bad kids." He did numerous stints at the local juvenile detention center. At sixteen, he started using marijuana and cocaine and found himself back in jail, charged with possession of narcotics. While driving with his older brother Lorenzo, whom Anthony considered a father figure, the police stopped them. Unbeknownst to Anthony, Lorenzo, who already had an extensive criminal record, had some drugs with him. Anthony took the charge for his brother to prevent Lorenzo from serving a long sentence. Out of love for his brother, Anthony threw himself again into an existence of suffering behind bars, a place where human pettiness leads to death and where, in the presence of constantly frustrated desires, people take out their anger on each other.

In effect, Anthony's entire family was in disarray. Not only was Lorenzo repeatedly in and out of jail, but his other brothers and a great aunt were heavy drug users also. All of that Anthony may have been able to deal with, but what affected him most deeply was the character of his mother. She was a prostitute and a drug user. The "dude" living with her pimped the woman for many years and she seemed unable to detach herself from his vicious treatment. Hooked on drugs, she was unable to resist the binding power of that urge. The whole purpose of her life seemed to be the avoidance of pain. Compounding her shame was the fact that Anthony's brothers at times would give her the drugs. They would rather see her doped than walking the streets.

When he recounted this past to me, Anthony tried to justify the actions of his loved ones, but I could tell how uncomfortable and disgusted he was with the whole mess. Still, his humanity survived. He told me without hesitation how much he loved his mother. "Mr. Ismael," he said, "in spite of it all, I always treat mother with respect." Anthony is a noble soul. He has weaknesses and continues to struggle—as he is the first to admit—but I am convinced of his fundamental integrity.

Besides the turmoil of his painful domestic world, Anthony has experienced another world of happiness, an escape valve allowing the pressures of life never to totally overwhelm his young psyche. This place is the tiny

St. Peter Claver Catholic Mission where I first met him. Church was for him a good place to be, with decent people to love, especially Mrs. Judy. When he talks of her, you can see his face light up.

Judy Peck is a middle-aged white woman who served as the youth minister and do-it-all employee at the mission. A living saint, in my view, Judy was beloved by all in the housing projects and deeply respected by us at the mission. To this day Judy receives letters of gratitude from many inmates she met at the local jail where she ministered. Her work in the black community spans more than twenty years and has brought comfort to many families in desperate need.

Anthony met her when he was about ten years old. She was handing out Christmas cards and inviting people to church. She would pick him up every Sunday for mass, counsel him, and treat him like a son. At times, Judy would take Anthony to her home so that her family became the one he never really had. The domain of darkness that encircled Anthony had no power over the light of love that Judy and her family offered. Anthony's face is radiant when he recalls the horseback riding, the family gatherings, the trips, and all the activities wholesome families do. Judy and her home were for Anthony a deep river of peace whose powerful flow washed away the pain.

The incidental nature of the encounters, however, could not totally remove the deleterious influence of the projects. When Anthony was seventeen, he was back in jail to serve another sentence. Mrs. Judy was there to console and counsel him. He enrolled in one of Judy's classes at the jail and made a concerted effort to get away from a life of crime.

People often prefer to keep their vices in full bloom rather than do the hard work it takes to detach from them. A profound aversion to anything that smacks of effort prevents many from ever experiencing a different way of life. Why is this? I think that refusing to change offers the psychological advantage of alibi. It enables people to continue in the fiction of incapacity and victimization. If the world is unjust and I must resign myself to an imposed fate, I need not attribute my misfortunes to myself. We see this clearly when a drug user tries to convince his "banging" partner not to go to treatment because his possible success places a shadow over other users.

Yet, at times, men find the courage to choose otherwise, and Anthony was one. He had to survive life behind bars first—not an easy task. There he saw a man stabbed in the eye with a pen for a simple disagreement, mortal fights to avenge old and often petty street debts, and brutal beatings for the infraction of "disrespects." Ironically, he survived incarceration due to his brother Lorenzo's bad reputation. Other inmates well knew who Lorenzo was and offered the brother respect due to his connection to a "bad dude."

When he was released from prison, Anthony began to take steps toward a better life. In spite of his resolve, the inner man at times needs to fight the errors of ill-thought government "solutions" to inner-city problems. After leaving the ghetto, Anthony moved to an area not far from where I live. It is poor but clean and peaceful. Unfortunately, because of the Department of Housing and Urban Development (HUD) and its ongoing Hope VI initiative—the latest failed attempt at a new model for subsidized housing—the inner city was brought back into Anthony's life. HUD tore down the old projects and replaced them with new townhouses. In the meantime, they offered worthless Section 8 vouchers to former residents. Because most landlords shy away from Section 8 tenants, afraid that they will destroy their apartments, only the owners of hard-to-rent properties in marginal neighborhoods are willing to accept the vouchers. Those trying to maintain the decorum of the area find themselves in a bind.[2]

The area where Anthony lives now has been inundated with people from the projects who brought with them the very temptations and perils he had been fighting so hard to avoid. They bring a set of values that end up destroying good communities inhabited by people, such as Anthony, who are achieving on their own what the bureaucrats of victimhood say is not possible. His home has been robbed. Once he came back home to find three strangers in his garage and his door tampered with. A few houses down, two neighbors were murdered by intruders. All of this turmoil was made possible courtesy of the fake compassion of government bureaucracy.

The importation of social pathology hurts Anthony and those like him who try to leave the inner city behind. Built on the deterministic ideology of victimhood, the system assumes that the market cannot provide unsubsidized housing for the poor. Vouchers then allow residents of subsidized housing to get a better home in better neighborhoods. The central planners tell us that, in turn, those with dysfunctional lifestyles will learn from those who are functional and successful and then turn their own lives around. The analysis buys into the lie of environmental determinism, which assumes that granting a better home in a better neighborhood is uplifting. In reality,

[2] See Howard Husock, *America's Trillion Dollar Housing Mistake* (Chicago: Ivan R. Dee, 2003), 50–51.

it is the individual's effort and determination to achieve the purchase of a home in a better neighborhood that is truly uplifting.[3]

Anthony is now a handsome twenty-three-year old man. The last time I saw him, he received me with joy and kindness. His apartment is small and modest, but very clean. After conversing for a while about his past, Anthony told me, "Life is what we make of it." For someone like him, who could easily excuse himself of responsibility at every turn, his wisdom is a powerful witness against victimhood. He tells me that one of the first things he needed to do to save his life was to leave the projects: "You need to leave that place, break the cycle, move somewhere, anywhere, and stay away." Another important decision was to go back to church. He has described with pride the pains he has taken to travel to church services on Sunday.

Yes, at times our intention to change is a weak and momentary impulse lacking true determination. I have many times witnessed the rousing decisions to change, only to observe that those who made the optimistic declarations soon return to their destructive ways. Yet, I think Anthony can make it. His determination seems to be steady, and his inner self appears to possess the necessary strength. More importantly, his actions confirm his expressions of resolve. He is working two jobs, wants to go back to study at a vocational school, and dreams of one day opening his own restaurant.

COUNTERCULTURE AND ITS EFFECTS

Today's poor black communities suffer from such devastation that facile externalist explanations cannot account for the debacle. The breakdown of civic order, and the all-encompassing hopelessness we observe in some segments of the community are not merely the results of discriminatory treatment. A cultural shift partially explains the changing prospects of black inner-city life. The sparks of change that the civil rights movement made possible also opened the door to new approaches to victimhood. This cultural shift had its roots in two different historical realities: the counter-cultural mood of the 1960s (the great disruption) and a new antagonism that gives rise to a culture of incivility within black inner cities.

For ancient civilizations as diverse as the Greek, the German, and the Roman, there existed a holy order rooted in the divine. They recognized a divine order that transcended their limited human undertakings and

---

[3] Husock, *America's Trillion Dollar Housing Mistake*, chaps. 3–4.

even their traditional understanding of tribal deities. As Heinrich Rommen tells us, "if an eternal, immutable law obliges men to obey particular laws, behind the popular images of tribal deities exists an eternal, all-wise Lawgiver who has the power to bind and to loose."[4] The spirit of inquiry by which searchers in these civilizations tried to discover the transcendent took diverse pathways, yet all roads led to the idea of universality.

As men contemplated the differences in laws among them and the diversity of mores and institutions of tribes and city-states, they began to perceive a distinction between divine and human law; between what was godly and what was merely a human construct. This awareness brought about further questions. What is the nature of divine law? How can we know it? What is the moral basis for human law? The impulse toward a common truth in the face of diverse human cultures nonetheless persisted. This truth, which C. S. Lewis calls the *Tao*, "is the doctrine of objective value, the belief that certain attitudes are really true, and others really false, to the kind of thing the universe is and the kind of things we are." Against the enthronement of appetite as king, the *Tao* insists that "[t]he heart never takes the place of the head: but it can, and should, obey it."[5] For centuries, a consensus prevailed in the West concerning the doctrine of objective value and its implications for behavior; this consensus was the context for the birth of our nation. The old-fashioned liberalism of the Founders was a unique expression of a social order immersed in the assumptions of this consensus.

Liberalism transformed America in the 1960s and, in the process, was itself transformed. The antiwar, feminist, gay activist, and later civil rights movements are all symptoms of this transformation, which was provoked by the virus of collectivism. In a sense, such movements were a reaction against nature, a condemnation of the way things actually are, and an attempt to overthrow the social consensus. They were a reaction against the moral order that the ancients took for granted. In collectivism, the new breed of liberalism found a way to escape reality by preaching a new order for the coming ages. The new consensus will reject an objective order in favor of a subjective one—one built on the assumption that men have an "inner freedom" that can establish what is true "for them." All we have is contin-

---

[4] John McWhorter, *Winning the Race: Beyond the Crisis in Black America* (New York: Gotham Books, 2006), 4–5.

[5] C. S. Lewis, *The Abolition of Man*, (San Francisco: HarperSanFrancisco, 2001), 18–20.

gency, emotive appetite, and inner truth. As modern liberalism came to believe that human beings are good by nature, traditional morality became an oppressive imposition they committed themselves to fight against with the weapon of a new egalitarian paradigm.

The great disruption of the 1960s, aptly detailed in Mona Charen's *Do Gooders*, established society as the carrier of stigma: the stigma of being the cause of individual and group demise. No longer would the use of shame as a barrier to bad behavior be tolerated. Because morality is subjective, shame is blaming the victim. (Of course, shame remains an acceptable tactic against violations of the new morality, as we have seen.) Therefore Victorian differentiation between the *working poor* and the *hoodlum* loses its validity because it is judgmental, and being judgmental is a cardinal sin.[6] What was once kept at bay through shame is now celebrated as authentic and liberating. If in the past it was shameful to depend on government, now this dependency is a never-sufficient entitlement along with a rights claim for the people against the social order. Under the new morality, out-of-wedlock births or dependency on welfare is no longer stigmatized—such conditions are the reflection of the strength of a people always adapting to unjust social structures. The cultural mood ignited in the 1960s had devastating consequences on the inner city.

THE NEW ANTAGONISM

Commenting on the American notion of rights, Tocqueville wrote, "It cannot be doubted that the moment at which political rights are granted to a people that had before been without them is a very critical one, although it be a necessary one." How a people appropriate rights, what mood they adopt, and how they interpret the meaning of the path placed before them is crucial to their future development.[7]

The new antagonism understood liberty as the opportunity for reprieve, demand, and reparation. It is, in fact, a duty of man to raise and exert fundamental rights. It is likewise true that oppressors may attempt to use the language of the virtue of prudence to stifle the cries of justice, as in perennial

---

[6] Mona Charen, *Do-Gooders: How Liberals Hurt Those They Claim to Help (and the Rest of Us)* (New York: Sentinel, 2004), 89.

[7] Alexis de Tocqueville, *Democracy in America* (1835; repr., New York: Bantam, 2000), 284.

calls for restraint even in the face of great evil. However, we must be careful of the explosive combination of undirected anger and the pursuit of justice. The acquisition of a right is a political entitlement that finds its foundation in, and is preceded by, virtue. Tocqueville defines political rights as "[the idea of] virtue introduced into the political world."[8]

We go wrong in trying to advance human goods when our feelings take over and impair our reason as it attempts to guide our actions. As Aquinas repeatedly states, the essence of wrongful doing is found in the "repugnance" of feelings toward "reason's commands."[9] It is when the passions fetter reason and make it their slave that the guidance of reason is impaired. Against the reign of passions, unfettered reason acknowledges two principles, both included by Aquinas as a second set of the first principles of practical reasoning: (1) the Golden Rule ("Do to others as you would have them do to you"), and (2) "Do not answer injury with injury."[10]

How easy it is for man to resort to injustice and violence when he has good reasons. The later stage of the civil rights movement with its call for black power and purposeless antagonism is a prime example of reason enslaved to appetites. In terms of irrationality, the black power and race-struggle movement that dominated the civil rights movement did not differ much from the oppressive racist regime it attempted to conquer.

The resistance of feelings to obey reason's directives may at times be appropriate. They may rightfully resist when, instead of sweeping reason away and making it its servant, they help one to act intelligently against perverse reasons and to "enhance the goodness of good choices and actions."[11] After all, we are not disembodied minds. No truly human act is negligent of the effects of the emotions; we must be attracted to the good before we can reason our way into action. The key is which faculty controls the other.

The new antagonism denied that life was gradually becoming better for blacks and social constraints were actually fading. Thus it acquired a different nature from the antagonism that was necessary during the early civil rights

---

[8] Tocqueville, *Democracy in America*, 282.

[9] Thomas Aquinas, *Scriptum super Libros Sententiarum Petri Lombard—iensis*, distinction 42, question 2, article Ic; *Sententia Libri Ethicorum*, II, 8 n. 3, cited in John Finnis, *Aquinas: Moral Political, and Legal Theory* (Oxford, U.K.: Oxford University Press, 1998), 73.

[10] Aquinas, *Summa Theologiae*, 94, 4. and 95, 2.

[11] Aquinas, *Summa Theologiae*, II-II, q. 155 a. I ad 2. There, Aquinas states that "good desires work against a perverse reason." See Finnis, *Aquinas*, 74–75.

movement. The early movement had antagonized the mainstream with a purpose: claiming just rights, exerting black moral dignity, leading the nation toward the recognition of objective values, and lifting the veil of invisibility that hid black life and black suffering. Such opposition was grounded in the very consensus of an objective order upon which the nation was founded. This was an antagonism leading us toward protagonism, toward healing.

Early in this movement, Martin Luther King Jr. approached the microphone of Holy Street Baptist Church in Montgomery, Alabama, to proclaim black dignity and to call that generation to elicit change. "When the history books are written in future generations," he declared, "the historians will have to pause and say, 'There lived a great people—a black people—who injected new meaning and dignity into the veins of civilization. This is our challenge and our overwhelming responsibility.'"[12] The early struggle was formulated in terms of blacks' responsibility to claim their place in the history of their country. It was not a black-white struggle. It was black dignity bursting forth in all its glory for the entire world to see. King explained that "this is not a war between the white and the Negro but a conflict between justice and injustice." His "Letter from Birmingham Jail" was squarely in line with the normative consensus of the natural-law tradition:

> How does one determine whether a law is just or unjust? A just law is a man-made code that squares with the moral law or the law of God. An unjust law is a code that is out of harmony with the moral law. To put it in the terms of St. Thomas Aquinas: An unjust law is a human law that is not rooted in eternal law and natural law. Any law that uplifts human personality is just. Any law that degrades human personality is unjust. All segregation statutes are unjust because segregation distorts the soul and damages the personality.... Hence segregation is not only politically, economically and sociologically unsound, it is morally wrong and sinful.[13]

Unfortunately, what followed was a new form of antagonism, purposeless opposition that, instead of lifting the veil to show self-worth, put a new mask in place that turned blacks back to the stereotype. That mask was victimhood as identity. The new antagonism replaced honorable struggle

---

[12] Cited in David R. Goldfield, *Black, White, and Southern: 1940 to the Present* (Baton Rouge: Louisiana State University Press, 2015), 99.

[13] See http://www.africa.upenn.edu/Articles_Gen/Letter_Birmingham.html.

with the politics of anger. If racism was so pervasive and blacks were simply victims, then blacks were not protagonists of a struggle to effectively change America but were scenery in the drama of white omnipotence. They could create a disruptive and antagonistic situation, but they were not truly powerful enough to change reality. Accepting few limits to their rhetorical claims of oppression, and now able to vent them with increased openness, the movement went from being a catalyst to becoming an obstacle.

THE PERENNIAL "ETIQUETTE OF RACE"

As we have seen before, *racial etiquette* in America made blacks invisible. The etiquette, as a response to southern defeat and humiliation, attempted to stereotype blacks as inferior and decadent. The code of conduct in southern serfdom demanded blacks' deferential behavior toward whites and emphasized black irresponsibility, propensity to crime, violent temper, and dependency on white benevolence. As David R. Goldfield observes, this was a kind of "stage Negro," a phantom of white imagination. Whites thought they understood blacks, but they were actually ignorant of black life and behavior. That is why southerners at times seemed astounded by Northern calls for change.[14] In creating the lie of black inferiority, they circled the wagons to protect their insecurity. No one has expressed the sense of black invisibility and white blindness better than Ralph Ellison: "I am invisible, simply because people refuse to see me.... When they approach me, they only see my surroundings, themselves, or figments of their imagination—indeed, everything and anything except me."[15]

Goldfield adds: "Racial etiquette turned the American Dream on its head; it devalued education and ambition, and rewarded its opposite. When blacks fulfilled these low expectations, they merely reinforced white

---

[14] Goldfield, *Black, White, and Southern*, 3–4.

> In 1948, for example, when pressure for modest racial adjustments began to build in Washington, a perplexed congressman from Mississippi, John E. Rankin, extended an invitation to his colleagues: "Go down South where I live ... where more Negroes are employed than anywhere else in the country, where they enjoy more happiness, more peace, more prosperity, more security, and protection than they ever enjoyed in all history."

[15] Ralph Ellison, *Invisible Man* (New York: Random House, 1947), 3.

perceptions."[16] This etiquette created the illusion of white superiority and blinded them to blacks' true identity. Thus, today's image of the "thug" as the authentic black is the opposite: it is the actualization of the white etiquette of race. The degradation of inner-city life is simply the internalization of white mythology about black identity, and not the inevitable result of oppression. To adopt degradation and thuggishness as identity is to make real the white dream world.

A new "etiquette of class struggle" demands that blacks be on the stage again: to be defined by victimhood, to be lifted up by bureaucratic initiative and government largesse, to be the tokens of recognition serving as a model for class-struggle purposes. The nefarious southern etiquette of race that created the stage Negro survived and re-emerged amidst the turbulence of an era of revolt and conflict of values. The leftist-influenced later civil rights movement and its etiquette of class struggle adopted as the "real black" that same stage Negro, rebellious but still determined by collective forces; angry, but still absorbed by a conflict of structures. Only now, the thug has become more than an aberration or a performance: It has been confused with identity, and it is still hurting the life of the community.

We see then that the degradation of life and the pathologies identified with the inner city are not the predetermined fate of a people affected by binding externalities nor the adaptive response of a people who have always adapted but the internalization of an identity that denies the reality of black self-worth. The oppositional culture of the late 1960s made possible the blindness that could confuse true identity with a "new awareness." By exalting discontinuity with traditional patterns of behavior and inaugurating a mood of opposition to traditional morality, the late 1960s movement channeled the struggle toward defeatism and dependency, inadvertently bringing back the demons it was supposed to expel.

FROM "STAGE NEGRO" TO "STAGE WHITE"

An additional fundamental phenomenon has emerged, the phenomenon of the "stage white." The former etiquette of race, where whites could be themselves but blacks had to perform, has been inverted. As the new boundary of civility for white America is the avoidance of even the appearance of racial prejudice, whites intentionally shun behavior that might be called

---

[16] Goldfield, *Black, White, and Southern*, 6.

racist. "White Americans," Shelby Steele surmises, "became a stigmatized group after the civil rights victories of the sixties. They became identified with the shame of white racism that the nation had finally acknowledged, and they fell under a kind of suspicion that amounted to a stigma."[17] Forced to prove a negative (that they are not racist) their public persona acquired a pattern of assent to whatever a black person acknowledged as racist, whether or not such statements were even faintly true. In fact, if the modern theories of racism as equivalent to the ownership of power are correct, blacks today can be just as racist as whites. Guilt in white America provides incredible power to those claiming historic victimization.

In the process, blacks are now the ones ignorant of the true content of white opinions and postures. Blacks now suspect—or think they know—that the roots of every white thought and every white action are overtly or covertly racist. Seeing that whites often assent to every conceivable claim coming from blacks but seldom give a hint of what they are truly thinking, blacks *assume* hidden racism. A more open but still racialized public forum remains closed to true encounter and honest exchange. The realization that race as a category is oppressive—whether it is utilized as a formula for exclusion or for collectivized inclusion—still escapes us. Because in a racialized public forum individuals can never discover each other's inner thoughts in honest interaction, the solution is a kind of strategy of containment. Whites contain black anger by monotonous assent to an expanded array of entitlements while blacks, assuming the pervasiveness of white racism, continue to look to government to attain a sense of security while expecting a white onslaught.

The new antagonism is empty as a tool for racial redemption and social change. We can now even elect black presidents and still race looms over all. The new antagonism impedes true encounter as it sees blacks as tokens in a collection. It is eminently *amoral* in the sense of obviating or minimizing personal responsibility and individual human encounter. In fact, the new race etiquette that sprang from the politics of the new antagonism demands that whites see blacks as *not* responsible for themselves. Whites are forbidden to judge "a lack of responsibility as even a partial cause of black problems or a seizing of responsibility as even a partial solution to those problems."[18]

Manning Marable's account of inner-city reality after the end of segregation is paradigmatic: "Trapped in the urban ghettoes of America's decaying

[17] Shelby Steele, *A Dream Deferred: The Second Betrayal of Black Freedom in America* (New York: Harper Collins, 1998), 156.

[18] Steele, *A Dream Deferred*, 158.

inner cities, plagued with higher unemployment rates, disease, bad housing, poor public schools, and inadequate social services, young blacks were filled with a sense of anger, self-hatred and bitterness."[19] Blacks are "trapped" and "plagued" by every social evil inflicted on them, and that externality binds their character and explains their psyche. Therefore, racism is the culprit of every evil that emerges from within a community under siege.

The collectivism of the new antagonism exalts political man over moral man; structural change over personal initiative; class and race struggle over personal encounter; and the quest for absolute equality over fraternity. Socialism emerges brighter than in any utopian arrangement we could have ever imagined. The new antagonism sees white society as irremediably oppressive.

BLACK REDNECKS AND WHITE LIBERALS

There has always been an element of dysfunction in black communities. Although pathological behavior is certainly not exclusive to black culture, it is important to understand the roots of this problem to better discern the reality of today's inner cities. The conventional explanations of today's condition focus on economic factors. As factories relocated beginning in the 1970s, poverty became ingrained. Works such as William Julius Wilson's *When Work Disappears* have solidified the consensus that fingers the economics of job availability as the main culprit for the devastation of inner city life.[20]

The economic determinism behind such explanations, however, cannot fully explain the human response to changed conditions. The Great Migration teaches us much about the quality of the human response to altered surroundings and about the impact on behavior and mores resulting from merging cultures. From 1916 to 1970, approximately seven million blacks moved from the southern to the northern United States.[21] The Great Migration was not just a geographic shift but also "a mass uprooting from a rural southern way of life and a transformation into a modern industrial and urban ethos. It was, in short, the kind of traumatic social change that took

---

[19] Manning Marable, *Race, Reform, and Rebellion: The Second Reconstruction in Black America, 1945–1990* (Oxford, MS: University Press of Mississippi, 1991), 155.

[20] William Julius Wilson, *When Work Disappears: The World of the New Urban Poor* (New York: Vintage, 1997). See McWhorter, *Winning the Race*, chapter 1 for a discussion of jobs and inner-city life.

[21] Some historians differentiate between a First Great Migration (1910–1930) and a second (1940–1970).

other ethnic groups generations to adjust to." Such a momentous clash of cultures expedited the development of a black Northern ghetto, one where the evils experienced by diverse groups "reappeared in the transplanted black populations of the cities."[22]

We must not substitute economic with cultural determinism but an examination of cultural trends and influences is essential to understanding present developments. A particular kind of subculture tied to southern whites and having its roots in the British Isles survived in the worst segments of black neighborhoods and today has been given all the necessary nutrients to grow and profoundly transform inner-city life. Failing to survive among most black and white southerners, this subculture found a feeding ground among mostly isolated populations who were susceptible to its influence. What is most remarkable is how that subculture took root within the inner cities and became associated with authentic black culture when, in effect, it existed among white southerners and their British ancestors long before it insidiously metastasized in black life.

Cracker Culture in America

Outside the English heartland, certain areas suffered backwardness and cultural deprivation for centuries. As Sowell explains, British migration to the American South proceeded mainly from Northern fringe areas of the isles, a no-man's land between Scotland and England where lawlessness and turbulence reigned. The inhabitants of these lands were called "rednecks" and "crackers" long before they migrated to America. Although areas such as Scotland eventually progressed substantially, most of the migration to the American South took place before those sweeping social and cultural improvements. [23]

Migratory patterns from the British Isles influenced the development of different cultures in varied parts of America. In *Cracker Culture*, Grady McWhiney tells us:

> Fundamental and lasting divisions between Southerners and Northern-
> ers began in colonial America when migrants from the Celtic regions

---

[22] Thomas Sowell, *Ethnic America: A History* (New York: Basic Books, 1981), 211.

[23] See David Hacket Fischer, *Albion's Seed: Four British Folkways in America* (New York: Oxford University Press, 1989), 634–35. See also Grady McWhiney, *Cracker Culture: Celtic Ways in the Old South* (Tuscaloosa: University of Alabama Press, 1988), 16–18.

of the British Isles—Scotland, Ireland, Wales, and Cornwall—and from the English uplands managed to implant their traditional customs in the Old South. From a solid eighteenth-century base in the Southern backcountry, these people and their descendants swept westward decade after decade throughout the antebellum period until they had established themselves and their anti-English values and practices across the Old South.[24]

The Celtic people were characteristically violent. McWhiney tells us that their "propensity to fight led them to hostilities on very slight occasions."[25] These peoples were prone to duel and combat at the slightest perceived offense infringing on their "honor."[26] In his treatment of English influence on America, historian David Hackett Fischer relates the development of this propensity to violence to the lawlessness caused by constant wars: "This incessant violence shaped the culture of the border region and also created a social system which was very different from that in the south of England."[27]

The North was mostly influenced by settlers migrating from the English lowlands while the South had, as one important migratory group, Scottish-Irish settlers. These were not like the English but "strangers to our laws and customs, and even to our language."[28] These people "in whose dialect a cracker was a person who talked boastingly" brought the term and the mores to the Old South.[29] Associated in the colonial period with herdsmen of Celtic origins, "cracker culture" developed and moved southward. Early on, Crackers are described as "rude and nomadic, excellent hunters but indifferent farmers ... and as people who kept themselves beyond the reach of all civilized law."[30] Many were desperately poor, "but even in their poverty they carried themselves with a fierce and stubborn pride that warned

---

[24] McWhiney, *Cracker Culture*, xiii.

[25] McWhiney, *Cracker Culture*, 149–51.

[26] James Logan, *The Scottish Gael; or Celtic Manners, as Preserved Among the Highlanders*, 2 vols. (1876; repr., Edinburgh: Inverness, 1976) I:116–17; and Alwyn Rees and Brinley Rees, *Celtic Heritage: Ancient Tradition in Ireland and Wales* (London 1961), 122–23.

[27] Fischer, *Albion's Seed*, 626.

[28] See Fischer, *Albion's Seed*, 605 (citing a Philadelphia Quaker, Jonathan Dickinson).

[29] Fischer, *Albion's Seed*, xiv.

[30] James A. Lewis, "Cracker-Spanish Florida Style," *Florida Historical Quarterly* 63 (1984): 188–91.

others to treat them with respect."[31] This pride "was a source of irritation to their English neighbors, who could not understand what they could feel proud about."[32] Stubborn pride and ferocity would be important traits in the development of Southern culture, which can be traced back to these early settlers as they spread and dominated the backcountry.[33]

Patterns of behavior prevalent in the British Isles continued to recur and further develop in America as the immigrants settled in the backcountry and deeper through the South. Cracker culture, although often associated exclusively with poor people, was not exclusive to that social stratum. Crackers were both rich and poor. Frederick Law Olmstead noted that some Crackers "owned a great many Negroes, and were by no means as poor as their appearance indicated."[34] Early on, Northern travelers described Southerners in general in ways similar to English descriptions of Celtic people.[35] Of Mississippians, a traveler said, "The men are generally idle, devoted to hunting, and the attention of their numerous herds, while their slaves till the ground. The poorer sorts ... are fond of drinking, gambling, and horse rising. From these sports quarrels often arise, which are sometimes ended by the dirk or pistol."[36]

Violence was not characteristic of all Southerners, and rejection of cracker attitudes was not limited to Northerners. Southern plantation owners with poor whites living on adjoining land would often offer to buy their land for more than it was worth, in order to get rid of such neighbors.[37]

Further negative descriptions associated Southern cracker culture with profanity, licentiousness, perjury, promiscuity and prostitution, and disregard for education. Wealth, instead of learning, was the primary determinant

[31] Fischer, *Albion's Seed*, 606.

[32] Fischer, *Albion's Seed*, 615.

[33] The first US Census confirms that these British Isles borderers settled prominently in Western Maryland and Virginia, North and South Carolina, Georgia, Kentucky, and Tennessee. See Fischer, *Albion's Seed*, 634.

[34] McWhiney, *Cracker Culture*, xvi.

[35] "The English, in general, found Celtic ways barbarous and disgusting; they spoke of Scotland, Ireland and Wales as 'frightful' places and the Celtic people as being 'wicked,' 'savage' and 'indolent drunkards.'" McWhiney, *Cracker Culture*, 105.

[36] McWhiney, *Cracker Culture*, 106.

[37] Lewis C. Gray, *History of Agriculture in the Southern United States to 1860*, vol. 1 (Washington, DC: Carnegie Institution, 1933), 484.

of status in a highly stratified and hierarchical society. The rates of out-of-wedlock births among the inhabitants of the backcountry were higher than in most other regions of the American colonies. "Rates of illegitimacy and prenuptial pregnancy," Hackett notes, "had long been higher in the far northwest of England than in any other part of that nation.... Rates of bastardy in the northwest were three times higher than in the east of England during the 16th and 17th centuries."[38]

Today's Black Redneck Culture

Why is this relevant? First, it shows us how crucial cultural patterns are to understanding the realities we now see in the inner city. The sharing, modeling, and passing of behavioral patterns is often reflexive. When people live in proximity, they influence each other even when the groups are diverse—and at times *averse* to each other.

Curious grammatical constructions in southern backcountry and in black English can be traced all the way to the British Isles' Northern border areas. Borderers arriving on our shores mainly settled in Western Maryland, Virginia, North and South Carolina, Georgia, Kentucky, and Tennessee and spread such linguistic usages throughout the South.[39] Expressions such as "he come in," "she done finished," and the double negative ("he don't have none") can all be traced to the British Northern border areas.[40]

The potential for intellectual transformation is relevant to race relations for a number of reasons. In resisting slavery by cultural appropriation, those enslaved may become moral rebels through their courageous personal stance. Here we are not referring to public rebellion and protest but to an affirmation of individual autonomy. In moral rebellion, the enslaved ironically take possession of cultural aspects coming from the oppressor. In observing the ruling group's behavior and patterns of success, the enslaved

---

[38] McWhiney, *Cracker Culture*, 171–72, 206. Fischer, *Albion's Seed*, 756; quote at 681.

[39] Fischer, *Albion's Seed*, 626.

[40] Fischer, *Albion's Seed*, 653–4. "Scholars generally agree that this language developed from the 'Northern' or 'Northumbrian' English that was spoken in the lowlands of Scotland, in North Ireland, and in the border counties of England during the seventeenth and early eighteenth century." See also J. H. Combs, "Old Early and Elizabethan English in the Southern Mountains," *Dialect Notes* 4 (New Haven, CT: American Dialect Society, 1913–1917) 283–97; Thomas Pyles, *The Origins and Development of the English Language* (New York: Harcourt Brace & World: 1964).

use them as role models for their own advancement. Cultural conquest is emotionally and intellectually demanding and is observed the most among the more sophisticated members of oppressed groups.[41] Conversely, cultural appropriation of *negative patterns* can become a moral rebellion against the enslaved condition where, in desperation, the oppressed adopts much less demanding coping mechanisms in a kind of "cultural suicide." Those with less emotional strength may be driven to despondency and despair by imitating and adopting negative behaviors coming from the oppressor's group.

Second, it shows how closely tied blacks and whites are, even in areas where some try to find radical differences. It is ironic that much of what some elites associate with authentically black culture may have more to do with white Celts than with Mother Africa. Intellectuals serving as surrogates for the oppressed have made redneck culture the archetype of true black consciousness without realizing that the dysfunctions they defend are vestiges of a negative white subculture.

Third, social pathologies are not inherent but can be inherited. They are not intrinsic to any race but can be passed on among racial groups. For too long, we have been offered false choices. Some have presumed innate racial inferiority on the part of blacks as the source of the problem. Others have pointed the finger at intentional discrimination and exclusion. The choices have been between externality and essentialism, between blaming "them" and blaming God for making us this way.

Migratory and cultural patterns go hand in hand. Inner-city blacks did not adopt negative patterns of behavior due to economic factors alone. Southern blacks who migrated to cities carried a culture different from that of blacks who were already there. As Sowell says,

> There have always been large disparities within the native black population of the U.S. Those blacks whose ancestors were "free persons of color" in 1850 have fared far better in income, occupation, and family stability than those blacks whose ancestors were freed in the next decade by Abraham Lincoln.[42]

The culture of black migrants was influenced by white southern culture, which in turn was shaped by earlier white migratory patterns.

---

[41] Patterson, *Ordeal of Integration*, 104–5.

[42] Thomas Sowell, "Crippled by Their Culture," *Wall Street Journal*, Tuesday, April 26, 2005.

Absorbed patterns can be positive or negative. Contact among individuals and cultures facilitate the introduction of certain patterns of behavior that can be eventually absorbed and adapted. The mechanisms of borrowing can occur even among antagonistic cultures as certain individuals may acquire elements of behavior whose origin can be gradually forgotten. In the case of negative cultural patterns, the resulting amalgamation produces socially unstable communities. For displaced people such as slaves with weak ancestral traditions, the deep-seated human tendency toward cultural conservation is not as strong as it would otherwise be.

African slavery likewise required slaves to acculturate to the mores of their masters. They had to "bond" or at least "normalize" their condition if they were to survive. Finding themselves away from the parent group, they needed to create a new identity within the society to which they now forcibly belonged. One of the reasons for the need was that kidnappers sought to place insuperable geographic distances between the parent community and the host. The trend toward exportation of slaves made slavery a major African institution as both domestic (African) and foreign markets found a ready supply of slaves. Slaves in turn had to find a way to merge with new communities.[43] Legal means were mostly out of their control, but cultural ones were not.

The enslaved understood that, somehow, they had to find a way to attach to the new group. As Miers and Kopytoff explain, the opposite of "enslavement" for the African was not "freedom" qua autonomy but the concept of "belonging."[44] Imitating cultural patterns springing from the enslaving group was a natural way of reducing marginality—a pattern learned well during their African experience. For the African enslaved in Africa, the future consisted in creating a new identity within a new group, not in pipe dreams of returning to a kin group where they may well be reduced again to marginality. This underlines how foolish it is for Afrocentrists to insist on foreign African identity as our true identity. American slaves renounced it quickly enough.[45]

---

[43] See Paul E. Lovejoy, *Transformations in Slavery: A History of Slavery in Africa*, 3rd ed. (Cambridge, UK: Cambridge University Press, 2012), chap. 1.

[44] Suzanne Miers and Igor Kopytoff, *Slavery in Africa: Historical and Anthropological Perspectives* (Madison: University of Wisconsin Press, 1979), 17–18.

[45] This renunciation was not a direct and conscious abandonment or rejection. It was simply the result of cultural adaptation in the face of new realities.

The problems of the inner city, of course, cannot be explained only by reference to cultural influence. Modern inner-city culture had influences besides early migrations. American society as a whole, as well as other factors such as the welfare state, the moral ethos of society, and diverse public policies, continue to influence what happens there. Still, the black/white redneck culture of the South has contributed to the inner-city subculture. Internal black cultural differences highlight the point. Free northern blacks exhibited great differences in educational achievement, sexual mores, rates of crime, and economic stance as compared to southern freedmen. These differences mirrored the differences between white rednecks and other whites.[46]

Moreover, redneck culture still plagues us under the guise of the authenticity of inner-city life and mores. Now celebrated and condoned, this culture remains an obstacle to black success. Regardless of the ultimate source of diverse cultural patterns, we must clearly understand that the moral dysfunction common in today's inner city is not representative of authentic black culture nor is it a badge of honor to most black Americans. Black and white intellectuals who defend such cultural memes by blaming poverty and oppression are using blacks as tokens in a political game.

[46] Sowell, *Black Rednecks and White Liberals*, 33–34, 40–43. One reason that might have contributed to the extent and permanence of the negative redneck culture in the inner city is that large numbers of one group were concentrated in narrow geographical confines consistently isolated by an antagonistic larger culture. It is not difficult to see how people can bond, even around faulty cultural elements, in the presence of a major common threat.

11

THE FAMILY

It takes a family to raise a village.

—Jennifer Roback Morse

I have already mentioned my friend and coworker, Judy Peck, who works in ministry at the African Caribbean American Catholic Center. Two sad incidents from her experience reveal the devastating situation of the black family. A few years ago, Judy was trying to assist a young black woman with an issue related to her children. To assist her, Judy needed the name of the father. To Judy's astonishment, the young lady only knew the father's first name—in fact, only the father's nickname. Although she and the father had known each other for quite some time, she had never bothered to learn much about who the man really was.

But she knew how to find the information. She approached a police car and asked if the officer could help her. By using the police computer on board the vehicle and examining the man's criminal record, the woman obtained the information that Judy needed.

In the other episode, Judy was driving black children to church on a Sunday morning when the conversation turned to their parents. There were questions about when during the day the children saw them and what kind of activities they enjoyed doing with them. Although most of the kids did not live with their fathers, they delighted in recounting instances of joyful experiences with their mothers and occasional fond memories of interaction with their fathers. One child spoke about seeing his dad every Sunday. "In fact, I'll see him today," he said with excitement. Happy to hear it, Judy continued the conversation so as to know more about what they were going to do together.

Just a few minutes down the road the child located someone in a crowd. "See, I told you, there is my dad!" he blurted while happily waving to a man hanging out on a notorious street corner. The only time he ever saw his father was for a few seconds on some Sundays while the man sat with friends at a site where alcohol, drugs, and prostitution were common.

There Is Nothing Wrong with Us!

Faced with marginality in Africa, the brutality of bondage in America, and the oppression of racism after emancipation, blacks held on the best they could to institutions such as the family and the church as their tools for survival.[1] The family was the most nurturing and comforting institution that most slaves ever came into contact with.[2] Even so, the black family as it came out of slavery was not entirely healthy. Scholars such as E. Franklin Frazier, Stanley M. Elkins, Kenneth M. Stamp, and Daniel P. Moynihan have found in "the legacy of slavery" the cause of the present pathologies in black family structure.[3] Moynihan's *The Negro Family in America*, based on the conventional academic wisdom of the day, attributed the problems to "centuries of injustice." He asserted that "a tangle of pathology" in the

---

[1] For an account of the importance of family and church in black history, see Alan Keyes, *Masters of the Dream: The Strength and Betrayal of Black America* (New York: Harper Perennial, 1996), chap. 3.

[2] Every study clearly proves that one of the most important reasons for slaves to attempt to escape was to be reunited with family. Some freed slaves even remained as if in slavery so as to stay close to loved ones. See Eugene D. Genovese, *Roll, Jordan Roll* (New York: Vintage Books, 1975), 451.

[3] E. Franklin Frazier, *The Negro Family in the United States* (Chicago: University of Chicago Press, 1939). One of Elkins' controversial arguments was that the experience of slavery was psychologically devastating to blacks to the point of infantilizing them. See Stanley M. Elkins, *Slavery: A Problem in American Institutional and Intellectual Life* (Chicago: University of Chicago Press, 1976). For his views on slavery and the family, see Kenneth M. Stamp, *The Peculiar Institution: Slavery in the Antebellum South* (New York: Vintage, 1964). Daniel P. Moynihan, *The Negro Family: The Case for National Action* (Washington, DC: U.S. Department of Labor, 1965).

black family was the result of black victimization: "It was by destroying the Negro family that white America broke the will of the Negro people."[4]

This dysfunction was certainly due in part to the experience of slavery in this country but that was not the only influence. Other factors must be taken into consideration. One is that slaves were influenced by patterns of family life going back to West Africa, where slavery compromised family stability and polygyny was widespread.[5]

If a slave was captured with the intention of selling him to other African tribes, Arab traders, or European buyers, that person was often treated as an object or commodity—not as a human being. "It is scarcely surprising," write Myers and Kopytoff, "that most reports emphasize that the 'trade slave'—the one bought or captured for barter—was the worse treated of all."[6] Those who came to our shores were already in a social limbo from being marginalized and commoditized in Africa. Belonging to weaker tribes, they lived in a fearful state, always expecting the raid or the trade at any moment.

W. E. B. Du Bois similarly focused on how slavery weakened the black family in *The Negro American Family* (1908). His research on the black family presents a picture of a damaged but by no means destroyed family with a clear dichotomy between family life among house servants and among the most oppressed segment of field slaves. Du Bois attributed the disorganized black family—"a fortuitous agglomeration of atoms" as he called it—to the crippling effects of slavery. After painstakingly detailing the legal constraints facing the black family in bondage, he refers to the black family of his own time in a hopeful fashion:

> The broken families indicated by the abnormal number of widowed and separated, and the late age of marriage, show sexual irregularity and economic pressure. These things all go to prove *not the disintegration of Negro family life* but the distance which integration has gone and has

---

[4] Moynihan, *Negro Family*, chap. 4; see also Herbert G. Guttmann, *The Black Family in Slavery and Freedom, 1750–1925* (New York: Pantheon Books, 1976).

[5] According to Professor Mwizenge S. Tembo, "Polygyny was widely practiced in Africa and it often formed the backbone of the traditional African family patterns. Studies conducted from the 1930s to 1950s indicate that polygyny was common virtually in all regions of Africa." Mwizenge S. Tembo, "Traditional Family Patterns in Africa," unpublished paper, Institute for African Studies, University of Zambia, 1988.

[6] Suzanne Miers and Igor Kopytoff, *Slavery in Africa: Historical and Anthropological Perspectives* (Madison: University of Wisconsin Press, 1979), 15.

yet to go. Fifty years ago, "family" statistics of nine-tenths of the Negroes would have been impossible. Twenty-five years ago they would have been far worse than today, and while there is no perceptible change ... in the statistics of 1890 and 1900, most of the tendencies are *in the right direction*, and a healthier home life is in prospect.[7]

Du Bois saw positive signs of improved moral standards among the masses of freedmen: "Of the raising of the sex mores of the Negro by these classes the fact is clear and unequivocal: they have raised them and are raising them. There is more female purity, more male continence, and a healthier home life today than ever before among Negroes in America. The testimony supporting this is overwhelming."[8] In spite of the devastating attack on the black family from slavery, Du Bois placed the illegitimacy rate among blacks at about 25 percent.[9] If the black family was improving in the years after slavery and then became worse in later decades, then the assertion that the weakness in contemporary African-American family life is entirely due to slavery loses its force.

In his seminal research on the black family, Herbert Guttmann defends the idea that the problems in the black family structure as he perceived in the mid-1970s had no serious causal relationship with slavery or Jim Crow. Guttmann found that during slavery, and for decades after emancipation, the black family structure was not "fatherless matrifocal" but father-present, double-headed, and kin-related. Throughout the times of slavery and afterward, a father was present in most black families, ranging from 82 to 86 percent in rural areas and 69 to 74 percent in urban areas. The primary reason for the absence of fathers was not abandonment but death.[10] Although the enslaved father was constrained by the ignominy of his condition, he sought to be a good father and often jeopardized his own well-being for

---

[7] W. E. B. Du Bois, *The Negro American Family* (Atlanta: Atlanta University Press, 1908), 21–25, 31, emphases mine.

[8] Du Bois, *Negro American Family*, 38.

[9] Robert William Fogel, *Without Consent or Contract: The Rise and Fall of American Slavery* (New York: Norton, 1991), 164.

[10] Guttmann, *Black Family in Slavery and Freedom*, xviii–xix, 32, 45, 444, 449; David Blankenhorn, *Fatherless America: Confronting Our Most Urgent Problem* (New York: HarperPerennial, 1995), 22.

the sake of his family.[11] If after centuries of African bondage and instability, over two hundred years of chattel slavery, and many direct attacks against the black family black children were mostly still living in two-parent homes, then what we have is a remarkably resilient family system. To expect the black family to have exhibited the same integrity as white families at the time would be naïve.

The adaptive capacity of blacks by which they prevented destruction of their family structure points not toward pathology but toward resilience. However, again, we cannot simply deny the effects of contrary forces affecting the black family. After rejecting the more assertive views coming from Guttmann, James Q. Wilson analyzes single-parent homes as "a bit more normal among black than white Americans. By normal I do not mean widely accepted or generally endorsed; I mean instead that they will involve people who are less different from other members of their race or ethnicity."[12] The record of such problems, as Guttmann says, "is not evidence that the black family crumbled or that a 'pathological' culture thrived."[13] The assertion that the experience of slavery weakened the black family is correct, but its influence cannot be presented as binding in the absolute. Theories based on a weakened and pathological black family do not "misperceive the oppressive nature of enslavement but underestimate the adaptive capacities of the enslaved and those born to them and to their children."[14]

It is also mistaken to minimize the importance of evidence of familial disintegration. We should not rationalize the dissolution of the family as a strategy of adaptation, as writers such as Andrew Billingsley do:

> The traditional two-parent, or simple, nuclear family which arose at the height of the industrial era has given way dramatically in relative ways to various alternative family structures.... It means ... that families are doing what they always do. They are adapting as best they can to the pressures exerted upon them from their society in their gallant

---

[11] Keyes, *Masters of the Dream*, 35.

[12] James Q. Wilson, "Slavery and the Black Family" *Front Page Magazine*, Thursday, June 27, 2002.

[13] Guttmann, *Black Family in Slavery and Freedom*, 465.

[14] See Guttmann, *Black Family in Slavery and Freedom*, xxi.

struggle to meet the physical, emotional, moral, and intellectual needs of their members.[15]

Are we to believe that in a few decades the traditional black family "adapted" to the point of radical transformation after centuries of resistance to oppressive social conditions? Black families that are falling apart, that have increased out-of-wedlock births by teen girls, that have fathers who abandon their children, and that have single mothers who struggle to survive are signs of devastation, not adaptation.

MOST SOCIOLOGISTS GET IT WRONG

As Elisabeth Lasch-Quinn observes, radical sociologists and other behavioral scientists who immersed themselves in the 1960s countercultural movement began to dominate the professions in the decades following, examining black reality with an overemphasis on the internal states of persons seen as emotionally oppressed. In place of the goal of colorblindness, the radicals advocated color-consciousness.[16]

Theodor Adorno's *The Authoritarian Personality* had momentous influence on views that racism was a pathological condition of a repressive society. The Black Panther Movement and other radical groups were viewed by many in the field as epitomizing a quest for identity. Influenced by Adorno, Erik Erickson, and the radicalism of the 1960s, behavioral scientists rejected the description of pathology among blacks, preferring to see black reality as resisting white oppression in a quest to forge a positive black image as a useful therapeutic model. A balanced and realistic consideration of the realities of black life gave way to the binary of oppression-resistance. Blacks were victims of great oppression and were resisting such impulses by any means available to them.[17] Therapy was not needed for behaviors that were part of resisting white oppression.

[15] Andrew Billingsley, *Climbing Jacob's Ladder* (New York: Simon & Schuster, 1992). 44.

[16] Daryl Michael Scott, *Contempt and Pity: Social Policy and the Image of the Damaged Black Psyche, 1880–1996* (Chapel Hill: University of North Carolina Press, 1997), 161–63.

[17] Elisabeth Lasch-Quinn, *Race Experts: How Racial Etiquette, Sensitivity Training, and New Age Therapy Hijacked the Civil Rights Revolution* (2001; repr., Lanham, MD: Rowman and Littlefield, 2002), 120–23.

Many scholars remain committed to blaming a racist society that rejects the development of strong black men through consistently denigrating media depictions and enforced marginalization. Patricia Dixon states: "It is difficult to gauge the status of African American fatherhood. However, considering African American male marginalization in the economic sector, the tenuous status of American manhood, and the adaptive strategies that African American males use to attain masculinity, it is not surprising that there are so many absent fathers."[18] Theories of oppression are formulated, and entire university departments are focused on investigating every possible externalist explanation. The capacity of blacks as persons to transcend antecedent factors is forgotten in a sea of excuses. The possibility that negative cultural patterns influence behavior is minimized and at times rejected as racist.

The moral cost of trying to protect blacks from being blamed is to make them objects of our affection instead of recognizing them as centers of subjectivity. As philosopher Lloyd Weinreb puts it, "An attribution of responsibility requires that we regard a person as *duly* constituted, that is, as having with respect to the conduct in question the attributes that are *rightfully* his and not merely the effects of circumstances beyond his control."[19] What truly infantilizes blacks is the condescension of scholars always ready to give them a pass by devising ever-changing externalist excuses for bad behavior.[20]

The social pattern of out-of-wedlock births—70 percent by 1994[21]—with its devastating socioeconomic implications for the black community is,

---

[18] Patricia Dixon, *African American Relationships, Marriages, and Families: An Introduction* (New York: Routledge, 2006), 111.

[19] Lloyd Weinreb, "The Moral Point of View" in *Natural Law, Liberalism and Morality*, ed. Robert P. George (Oxford, UK: Oxford University Press, 1996), 205.

[20] The fact that similar patterns of pathology are observed within other ethnicities that did not experience the type of racist oppression that blacks experienced supports the idea that there are universal patterns at play and that positive change is possible without dwelling on long-gone historical circumstances that are often interpreted with a glaze of ideology.

[21] Stephan and Abigail Thernstrom, *America in Black and White: One Nation, Indivisible*, 240, 254–55. The Thernstroms convincingly argue that the enormous increase in out-of-wedlock births cannot be explained by economic criteria. Scholars such as William Julius Wilson, (*The Truly Disadvantaged: The Inner City, the Underclass, and Public Policy* [Chicago: University of Chicago Press, 1987]) have argued that the "black-male marriageable pool" was reduced by the negative financial position of single black

I contend, not *primarily* a legacy of slavery and racism but a disease that thrives in a culture promoted by collectivist policies—the changing values of American civil society previously detailed in this book. By portraying our present family problems as a legacy of slavery and perennial racism, we can relinquish responsibility for the crisis and place it in the hands of whites or in the hands of the state.[22] This attitude supports increased demands for government intervention and feeds the myth that racism is the only explanation for our present situation.[23]

Cultures that successfully resist evil do so by adapting while retaining certain basic values. However, cultures can and do change, at times for the worse, when certain core values are abandoned. Daniel Patrick Moynihan stated clearly fifty years ago that the culture of the inner city was dangerous. Although I have taken issue with Moynihan's implication that slavery was largely to blame for black familial dysfunction in the 1960s, he was entirely correct in pointing to family breakdown as the source of other social and economic problems. The reaction against the Moynihan Report signaled a refusal by liberals, radical intellectuals, and civil rights leaders to honestly deal with two important truths: first, cultural life determines economic reality, not the other way around; and second, "ghetto families were at risk of raising generations of children unable to seize the opportunity that the civil rights

---

men. During the Great Depression, marriage rates for blacks were higher than for whites and during the 1940s and 1950s. During the 1970s, the unemployment rise was too small to explain the massive rise in out-of-wedlock births.

[22] Kay Hymowitz, "An Enduring Crisis for the Black Family," *Washington Post*, December 6, 2008, A15.

> In 1950, at the height of the Jim Crow era and despite the shattering legacy of slavery, the great majority of black children—an estimated 85 percent—were born to their two married parents. Just 15 years later, there seemed to be no obvious reason that that would change. With the passage of the Civil Rights Act and the Voting Rights Act, legal barriers to equality were falling. The black middle class had grown substantially, and the first five years of the 1960s had produced 7 million new jobs. Yet 24 percent of black mothers were then bypassing marriage. Moynihan wrote later that he, like everyone else in the policy business, had assumed that "economic conditions determine social conditions." Now it seemed, "what everyone knew" was evidently not so.

[23] See James Mellon, ed., *Bullwhip Days* (New York: Avon Books, 1988), 15.

movement had opened up for them."[24] Those who denounced Moynihan refused to look within the community itself to begin to grapple with reality.

SEMPER FI?

As we have seen, some liberal scholars have tried to minimize the impact of the erosion of the traditional black family structure by presenting it as a positive survival tool or by asserting that fatherlessness is a general cultural pattern that does not affect the black family more than any other group.[25] They try to dissociate present pathologies from the breakdown of the black family after the 1960s.[26] Some modern scholars go further, joining the movement to dethrone the traditional marriage arrangement itself as a mere bourgeois convention with no inherent value worth preserving.

The traditional view of marriage might be described as "a two-in-one-flesh communion of persons that is consummated and actualized by sexual acts of the reproductive type" and "an intrinsic ... human good; as such marriage provides a non-instrumental reason for spouses, whether or not they are capable of conceiving children in their acts of genital union, to perform such acts."[27] Marriage is a union of spouses, male and female, which is good in itself. The unitive nature of their sexual union is intrinsic to what marriage is and not merely an instrumental tool for desire-satisfaction or for "producing" children. The reality that sexual acts must be of a reproductive type, even though they may not in effect become reproductive, gestures toward another good of marriage: the procreation and rearing of children. Children

[24] Kay S. Hymowitz, "The Black Family: Forty Years of Lies," *City Journal* (Summer 2005).

[25] See Billingsley, *Climbing Jacob's Ladder*, 44. This assumption flies in the face of the reality of poverty experienced by most single-parent families. In 1995, 62 percent of black children in female-headed families lived in poverty and only 13 percent of black children from intact families lived in poverty. See also Thernstrom and Thernstrom, *America in Black & White*, 236–37.

[26] Examples of this view are Maxine Baca Zinn, "Family, Race, and Poverty in the Eighties," in *Black Women in America: Social Science Perspectives*, ed. Micheline R. Malson et al. (Chicago: University of Chicago Press, 1990), 245–64; and Alvin L. Schorr and Phyllis Moen, "The Single Parent and Public Policy," in *Family in Transition*, ed. Arlene S. Skolnick and Jerome H. Skolnick (Boston: Little Brown, 1983).

[27] Robert P. George, *In Defense of Natural Law* (Oxford, U.K.: Oxford University Press, 2001), 139.

are gifts, not objects or products of intercourse. This is profoundly important in order to understand why a proliferation of single-parent homes and the boyfriend-girlfriend paradigm are deeply damaging to any community. Because marriage, as described, is a human good, any other arrangement tends to instrumentalize the spouses. Partners become tools for the given purpose of desire satisfaction, and children become trophies.[28]

In my work with black women in crisis, it is very common to hear the phrase, "I made x number of children *for* him." The expression carries either the pride of being fecund as a hook to keep a long-gone man still involved, or the bitterness of betrayal. A child becomes a sign of fertility, a billboard of manhood or womanhood, a tool for the purpose of "keeping a man"; or, obversely, a kind of comfort doll, someone to hold on to and "love" as the only tangible memory of a lost relationship.

Relationships built on instrumental goals are as fleeting as the feelings that initiated them. The integrity of the human person is violated every time their sexual organs are considered mere equipment for the purpose of intercourse rather than as part of the integral reality of the human person, making marital sex a truly interpersonal encounter.[29] The unity of bodies signals, or ought to signal, a real unity of spouses.

Marriage is an essential building block of a healthy community. No other arrangement can equal marriage, and no other arrangement can better serve the good of children. Men abandoning children and women living alone while trying to raise their children are deviations, not positive developments. The relevance of commitment explains why cohabitation does not lead to more successful marriages. The "30-day guarantee or your money back" kind of arrangement that springs from cohabitation is not very effective because it does not adequately prepare people for a committed relationship. That is why marrying after cohabitation results more often in divorce than does marrying without cohabitation.[30] In a boyfriend-girlfriend

[28] George, *In Defense of Natural Law*, 141–42, 155. According to George, there may be instrumental purposes in marriage that can be harmonized with the non-instrumental purpose of the relationship without altering the basic noninstrumental nature of the relationship.

[29] George, *In Defense of Natural Law*, 147–48.

[30] Steven L. Nock, "A Comparison of Marriages and Cohabiting Relationships," *Journal of Family Issues* 16 (January 1995); Georgina Binstock and Arland Thornton, "Separations, Reconciliations, and Living Apart in Cohabiting and Marital Unions," *Journal of Marriage and Family* 65 (May 2003): 432–43; Jay Teachman, "Premarital Sex,

cohabitating relationship, partners enter the arrangement with conflicting expectations (seldom verbalized). Men like the opportunity for sex and shared expenses without the pressures of a commitment while women often see the mingling as a first step toward marriage. If marriage occurs, the rules change as the institution has specific religious, cultural, and legal stipulations that conflict with the previous ones. All of a sudden, the partners begin to reveal hidden intentions.

An even more difficult situation for black America is that many black women are simply not marrying at all; cohabitation is all there is for them.[31] The only relationships they will ever experience are short and often tumultuous ones, where long-term commitment is not even expected. There is in those relationships a built-in expectation of sadness and heartache. Cohabitation is not only poor preparation for marriage, but it is in itself also a stressful and painful arrangement. An array of negative effects are associated with cohabitation: depression, physical abuse, alcohol-related problems, infidelity, and lower income levels.[32] Again, this is not a so-called adaptation to be celebrated.

Premarital Cohabitation, and the Risk of Subsequent Marital Dissolution among Women," *Journal of Marriage and Family* 65 (May 2003): 444–55; Susan L. Brown, "The Effect of Union Type on Psychological Well-being: Depression among Cohabitors Versus Marrieds," *Journal of Health and Social Behavior* 41 (September 2000): 241–55.

[31] According to the Administration for Children and Families African American Healthy Marriage Initiative:

> Studies show that while 35% of Americans between age 24 and 34 have never been married, that percentage increases to 54% for African Americans in the same age group. Additionally, married couples head 76% of our American families, while African American married couples head only 47.9% of [African] American families.

> While the overall rate for single-parent households in America has increased for all children, it is especially alarming among African Americans. Between 1960 and 1995, the number of African American children living with two married parents dropped from 75% to 33%. At this moment, 69% of African American births are to single mothers, as compared to 33% nationally.

Quote is available at http://www.aahmi.net/focus.html, under the heading Statistics.

[32] Susan L. Brown, "The Effect of Union Type on Psychological Well-being: Depression Among Cohabitors Versus Marrieds," *Journal of Health and Social Behavior* 41 (September 2000): 241–55; Wendy D. Manning and Daniel T. Lichter, "Parental Cohabitation and Children's Economic Well-Being," *Journal of Marriage and the Family* 58 (November 1996): 998–1010; Allan Horwitz and Helene White, "The Relationship

At times, we are told that for black single mothers raising children is a common marital arrangement rooted in an African matrilineal family structure where the female and the extended family fulfilled the needed roles for the rearing of children. Others see marriage as a utilitarian arrangement that admits a variety of types. In one social-work textbook, we learn that a family is "a group of people who choose to live together, or at least have regular contact, for the purpose of performing specific functions." The same text asserts that there is no such thing as a "normal" family, seeing that "normalcy is an idea located in the eye of the beholder."[33]

Nothing is more normal about single parenthood than this: poverty. Kay S. Hymowitz shows that single parenthood has created a caste system of poverty with blacks figuring prominently. While 6 percent of married families live in poverty, 36 percent of single-parent ones are poor. An astonishing 92 percent of children whose families make above $75,000 come from two-parent homes, and only 20 percent of children in two-parent families are in households making $15,000 or less.[34]

Married-parent homes have incomes that are significantly higher than single-parent homes. One indirect reason is the marriage-wage premium. Married men earn more, work longer hours, and seem to engage more in productive activity, probably out of a sense of increased responsibility. Another reason seems obvious: there can be two incomes instead of only one. For example, according to the US Census Bureau, the 2007 poverty threshold for a single-parent home with two children was $16,705. For a two-parent home with two children, it was $21,027, a difference of $4,322.[35] In times of economic downturns, the two-parent home is obviously advanta-

of Cohabitation and Mental Health: A Study of a Young Adult Cohort," *Journal of Marriage and Family* 60 (May 1998): 505–14.

[33] Cynthia Crosson-Tower, *Exploring Child Welfare: A Practice Perspective* (Boston: Allyn & Bacon, 1998), 21, 28.

[34] Kay S. Hymowitz, "Marriage and Caste in America: Separate and Unequal Families in a Post-Marital Age," Heritage Foundation Lecture #1005 (March 23, 2007). Statistics come from the research of Christopher Jencks and David Elwood. See also Kay S. Hymowitz, *Marriage and Caste in America: Separate and Unequal Families in a Post-Marital Age* (Chicago: Ivan R. Dee, 2006).

[35] *Poverty Thresholds for 2007 by Size of Family and Number of Related Children Under 18 Years* (US Census Bureau, Housing and Household Economic Statistics Division).

geous: If one income is lost, the family still receives income comparable to that of the single-parent home.[36]

Studies reveal that a traditional mother-father arrangement is better for black children for many other reasons. According to the Institute for American Values, "Black children of married parents typically receive better parenting, are less delinquent, have fewer behavioral problems, have higher self-esteem, are more likely to delay sexual activity, and have moderately better educational outcomes."[37]

Studies signal that the presence of fathers is essential for the better development of their children, especially for boys: "[W]hen African-American boys live with their father in the home—particularly their married father—they typically receive substantially more parental support. As a result, black boys of married parents tend to do better in school and are less likely to become delinquent."[38] Debates about matriarchy and patriarchy do not impinge on the marital norm. Matriarchy may speak of the relative power of the female in the family structure, but it does not mean the mother's role is exclusive. Similarly, even in a patriarchal system, the mother had a very important function, one that, in her absence, could not be easily fulfilled by the father. Single-mother (or single-father) homes are not better off because ancestral African arrangements were matriarchal or because black women have the capacity to adapt to changing conditions. The best situation for children of any race is in the traditional- or nuclear-family structure.[39]

Regrettably, the chances of living in a two-parent home were higher for black children during slavery than they are today.[40]

---

[36] Michael D. Tanner, *The Poverty of Welfare: Helping Others in Civil Society* (Washington, DC: Cato Institute, 2003), 138.

[37] Lorraine Blackman, et.al, *The Consequences of Marriage for African Americans: A Comprehensive Literature Review* (New York: Institute for American Values, 2005), 5.

[38] Cheryl Wetztine, "Marriage Found to Improve Blacks' Lives," *Washington Times*, October 25, 2005; William Raspberry, "Poor Marriages, Poor Health," *Washington Post*, October 24, 2005.

[39] Prominent sociologist David Popenoe states: "Fathers are far more than just 'second adults' in the home.... Involved fathers bring positive benefits to their children that no other person is as likely to bring." David Popenoe, *Life without Father: Compelling New Evidence That Fatherhood and Marriage Are Indispensable for the Good of Children and Society* (New York: Free Press, 1996), 163.

[40] Andrew J. Cherlin, *Marriage, Divorce, Remarriage* (Cambridge, MA: Harvard University Press, 1992), 110; Herbert G. Guttmann, *The Black Family in Slavery and Freedom.*

THE "BLACK DEATH" AND LIVING IN PERPETUAL CRISIS

Although some claim that the number of children growing up in single-parent homes has remained constant, better research indicates that the number has in fact increased significantly since the early twentieth century.[41] This is not a morally or culturally neutral development. Evidence suggests that poverty in black America is directly related to the proliferation of families headed by single mothers. In 1959, two-thirds (66 percent) of all black children lived in poverty. By 1995, that number had fallen to 42 percent. However, in 1995, 62 percent of children in female-headed families lived in poverty while only 13 percent of children in intact families were poor. Of all black children in poverty, 85 percent lived in fatherless families.[42]

Abigail and Stephan Thernstrom point out that even when you control for income, "Family structure has an independent effect that is measurable, and that, in important ways, the effect of growing up in a single-parent family is negative."[43] If we turn to the interesting case of new immigrants, we find that low birth weight and infant mortality are higher among babies born to US mothers than among babies born to immigrants. This happens in spite of the fact that, typically, immigrant women come from poorer backgrounds and receive less prenatal care. Adolescents from immigrant families experience fewer health-related school absences and engage less frequently in risky behaviors. Hence, economics does not explain the problems of single-parent homes. There is something lacking in the human interaction in these homes that affect connectedness at the earliest foundations of child rearing.[44]

Even if we were to grant that the number of children in single-parent households is the same today as it was fifty years ago, there are profound differences that must be accounted for. Fatherlessness due to death and fatherless due to abandonment are not the same thing; nor is fatherless due to death equivalent to the lack of a father *from the beginning* of childhood. Death brings finality and affirms the idea of fatherhood while abandonment

---

[41] In 1900, the percentage of children living in single-parent homes was 10 percent and in 1992, it was 27 percent. See Blankenhorn, *Fatherless America*, 23.

[42] Thernstrom and Thernstrom, *America in Black and White*, 236–37.

[43] Thernstrom and Thernstrom, *America in Black and White*, 241. The authors of *America in Black and White* point out that controlling for income is not justifiable due to the strong connection between poverty and single-parent family structure.

[44] The Commission for Children at Risk, *Hardwired to Connect: The New Scientific Case for Authoritative Communities* (New York: Broadway Publications, 2003), 10.

creates anxiety, resentment, continual insecurity, and turmoil, diminishing the image of the father. Abandonment damages the image of a father, while the death of a father, in general, highlights and uplifts that image. In fact, what many children living with single mothers experience is the inconsistency of intermittent relationships with multiple men who often leave just when the child begins to hope for a long-term relationship.[45]

We are now confronted with the real possibility of the extinction of the *husband-father* stable male presence, substituted by the *boyfriend-father* intermittent presence. This prospect is tragic for our entire country but especially for black America. The relationship of the boyfriend with the mother is often sporadic and unstable. Many of these relationships are established with young mothers with very young children fathered by men who have no desire for permanence in the relationship. These young black men usually have offspring with several mothers and pay minimal attention to the children. Resentment, anger, and humiliation are common feelings between boyfriends and girlfriends in these situations and among the children against both parents. "As a result, the boyfriend-father frequently becomes a violent guy, using his fists or a weapon to grab for something—ultimately, perhaps, a sense of control and self-respect—that his situation renders almost inherently unattainable."[46]

The family has lost the fundamental idea of morality and virtue: to love your neighbor. It is only in love that we can ever find the answer to the problems of the family. We *learn* to love. If we do not train our children to love, they will instead pursue primarily the satisfaction of appetites, a poor substitute for real love. We cannot love if we are not loved, and we cannot train if we were not trained—a deadly cycle that prevents the realization of basic human formation: "The human child is talked into talking and loved into loving."[47]

The breakdown we see in the black family today is a microcosm of the entire society. Many black families, especially but not exclusively those on the bottom rung of the economic ladder, are "families in perpetual crisis." This crisis is an ongoing experience of frustration, despair, and disillusionment. As Richard Kagan and Shirley Schlosberg tell us, "Living in a crisis-oriented family is like riding a roller coaster 24 hours a day:

---

[45] Blankenhorn, *Fatherless America*, 23–24.

[46] Blankenhorn, *Fatherless America*, 36.

[47] Commission, *Hardwired to Connect*, 25.

terrifying, energizing, and addicting."[48] The grief process has been blocked in these families by deep personal hurts, unfulfilled dreams of meaningful relationships, traumatic and repeated experiences of loss, and incessant victim-focused propaganda about the roots of their condition. It is as easy to blame "my man" (or "that bitch") for all my troubles as it is to blame "the man" (or "Whitey") for the problems of the black community as a whole. In fact, both attitudes are two sides of the same coin of victimhood. Denial and rage are the escape valves and diversion tactics that protect the crisis-oriented family from facing real change; the same responses also feed the insatiable need to point the finger at society in general and whites in particular for every conceivable social problem.

Single mothers and heroic aunts and grandmothers, exhausted and lonely, are often victims of a painful reality of loss and despair. Yes, there are many heroines out there raising children on their own, but the broken family cannot be the ideal or the norm. Where it is, morality suffers. Children are born to attach, an essential condition to developing a conscience, to developing as moral beings. Scientist Barbara Stillwell writes, "[m]oralization is a process whereby a value-driven sense of oughtness emerges with specific human behavioral systems, namely the systems governing attachment, emotional regulation, cognitive processing, and volition." [49] As the child broadens his network of connectedness to the extended society, new factors will have formative influence on his character and his conscience. A child who cannot attach at home will not attach in the larger society.

Children in perpetual loss soon become adults in perpetual grief. Sometimes they become adults primed to lash out at others. The intrusion of death into the life of a child is a painful experience that may, however, bring with it the opportunity for the closing of a chapter. There are traditions, ceremonies, rituals, and even children's games providing true opportunities to grieve and move on.[50] In black America, abandonment of children

[48] Richard Kagan and Shirley Schlosberg, *Families in Perpetual Crisis* (New York: Norton, 1989), 2.

[49] Barbara M. Stillwell, "The Consolidation of Conscience in Adolescence," Commission of Children at Risk, Working Paper, no. 13 (New York: Institute for American Values, 2002), 2.

[50] For a discussion of such processes see Robert Kastenbaum, "The Kingdom Where Nobody Dies" in *Living with Grief: Children, Adolescents and Loss*, ed. Kenneth J. Doka (East Sussex, UK: Psychology Press, 2000).

by their fathers condemns black children to a long and profound state of grief. There is no ritualistic remedy for abandonment—no memories to cherish, no rites to close a chapter. We only get an open wound, always fresh, always hurting.

One of the outcomes is youth violence. David Blankenhorn describes the connection to fatherlessness:

> When this process of male identity does not succeed—when the boy cannot separate from the mother, cannot become the son of his father— one main result, in clinical terms, is rage. Rage against the mother, against women, against society. It is a deeply misogynistic rage, vividly expressed, for example, in contemporary rap music with titles such as "Beat that Bitch with a Bat."[51]

This dangerous course helps the individual evade the challenge of confronting reality and facing difficult human existence. It offers an escape valve into a pseudo-existence where self-pity and self-righteousness merge into confusion and anger. Instead of focusing on the opportunities and risks inherent in taking responsibility, crisis-oriented families "act out" the pain and inner void that are built on too many disappointments by hurting people and blaming "the system." Outsiders play the role of "enabler," "hero," and "scapegoat."[52] These roles are often played by government officials and agencies of the welfare state. As Kagan and Schlosberg observe, "Professionals caught up in 'enabling' roles often miss the context of a family's behavior and their own roles in an ongoing cycle of crises."[53]

In fact, at times, "helpers" become so involved in the turmoil of a crisis-oriented family that they become part of the cycle, taking sides and fighting with other "helpers" engaged in the dynamic. Family therapist Evan Imber-Black recounts a case where a single-parent family and other family members were engaged in a dispute, and professionals became involved. "Each side then began to enlist outside helpers, characterizing the other side

---

[51] Blankenhorn, *Fatherless America*, 30–31. Hyperactive masculinity and misogyny are often found in rap videos and in the behavior of young black men. Both are the result of problems with male identity caused in large measure by fatherlessness.

[52] Richard Kagan and Schlosberg, *Families in Perpetual Crisis*, 8.

[53] Kagan and Schlosberg, *Families in Perpetual Crisis*, 8.

as bad, intractable, unworkable, and so on. Mistrust among the helpers ran extremely high, replicating the pattern in the family."[54]

These professionals cannot help but serve as enablers due to the fact that the welfare state is an enabling system, and their professional training has primed them to become enablers. As authority and decision-making is moved from the individual and from whatever remnant of community is still present in the family system to the state, it momentarily becomes the hero. It is extremely tempting for the agents of collectivized state compassion to offer excuses for bad behavior and provide all sorts of tangible benefits so as to stabilize the family.

A family in crisis cannot support free individuals. Only leaving the plantation of dependency on state action will allow such families to break free from their slavery. Only a free and healthy family can teach children about trust and love, about intimacy and connectedness, and about how to thrive as free persons.

The "cultural hurricane of the 1960s," as Jennifer Roback Morse has called it, with its gospel of collectivism to lift up the poor by government action, with its commandments of sexual license, "authenticity" and tolerance for any self-regarding behavior regardless of its depravity, wounded true love in the black family. Soon, the tragic hero of the state became a scapegoat. The state as parent, as hero, as savior soon becomes the great enemy, reminding families of their deficits and providing benefits that induce them to remain dependent.

THE SOLUTION: AUTHORITATIVE COMMUNITIES

How do we solve the family crisis in black America? The Commission on Children at Risk speaks of the role of *authoritative communities* as an important element in arriving at a solution. These are "groups that live out the types of connectedness that our children increasingly lack."[55] The human person has been made by God for connectedness, for relationship. The family is that most basic community where children develop the innate capacity to love and learn; it is an institution where children learn "love, discipline, and permanence." In the family, children learn "standards of personal conduct that cannot be enforced by law, but which are indispensable traits

---

[54] Evan Imber-Black, *Families and Larger Systems: A Family Therapist's Guide Through the Labyrinth* (New York: Guilford Press, 1988), 19.

[55] Commission, *Hardwired to Connect*, 6–7, 33.

for democratic society."[56] If the family is not providing such an incipient moral ecology, then the most pressing moral imperative is the rebuilding of this intimate community.

The great temptation of government intervention must be resisted at all costs. The state cannot fix the family. The state has no special capacity to strengthen a community whose primary job is to build relationships. Government schools and affordable day-care centers are not the answer to rebuilding the foundations of the family. They are utilitarian tools to assist parents in acquiring needed material resources, but they do not restore lost relationships. Children from single-parent homes suffer disadvantages in many areas and have lost something essential: *a parent.*[57] No child care or government program acting as a surrogate will ever bring that parent back.

The absent parent is very often the father, and there is no good substitute for a father. A father present in the home is much more than another paycheck or another set of hands. As Morse states:

> The father's contribution to the moral development of children is something to which we are almost blind at this moment in our history. We scoff at the idea of gender-specific roles for parents.... The real question is not whether men and women are different but how the difference allows each to contribute something unique to the moral development of children.[58]

A father enforces discipline and models manhood. The father joins the mother in creating a strong team of authority. He provides the stability and protection of a male presence to help boys discover what being a man really

---

[56] Commission, *Hardwired to Connect*, 17–19, 40. As the report states,

> brain researchers and other scientists are now clearly mapping out what might be called the biochemistry of connection. The report makes clear that such scientific evidence is not leading toward biological determinism. They have also discovered that a social environment can alter genes. Thus, the "nurture vs. nature" question is a false dilemma. Nature and nurture are "not like boxers, with each one trying to knock the other out, but more like dancers, with each subtle move producing a reciprocating move."

[57] For a detailed account of the evidence of the great disadvantages experience by children from single-parent homes, see Jennifer Roback Morse, *Love and Economics: It Takes a Family to Raise a Village* (San Marcos, CA: Ruth Insitute Books, 2008), 90–91.

[58] Morse, *Love and Economics*, 97.

is, to help them navigate the troubled waters of growing up, and to discern between authentic and false manhood. Fathers offer girls a sense of security and protection. Fathers reinforce the importance of loyalty within the structure of the family. "Statistics show that young girls in fatherless families are at greater risk of abuse by men outside the circle of their families and their mother's friends. Children without a resident father are more vulnerable to predatory behavior, both sexual and physical, by people outside the family."[59] Recent studies have found that the presence of biological fathers at home delays the onset of puberty while the presence of a stepfather or a boyfriend hastens it.[60]

Although government policy, as stated, cannot find an answer to the family problem, it can do certain things to encourage family unity.

First, it can make divorce very difficult to get, especially for couples with children; eliminating no-fault divorce is one step in the right direction. Absent abuse, divorce ought to be expensive and a truly last resort.

Second, it can provide additional tax advantages to married couples and refuse to provide automatic economic benefits to single mothers. Such benefits not only deter couples from depending on each other but also from depending on family and friends.

Third, it needs to stay the course on welfare reform. As Professors June E. O'Neill and Sanders Korenman amply demonstrate, welfare reform accounts for at least half of the reduction of child poverty since 1996.[61]

There are also things we can do as a society, outside of public policy. For one, we can be more judgmental. By failing to denounce certain behaviors in an open and direct way, we hurt people and diminish the realm of true freedom. By making it easier for people to choose actions that are not good for them, we deprive individuals of what they need to complete their humanity. We must understand that there is a difference between the objective categorization of an act as good or evil and the subjective application of guilt to the person committing the act. To oppose certain *behaviors*

---

[59] Morse, *Love and Economics*, 99.

[60] Researchers attribute this effect to exposure to pheromones. Bruce J. Ellis et al., "Quality of Early Childhood Relationships and Individual Differences in the Timing of Pubertal Maturation in Girls: A Longitudinal Test of an Evolutionary Model," *Journal of Personality and Social Psychology* 77, no. 2 (August 1999), 387–401, cited in Commission, *Hardwired to Connect*, 18.

[61] June E. O'Neill and Sanders Korenman, "Child Poverty and Welfare Reform: Stay the Course" *Civic Report*, Manhattan Institute, no. 44 (December 2004).

as unworthy of persons is to love people. A culture where certain actions are rejected as evil protects our true freedom—our freedom has boundaries, or it is not freedom at all. Basic norms of morality help us guide our choices to maintain them within the boundaries of true freedom. When I was growing up, I knew that there were certain things I should not do if I wanted to avoid my parents' wrath. That moral reproach molded character. Individuals in local communities must take the risk of speaking out boldly and modeling good behavior openly.

In addition, basic communities must develop extensive nonprofessional and nonspecialist organizations. The formation of civic groups utilizing *moral reasoning* and led by family members and other local, concerned individuals must be encouraged.[62] The establishment of regional institutes dedicated to the dissemination of the ideas of a free and virtuous society informed by the principles of the American Founding is essential in renewing the foundations of civil society. Freedom must be defended *at the local level.* Many effective, quality institutes work at the national level. Often, however, such organizations cannot be present at the level of local communities. There is a desperate need to bring the ideas of freedom being developed and defended by national and international institutes to local communities through local efforts. In other words, we must apply the principle of subsidiarity by creating networks of "community activists for freedom." The number of collectivist local groups working in minority communities is overwhelming; we need viable alternatives to influence the thought of the younger generation.

In the end, however, only in a *personal* commitment to love will we find an answer to all our problems. Love properly understood is a decision for the good of the other, a morally binding decision to lay down our life for our friends. Our first friend in marriage ought to be our spouse; the best gift a man can give to his children is to love their mother. This truth reminds me of the inspiring speech delivered by John Nash as he received his Nobel Prize in Stockholm, Sweden, in 1994 (and replicated by Russell Crowe in the movie *A Beautiful Mind*). Looking toward his wife, Alicia, Nash says, "I have made the most important discovery of my career, the most important discovery of my life: It is only in the mysterious equations of love that any logic or reasons can be found. I'm only here tonight because of you. You are the reason I am. You are all my reasons."[63]

---

[62] Commission, *Hardwired to Connect*, 37.

[63] See http://www.americanrhetoric.com/MovieSpeeches/moviespeechabeauti-fulmind.html.

12

A PERSONALIST APPROACH

The heart never takes the place of the head:
but it can, and should, obey it.

—C. S. Lewis[1]

Taken from her biological mother at an early age, the only life my wife, Crystal, remembers is the one with Fred and JoAnne, her foster parents. The family also included younger sisters Angela and Lydia. They were a typical black family living in a blue-collar Southside Chicago neighborhood. Her father worked long hours as the sole provider, and JoAnne was an expert homemaker. She kept an immaculate household, with no tolerance for sloth or uncleanliness. JoAnne took good care of all the girls' physical needs, but she was emotionally detached, keeping at bay any expression of warmth or sentiment. Fred would hand his paycheck over to his wife, and she managed it with a tight fist.

As a young girl, Crystal used to help her foster dad with the garden and earned twenty-five cents for her efforts, a nice treat in the 1960s. Fred also offered his foster daughter much fatherly advice. Study hard. Do not get involved with married men. His natural daughters were promiscuous and Fred wanted Crystal to chart a better course. She listened attentively and enjoyed the time with her adoptive father.

---

[1] C. S. Lewis, *The Abolition of Man* (1994; repr., New York: HarperSanFrancisco, 2001), 19.

Early in life, Crystal developed a poor self-image. The origin of the angst in her interior life without a doubt was her alienation from her mother and the loss of her father, brutally murdered by his best friend during a petty workplace argument. Some psychological damage from this upbringing was to be expected. Yet, Crystal grew up to be pensive, considerate, and studious. The stability offered by the Crawford family helped her to survive the initial familial turmoil and provided more than a mere sense of belonging. She recalls her life with her foster family as a happy experience.

The family's life took an unexpected turn soon after Crystal entered Percy L. Julian High School. When JoAnne fell sick with breast cancer, everything seemed to fall apart. Angela, then fifteen years old, was in a relationship with an ice-cream truck driver in his thirties. Once, around midnight, the man appeared at the door and asked to see her. Fred was first dumbfounded, then furious. Relentless, the man blurted, "I am here for my woman!" Angela confessed her relationship with the man and decided to join him. Fred went for his gun, but JoAnne intervened and offered the young girl a Faustian option. It was up to Angela to choose whether or not to leave with the man.

In her immature happiness, the she began to pack excitedly. She asked Crystal to join her. "If you come with me, he will take care of you. He is very rich. He will drive you in his limousine and will give you $20 for school every day." Confused, excited, and scared for her little sister, Crystal asked JoAnne about it. "Well, if you go with her, you are not coming back," she replied. Persuaded of the possibility of a great life with her sister and unwilling to see her go alone, Crystal packed and left.

Of course, the man was not rich. He was a homeless bum living in a car, but he possessed a clever tongue and a remorseless conscience. On that hot summer night, Crystal's life turned into a hell.

The man took them to his brother's warehouse. "We need to stop here for a while. His brother owns this," Angela explained. Crystal insisted that they continue their journey to the promised mansion, but she feared the worst. The man's brother came outside and spoke ominous words, "I need a girlfriend." They finally convinced Crystal to come inside with the promise of allowing her to call home. Once inside, the nightmare turned worse. Her sister, for whom she had left the security of a trusted home, deserted her. Angela turned to Crystal and said, "He will take care of you. I changed my mind. We want our own thing."

In desperation, Crystal called home and pleaded with her foster mother to be allowed to return. "Crystal, what did I tell you before you left? You made your bed and now have to lie on it." The possibility of returning to the happy home of her upbringing seemed to vanish forever.

For over a year, Crystal lived with an old drunkard in horrendous circumstances. The man used her and controlled her. The darkness was total and fear ever-present. She continued to go to school without asking anyone for help. She would stay late and wander around the park asking God, "Why? Are you real? Can you help me?"

At times, she did feel the presence of God, even amidst the storm, but her oppression was merciless, offering no immediate sense of liberation. Ending her life to recover it seemed a reasonable option. She consumed a bottle of pills and awaited the freedom that the induced slumber refused to produce.

One day, Crystal came back to the apartment and he was drunk. He began to issue his usual threats: "If you ever leave me, I'll kill you!" Asking God for strength and summoning enough courage to stand up to him, she found herself emerging from lifeless weakness into a growing sense of existence. "I am leaving!" she cried. She grabbed her book-bag and began to walk out. As she exited the first set of apartment doors, he grasped the door close behind her. She struggled to hold the door closed. Despair alone seemed to urge her to fight—but it was grace, I say, that protected her. As he gained control and the door flew open, he fell backwards, enabling her to run downstairs, through the glass doors of the apartment complex, and into freedom.

Crystal walked toward the bus stop. As the unexpected realization of a newfound freedom dawned on her, she sat at the bus stop and asked herself, "Now what?" She began to cry.

Early in this book I wrote of the power and importance of memory and that to remember—to remember in light of right reason—is our salvation. Suddenly, Crystal remembered a counselor from a pregnant girls' home who had offered assistance. (Ironically, she had met the pretty, young woman while visiting Angela there. By then, Angela was no longer with "her man"; he discarded her when she became pregnant.)

Hurriedly, Crystal took the bus that promised a return to peace. The door of the home opened. "Crystal, what are you doing here?" the lady kindly asked.

"I have nowhere to go," Crystal mournfully replied.

"That is not true," the counselor said, and embraced her with love.

They talked long into the night. The counselor spoke of how God had told her to save a space there for Crystal even though it was a home for pregnant girls and not a shelter. The woman became her lifeline, her strength whenever the fear and emotional attachment to her captor tempted her to return—tempted her to doubt reality and immerse herself in the familiar normalcy of the nightmare.

Crystal seemed destined to fall into the maelstrom of despair. As one door after another closed, she could have grown attached to the taste of self-serving victimhood. Her life, after all, bore the stamp of imposed failure that collectivists present as benefit. However, in the midst of oppression that justified grievance, her inner self triumphed. Living on the edge of her life's doom, she refused to give up.

Crystal eventually graduated from the home for girls with a medical assistant certificate and went on to college to earn a master's degree in marriage and family therapy. The curriculum specialist at Pearce Julian, Ann Swilley, took an interest in Crystal and eventually adopted her, becoming the mother that Crystal desperately needed. That marked the start of her life in service to others: For twenty years Crystal has enjoyed a successful career affirming the goodness, potential, and worth of individuals, couples, and families from all walks of life in her roles as a marriage and family therapist, a relationship coach, and an executive directing non-profit programs. Today she devotes her time to family and helping others find peace through a life of faith and meaningful work.

Returning to True Self

How easily we blame others for our shadows. In our earlier exploration of the theology of the body, we found a boundary, a line of demarcation between wholeness and alienation. There we observed that nakedness deprived of shame signals the mystery of man's creation in integrity and love. Recapturing that state of wholeness requires a willingness to admit to our own demons, a readiness to look inside and recognize our lack as the first step toward healing. In so doing, we will discover that, regarding most obstacles we encounter in life, we are both the source of the problem and the solution.

As anthropologist Robert Ardrey made plain, Jean Jacques Rousseau initiated the "age of alibi" by assigning the origin of human corruption to society. From there sprang the pernicious habit of pointing fingers at others.[2] Modern man is constantly exposed to the esoteric ideas of complete wellness and harmony; man is good by nature and everything can be perfected by human action. We are masters of the world; we are gods! Gurus show us the path, relationship experts make us weep, and mega-church preachers exult that wealth and health are ours if we just ask. Heaven on earth is a real possibility.

Except, what if we fail to reach that ecstatic state of existence?

What we experience when reality crashes the party of ecstatic wonder is the *utopian syndrome*. One expression of this syndrome is readily apparent in the lives of many: self-pity. One may feel sorry for oneself as a victim of others and "drop out" of reality into a world of withdrawal, depression, and callousness. Such a loner often becomes the victimizer of others without any sense of regret. In effect, the more engulfed he is in the decadence of his condition, the more ready he is to blame others. A second expression of the syndrome goes in the direction of empty nihilism: the search for immediate gratification in momentary and meaningless euphoric experiences such as drugs, sex, and violence. The third expression of the syndrome is rabid activism. If I am unable to attain the goal of a contented existence, it is because I am being deprived by oppressive systems. It is "because my parents, or society at large, by their rules and limitations, have crippled me and are unwilling to concede to me that simple freedom needed for my self-actualization."[3] For blacks who succumb to the utopian syndrome, a system controlled by white privilege is seen as the major cause of dissatisfaction.

In a self-righteous crusade, we attack the system and rebel against reality. We will always find actual experiences of loss that can be adduced as examples of the effects of oppressive systems, for there is no perfection this side of heaven. The problem here is not the challenge of confronting evil (such is our duty) but the absolutization of victimhood—the clouding of reason that prevents us from seeing meaningful progress. When the premises on which we base our existence become more real than reality itself, radicalism triumphs. The subjective animus against society engulfs our view of reality and clouds the intellect. Thus, if interventionism has not proven to be effec-

---

[2] Robert Ardrey, *The Social Contract: A Personal Enquiry into the Evolutionary Sources of Order and Disorder* (New York: Atheneum, 1970), 3.

[3] Paul Watzlawick, John H. Weakland, and Richard Fisch, *Change: Principles of Problem Formation and Problem Resolution* (New York: Norton: 1974), 48–51.

tive in uplifting the poor, it is because we have not invested enough; if we have not yet achieved economic parity with other minority and majority groups, it is because structural racism prevents it; if the black family is in shambles, it is due to the lingering effects of slavery and segregation; if my life is not what I want it to be, it is because I am a victim.

John McWhorter is perhaps correct in saying that victim mentality, or victimology, is not consciously internalized.[4] He contends that victimology is the result of a combination of oppression and the forced court decisions regarding desegregation of the 1960s; a kind of "integration shock," as Shelby Steele describes it.[5] The powerful molding influence of historical forces cannot be denied, but the explanation remains externalist. I submit that victimology is a disease that spread during the collectivist phase of the civil rights movement and is not primarily a byproduct of slavery, Jim Crow, and integration, as damaging as those historical experiences were.[6] Victimology is rather the result of false premises and false visions of social causation that have remained unchallenged. The utopian syndrome demonstrates the errors of the anthropology at the heart of the social vision of racialism. The collectivist vision of our time, of which racialism is an important segment, builds on a false vision of man.

After taking into account the importance of history, geography, and culture in shaping human behavior, we must always come back to the person. Every choice shapes us for good or for ill. At the center of truly human choices resides a self-determining element that remains in us, giving us moral standing.[7] As phenomenologist Max Scheler observes, "The *whole person* is contained in *every* fully concrete act—without being exhausted in his being in any of these acts."[8] Our free choices are not merely physical events that "happen" to a person. Rather, our actions abide in us until we determine

[4] John McWhorter, *Losing the Race: Self-Sabotage in Black America* (New York: Free Press, 2000), 32–34.

[5] Shelby Steele, "Being Black and Feeling Blue," in *The Eighties*, ed. Gilbert T. Sewall (Reading, MA: Perseus Books, 1998), 111.

[6] See McWhorter, *Losing the Race*, 26–29.

[7] John Finnis, *Moral Absolutes: Tradition, Revision, and Truth* (Washington, DC: Catholic University of America Press, 1991), 71–72.

[8] Max Scheler, *Formalism in Ethics and Non-Formal Ethics of Values: A New Attempt Toward the Foundation of an Ethical Personalism* (Evanston: IL: Northwestern University Press, 1973), 377; cited in Samuel Gregg, *Challenging the Modern World: Karol Wojtyla/*

ourselves to transform our being by the adoption of other volitional acts.[9] Our reality evolves; it is never inexorable. The human person remains at the center of the drama, and our vision of man has a radically important place in understanding social causation.

As theologian Kevin L. Flannery, SJ, writes, "Anything one does involves projecting (as a good thing) a stretch of road ahead and taking it.... Free choice is an opportunity to go forward or away from the good and thus to become either virtuous or not."[10] According to Germain Grisez, character is "the integral existential identity of the person—the entire person in all his or her dimensions as shaped by morally good and bad choices—considered as a disposition for further choices."[11] Our capacity to choose may send us into the self-contradiction we call sin. As Reinhold Niebuhr puts it, in sinning, "[m]an contradicts himself within the terms of his own essence. His essence is for free self-determination. His sin is the wrong use of his freedom."[12]

None of this denies the influential forces around us. None of this fails to recognize how our environment and others press upon us to move in a certain direction. Nonetheless, the focal point of the challenge of true freedom is purposeful action within the boundaries of whatever degree of freedom we possess. "To the degree that our choices and actions are determined by [extrinsic] factors," Grisez and Shaw remind us, "freedom does not enter into the picture at all."[13]

John Paul II and the Development of Catholic Social Teaching (Lanham, MD: Lexington Books, 2002), 58.

[9] See William E. May, *An Introduction to Moral Theology* (Huntington, IN: Our Sunday Visitor, 1991), 29.

[10] Kevin L. Flannery, "Practical Reason and Concrete Acts," in *Natural Law and Moral Inquiry: Ethics, Metaphysics, and Politics in the Work of Germain Grisez*, ed. Robert P. George (Washington, DC: Georgetown University Press, 1998), 123.

[11] Germain Grisez, *The Way of the Lord Jesus*, vol. 1, *Christian Moral Principles* (Chicago: Franciscan Herald Press, 1983), 50.

[12] Reinhold Niebuhr, *The Nature and Destiny of Man*, vol. 1 (New York: Charles Scribner's Sons, 1949), 16, cited in Patricia Donohue-White et al., *Human Nature and the Discipline of Economics: Personalist Anthropology and Economic Methodology* (Lanham, MD: Lexington Books, 2002), 21.

[13] Germain Grisez and Russell Shaw, *Beyond the New Morality: The Responsibilities of Freedom* (Notre Dame, IN: University of Notre Dame Press, 1974), 151.

What theologian Johann Baptist Metz calls "evolutionary thought," however, dominates the modern mind in describing human agency. This evolutionary thought aligns well with the utopian syndrome of self-pity. Metz tells us that an evolutionary mindset has become a totalism, a comprehensive worldview where culture, human activity, and consciousness are predetermined by a constant evolutionary process. It is in the impersonal movement of evolutionary forces that we can both appreciate change and dismiss choice. Apathy is the logical response. Metz writes,

> Man is at the mercy of a darkly speckled universe and enclosed in an endless continuum of time that is no longer capable of surprising him. He feels that he is caught up in the waves of an anonymous process of evolution sweeping pitilessly over everyone. A new culture of apathy and lack of feeling is being prepared for him in view of his experience of fragile identity.[14]

A Return to the Person

A deep psychological and spiritual transformation is necessary to escape victimhood. A personalist understanding of social interaction is essential to discover the route we must take to begin a process of healing. The individual human person possesses ontological priority over any collective entity. All human capacities are unique and incommunicable in each human person. This emphasis on the human person is not atomistic but holistic. The human person requires intersubjectivity as relationships are an essential metaphysical component of being. We exist in relationship with others as an inescapable element of who we are. Yet, "the person appears to stand *sui juris* and *sui generis* in the midst of his or her common community."[15]

The penetrating personalist analysis of Dietrich von Hildebrand shows the path toward healing from the effects of victimization. Hildebrand says that an unqualified readiness to change is the prerequisite for acquiring the self-knowledge necessary for transformation. This unqualified readiness must

---

[14] Johann Baptist Metz, *Faith in History and Society* (New York: Seabury Press/ Burns & Oates, 1980), 6.

[15] In using the term *individual human person*, we recognize a methodological preference for the term *person*. This term more fully allows the dimension of intersubjectivity. See Gregory R. Beabout et al., *Beyond Self-Interest: A Personalist Approach to Human Action* (Lanham, MD: Lexington Books, 2002), 8–9.

suppose *recognition of our individuality*.[16] Our individuality has to be reasserted to counter the insidious damage of an identity based on collective victimization. The hopelessness of victimization in the black community has created what Hildebrand calls an "inward barrenness."[17]

By defining people by their race, we have given our individuality a mortal blow. Our authenticity as human persons is blocked by an inordinate group identification, which is defined against true self and against the social mainstream. Our group and racial identification has taken an expansive place in our definition as persons. The process de-humanizes us by encapsulating in partiality the infinite depth of the human person.[18] Race is but an element of who we are and collective identification cannot supersede the individual's uniqueness.[19] By deriving our meaning as persons from group victimization and transferring both value and guilt into external forces, we empty ourselves of the elements necessary for the self-knowledge required for inner transformation. We inevitably take a purely psychological interest in ourselves as victims of external forces.[20] Essentially, we renounce our reality as subjects. Assuming the role of spectators in the drama of our lives, we detach ourselves from full responsibility—without which we can never be free. In search of the innocence of a victim, we become invisible, empty.

Hildebrand explains:

---

[16] Dietrich Von Hildebrand, *Transformation in Christ: On The Christian Attitude* (San Francisco: Ignatius Press, 1990), 8–10; "For the essence of every human person supposes a unique and incommensurable task; it is destined to unfold and to operate in a direction inalienably proper to it" (23).

[17] Hildebrand, *Transformation in Christ*, 23.

[18] For a critical discussion of how exhaustive classifications destroy personhood, see Emmanuel Mounier, *Personalism* (Notre Dame, IN: University of Notre Dame Press, 1952).

[19] Beabout et al., *Beyond Self-Interest*, 46. "People may be classified in a myriad of ways (by gender, height, ethnicity, nationality, occupation, marital status, and so forth), but these classifications never fully exhaust their being as persons."

[20] John Perazzo perfectly describes the attitude of many black leaders in dealing with black violence: "Civil rights leaders, academicians, and members of the media depict sadistic marauders who terrorize entire cities as reservoirs of sociological information, specimens to be examined so that society might learn how to better address its own 'injustices'"; *The Myths that Divide Us: How Lies Have Poisoned American Race Relations* (New York: World Studies Books, 1999), 121.

> Whenever we take a purely psychological interest in ourselves and thus analyze our character in the manner of mere spectators, we pursue a false and sterile self-knowledge. We then envisage our character not by any standard of good and evil, but in entire neutrality as though we were analyzing some phenomenon of exterior nature. We leave our solidarity with our character to one side, and look upon ourselves as though we were observing some odd stranger.[21]

We must become a mirror before we become a window. Self-knowledge based on psychological curiosity is not true knowledge of self. By extracting ourselves from the equation, we readily admit an unwillingness to change. Curiously, we are often willing to state publicly our vices and the malaise that infects our midst. However, this confession is performed with a self-righteous detachment from any responsibility. This unveiling is not done out of true self-consciousness but out of a need to decry the evils inflicted by others.

There is no transformational power in this kind of disclosure. Fear of peering into the dark abyss of our true selves and discovering our failures and weaknesses prevents us from ever looking too deeply. Without cognitive apprehension of our reality, we neglect a basic element for change. As Hildebrand correctly observes, "The radical extirpation of a defect of character requires an interior knowledge of that defect."[22] Only an honest look into the depths of existence can answer the universal question, "Who am I?" The answer cannot be delegated to a group or to a structure.

Conscious man is characterized by a self-awareness that offers continuity. "*Unconscious* man gives himself entirely over to the moment's experience," Hildebrand writes. "He allows the present impression (which, of course, is conditioned, in an extra-conscious sense, by many anterior experiences) to capture him."[23] How true is this assessment when applied to the condition of many in the black community. Only a renewal of our minds (Eph. 2:23) will bring the readiness to change and the true self-awareness necessary to counter the vicious and damaging effects of adopting victimhood as identity.

This, of course, is a process. There are no easy answers to the problems in the black community. Nevertheless, the first step is clear: an unqualified

---

[21] Hildebrand, *Transformation in Christ*, 44–45.

[22] Hildebrand, *Transformation in Christ*, 44.

[23] Hildebrand, *Transformation in Christ*, 63–64.

effort to weaken the negative aspects of extreme group consciousness and to foster self-knowledge by asserting our individuality.

That step taken, we must recognize that categorical solutions are not available to us.[24] The radical egalitarianism pervasive in the black community assumes that if racial discrimination is absent, equality of results is inevitable, but that is simply a phantom. Real advances in the law, which provided equality of opportunities, have been seen as political ploys to "keep us down" simply because they do not guarantee equality of results. It is assumed that because our problems are the result of unjust structures erected by racism the solutions require political battles to protect and expand government preferential treatment.[25] We remain immersed in a political battle that refuses to give way to the quest for true identity in individuality.

Although categorical solutions are illusory, we can present a partial alternative. There is a need for black Americans who reject the modern liberal/radical mindset to speak out boldly. We must challenge the monopoly and honor the need for a genuinely pluralistic community. The idol of government priority and racial etiquette must be overturned by a radical commitment to individuality and human liberty as well as staunch support for the idea of limited government.[26] This commitment must come especially from black voices. What we need today, more than at any other time in our history, is not merely justice but, even more, courage.

---

[24] Liberals tend to emphasize categorical solutions over incremental ones. Categorical solutions are seen as possible and, in the black community, they refer to the lack of political power. Incremental solutions are rejected and seen as always insufficient. See Thomas Sowell, *The Vision of the Anointed: Self-Congratulation as a Basis for Social Policy* (New York: Basic Books, 1995), 109–19.

[25] Terry Eastland counts 160 federal government programs that use racial preferences. Terry Eastland, *Ending Affirmative Action: The Case for Color Blind Justice* (New York: Basic Books, 1996), 40.

[26] Shelby Steele says, "There will be no end to despair and no lasting solution to any of our problems until we rely on individual effort within the American mainstream—rather than collective action against the mainstream—as our means of advancement"; The *Content of Our Character: A New Vision of Race in America* (New York: HarperCollins, 1990), 31.

ESCAPING THE PARADIGM OF VICTIMHOOD

Realities of race in America today impose on us a new set of commitments. Such commitments represent a departure from the one-dimensional explanations of the liberal/radical racial narrative. The departure is not simply methodological but foundational; not incremental but reconstructive. The thought of Thomas S. Kuhn on the appearance of scientific revolutions can enlighten our discussion here.

In his *Structure of Scientific Revolutions*, Kuhn tells us that scientists routinely operate within paradigms providing certain assumptions about the nature of the world. These assumptions retain an element of arbitrariness that enable the practitioners to suppress ideas that are inconsistent with the paradigm. In effect, "normal science research is directed to the articulation of those phenomena and theories that the paradigm already supplies."[27] The arbitrariness, however, also serves as a catapult for change once a given set of assumptions moves at least *some* practitioners to re-evaluate their commitment to the assumptions.

The momentous episodes when a new set of commitments appear is what Kuhn calls *scientific revolutions*. These episodes necessitate "the community's rejection of time-honored scientific theory in favor of another incompatible with it." They offer the opportunity to reframe at the level of metareality the change that takes place at the conceptual level. Because the assumptions of normal science are constructs of the mind to interpret reality but are not reality itself, reframing allows us to renew our minds and look at reality differently.[28]

We are at the crossroads of a great opportunity to reframe the racial debate. A generation invested heavily in the paradigm of eternal victimhood is slowly fading, not by the appropriation of a new paradigm but simply because of age. Most black intellectuals still cling to the old paradigm, unwilling or unable to shift. Yet, a new generation of blacks not scorched by the flame of segregation and more interested in universalism is emerging. The possibility of challenging the theory instead of simply elaborating on and reformulating it is real.[29]

---

[27] Thomas S. Kuhn, *The Structure of Scientific Revolutions* (Chicago: University of Chicago Press, 1962), 24.

[28] See also Watzlawick et al., *Change: Principle of Problem Formation and Psychotherapy* (New York: Norton, 1974), 97.

[29] Kuhn, *Structure of Scientific Revolutions*, 33.

Yes, ceasing to agree with the liberal radical consensus has its perils. As in normal science, to work under different premises is to cease to be a member of the community: "Work under the paradigm can be conducted in no other way, and to desert the paradigm is to cease practicing the science it defines." Nevertheless we are no longer in the time when the entire spectrum of scholars operating outside of the paradigm consisted of two men, Thomas Sowell and Walter Williams. Their desertion, I submit, was the "pivot about which scientific revolutions turn."[30] We are at the crossroads of the dawning of a new era when a growing sense that the existing ideologies of race and its messiahs cannot meet the needs of a community whose problems are precisely the result of an environment they created.

"Discovery commences with the awareness of anomaly, that is, with the recognition that nature has somehow violated the paradigm-induced expectations that govern normal science."[31] Sowell and Williams opened the eyes of a generation to the puzzling reality of the failure of the liberal/radical paradigm to effect real change. It is precisely the appearance of certain puzzles that creates the opportunity for qualitative leaps. Because those who operate within a given paradigm often insulate themselves from socially important problems not reducible to the assumptions of the system, they unwittingly open the opportunity to challenge the very assumptions that give life to normal science by the discovery of "pockets of apparent disorder."[32] These pockets, unanswerable by the accepted assumptions, can provoke a scientific—or social—revolution.

Before us we have three options. The first is to adhere to the old paradigm of victimhood and adopt its reactionary resistance. The second is to intellectually reject the old paradigm but accept its practical application by concluding that there are no real alternatives. That is the road already traveled. Third, there is the possibility of the emergence of a new paradigm with new rules and new expectations. We dare to hope that the last alternative has already been conceived in the minds of a few, such as Sowell and Williams, who were from the start not committed to the fundamental assumptions of racialism. There is now an opportunity to renew our minds and finally see anew:

---

[30] Kuhn, *Structure of Scientific Revolutions*, 34.

[31] Kuhn, *Structure of Scientific Revolutions*, 52.

[32] Kuhn, *Structure of Scientific Revolutions*, 42.

Led by a new paradigm, scientists adopt new instruments and look in new places. Even more important, during revolutions scientists see new and different things when looking with familiar instruments in places they have looked before. It is rather as if the professional community had been suddenly transported to another planet where familiar objects are seen in a different light and are joined by unfamiliar ones as well.[33]

Healing the Twoness

Forceful condemnations of racism must cease to be presented as war cries in the cause of separatist rebellion. They instead ought to be prudent statements recognizing the incidental nature of the problem. Yes, racism is alive, but not well, and its corrupt body fails to expire because some refuse to let the patient die. The racialists of today are the shamans of race consciousness, and their activist groups have become the tomb of our hopes for ever witnessing the end of racism. If we are ever going to find our way toward unity, the age of particularist racial identity "must give way to planetary unity" where, as von Balthasar reminds us, "[a] new consciousness of humanity as a whole would appear as one that takes man as its starting point and common denominator."[34]

We need to turn from the path of race consciousness, and then we may be able to perceive, even if only in the boundaries of possibility, the end of racial struggle. Man must not be sacrificed any longer to grandiose collectivist plans concocted by groups of people forever lost in the great sea of color. Purged of all the baggage of victimhood, the transcendent subjectivity of the human person will emerge.

It is undeniable, as we have previously stated, that *consciousness* of all the particularities of our being—including race—is essential for the recognition of our own subjectivity and the formation of conscience. However, it is in acting that we form our moral being. We must be careful not to absolutize consciousness, as we run the peril, as Samuel Gregg aptly points out in describing Karol Wojtyła's thought, of reducing *being* to *perception* and "[locking up] man in the inner fortress of idealism." In any event, there is an even higher truth. Man as a "dynamic subject" is the originator of both

---

[33] Kuhn, *Structure of Scientific Revolutions*, 111.

[34] See Hans Urs von Balthasar, "Anthropology and Religion," in *Modern Catholic Thinkers Anthology*, ed. Aloysius Robert Caponigri (New York: Ayer Publishing, 1970), 8.

recognition and action. Both are grounded in the human person as the superintendent of all their measures.[35]

More than a century ago, Du Bois spoke eloquently of the dichotomies of black existence in America. "It is a peculiar sensation," he noted,

> this double consciousness, this sense of always looking at one's self through the eyes of others, of measuring one's soul by the tape of a world that looks on in amused contempt and pity. One ever feels his twoness—an American, a Negro; two souls, two thoughts; two unreconciled strivings; two warring ideas in one dark body, whose dogged strength alone keeps it from being torn asunder.[36]

Du Bois's twoness is something every black American has felt to some extent. However, this tension can be either a prompt to reconciliation or a goad to destruction. Too often, we have chosen the latter.

A young and promising black student came back home from his first year in college. I remember "Charles" sitting there at an event in the Dunbar community and attentively listening to the discussions. As I got to know him better, Charles seemed angry at the white world and revealed a radical racial ideology. I liked the young man and saw much potential in him. Trying to help, I spent many hours discussing issues and trying to counsel him on the importance of his studies at a local university. I insisted that he needed to leave politics alone for a while, graduate, and then come back and pursue whatever he desired. Others did the same.

However, he refused the advice and continued his furious activism. He interrupted city hall meetings, verbally attacking people, and at times had to be escorted out. Confrontations with the police ensued, and Charles soon became a "community activist." Unfortunately, the stimulus of activism released demons difficult to control. It offered an immediate release of emotion that made smashing obstacles preferable to hurdling them. Activism seemed to consume his existence, bringing a glow of satisfaction, a high that eclipsed the less euphoric effects of reasoned engagement.

His college attendance became sporadic. Having practiced his brand of wild activism at the university, he was soon expelled. Some joined him to organize a new group to "fight for justice." Supporters insisted that we critics were missing something important about how vocal black men are treated

---

[35] Gregg, *Challenging the Modern World*, 58–61.

[36] W. E. B. Du Bois, *Souls of Black Folk* (1903; repr., Chicago: Bartlebys, 1999), 45.

in our country. The problem, they said, is racism and white intolerance of black men who express rightful anger.

In reality, Charles's approach gains nothing. A life that could have been one of authentic service has been sacrificed to the god of anger, and the community's gain in meaningless gesture is its loss in purposeful activity.

The time has come to openly reveal our frailty and self-doubt. We must no longer merely reflect the world as it acts on us but confidently open the doors of our soul to a future of both risk and opportunity.

Yet, fear lurks. Cowed into indecision, we still hang perilously over the abyss of existence. As Henry Ward Beecher preached long ago:

> Fear sat in the window and lied. And Pride cried, and Vanity cried, and Avarice cried—and ought to cry. Fear sat and told lies to them all. For there was not one of those things, probably, down there. Did Fear see them? Yes. But Fear has a kaleidoscope in its eye, and every time it turns it takes a new form. It is filled with broken glass, and it gives false pictures continually. Fear does not see right. It is forever seeing wrong.... So Fear sits in the window to torment the lower forms of all our good feelings and all our malign feelings. And under such circumstances how can a man do anything? He has smoked glass before his eyes when his feelings get before them, and they are in a morbid state.[37]

The old racialist orthodoxies are dying, yet they are still dangerous. Our transitional age, after all, could lead toward a reactionary future of untold racial turmoil and ruin. We must strive instead for a future in which our individuality finally ends the reign of race-consciousness. A future without the hold of race where the visionary dream of authentic personhood is realized is not impossible.

Now, it is time for us to accept our identity as black American individuals. It is time to reconcile the two identities that have become one through years of suffering, struggle, and commitment to the ideas of liberty and faith. Our ancestors worked hard in bondage so that we could work hard in freedom. They kept their faith in this beloved country of ours in the face of continual oppression so that we could embrace it without fear. James Cone describes the source of the strength and determination exhibited by generations of black Americans:

---

[37] Henry Ward Beecher, *The Sermons of Henry Ward Beecher: In Plymouth Church, Brooklyn* (New York: J. B. Ford, 1871), 144.

No reality was more important than God, in this life and the next. God, African-American Christians claimed, could make "the crooked roads straight" and the "rough places plain." They believe that God "builds you up when you are torn down" and "props you up on every leaning side." No matter what whites said about blacks or what wicked laws they enacted against their humanity, the people of Ebenezer believed that God had bestowed upon them a somebodyness, which had been signed and sealed by Jesus' death and resurrection.[38]

The only way to begin to accept the beautiful gift of our American identity is through the restoration of the place of the individual, the family, and the church in our communities. It will come from reclaiming the way of our ancestors and from taking to heart the values they embraced at such a high price. We must affirm that we are not, by any means, tragically colored.

---

[38] James Cone, *Martin & Malcolm & America: A Dream or a Nightmare* (Maryknoll, NY: Orbis, 1992), 25.

BIBLIOGRAPHY

Author's Note: The titles below represent important influences in shaping my thinking about the topics in this book, which is not to say that I agree with everything contained in all of them. I have arranged them topically rather than by chapter. A more comprehensive listing of references for quotations and ideas cited in the book can be found in the footnotes.

THEOLOGICAL AND PHILOSOPHICAL FOUNDATIONS: PERSONHOOD, FREEDOM, AND MORALITY

Adler, Mortimer J. *The Difference of Man and the Difference It Makes.* New York: Fordham University Press, 1993.

Aquinas, Thomas. *Summa Theologiae*

Augustine of Hippo, *Confessions*

Beabout, Gregory R. et al. *Beyond Self-Interest: A Personalist Approach to Human Action.* Lanham, MD: Lexington Books, 2002.

Colson, Charles, and Nancy Pearcey. *How Now Shall We Live?* Wheaton, IL: Tyndale House, 1999.

Donohue-White, Patricia, et al., *Human Nature and the Discipline of Economics: Personalist Anthropology and Economic Methodology.* Lanham, MD: Lexington Books, 2002.

Fern, Richard L. *Nature, God and Humanity: Envisioning an Ethics of Nature.* New York: Cambridge University Press, 1992.

Finnis, John. *Aquinas: Moral, Political, and Legal Theory.* Oxford, UK: Oxford University Press, 1998.

Finnis, John. *Fundamentals of Ethics.* Washington, DC: Georgetown University Press, 1983.

Finnis, John. *Moral Absolutes: Tradition, Revision, and Truth.* Washington, DC: Catholic University of America Press, 1991.

Finnis, John. *Natural Law and Natural Rights.* Oxford: Oxford, University Press, 1980.

Galston, William. *Liberal Purposes: Goods, Virtues, and Diversity in the Liberal State.* New York: Cambridge University Press, 1991.

George, Robert P. *In Defense of Natural Law.* New York: Oxford University Press, 2001.

George, Robert P. *Making Men Moral: Civil Liberties and Public Morality.* Oxford, UK: Clarendon Press, 1993.

George, Robert P. *The Clash of Orthodoxies.* Wilmington, DE: ISI Books, 2001.

George, Robert P., and Christopher Tollefsen. *Embryo: A Defense of Human Life.* New York: Doubleday, 2008.

Gilson, Étienne. *God and Philosophy.* New Haven: Yale University Press, 1941.

Grabill, Stephen J., Kevin E. Schmiesing, and Gloria L. Zuniga, *Doing Justice to Justice.* Grand Rapids: Acton Institute, 2002.

Gregg, Samuel. *Challenging the Modern World: Karol Wojtyła/John Paul II and the Development of Catholic Social Teaching.* Lanham, MD: Lexington Books, 2002.

Gregg, Samuel. *Morality, Law and Public Policy.* Sydney: St. Thomas More Society, 2001.

Gregg, Samuel. *On Ordered Liberty.* Lanham, MD: Lexington Books, 2003.

Grisez, Germain, and Russell Shaw. *Beyond the New Morality: The Responsibilities of Freedom.* Notre Dame, IN: University of Notre Dame Press, 1974.

Grisez, Germain. *The Way of the Lord Jesus*, vol. 1, *Christian Moral Principles.* Chicago: Franciscan Herald Press, 1983.

Gutierrez, Gustavo. *A Theology of Liberation.* NewYork: Orbis, 1973.

Hayek, F. A. *The Constitution of Liberty.* Chicago: University of Chicago Press, 1960.

Hayek, F. A. *The Road to Serfdom.* 1944; repr., Chicago: University of Chicago Press, 1994.

Hazlitt, Henry. *Economics in One Lesson: The Shortest and Surest Way to Understand Basic Economics.* New York: Crown Publishers, 1979.

Hittinger, Russell. *The First Grace: Rediscovering the Natural Law in a Post-Christian World.* Wilmington, DE: ISI Books, 2003.

Horowitz, David. *Left Illusions: An Intellectual Odyssey.* Dallas: Spence, 2003.

Jasay, Anthony de. *Justice and Its Surroundings.* Indianapolis: Liberty Fund, 2002.

John Paul II, Pope. Encyclical Letter *Centesimus Annus* (1991).

John Paul II, Pope. *The Theology of the Body: Human Love in the Divine Plan.* Boston: Pauline Books & Media, 1997.

Jouvenel, Bertrand de. *The Ethics of Redistribution.* Indianapolis: Liberty Fund, 1990.

Kant, Immanuel. *The Postulates of Practical Reason* (1788).

Kuhn, Thomas S. *The Structure of Scientific Revolutions.* Chicago: University of Chicago Press, 1962.

Lewis, C. S. *The Abolition of Man.* San Francisco: HarperSanFrancisco, 2001.

Marcel, Gabriel. *Mystery of Being: Reflection & Mystery*, vol. 1. South Bend, IN: Gateway Editions, 1950.

Maritain, Jacques. *Man and the State.* Chicago: University of Chicago Press, 1951.

May, William E. *An Introduction to Moral Theology.* Huntington, IN: Our Sunday Visitor, 1991.

Mises, Ludwig von. *Human Action: A Treatise on Economics.* San Francisco: Fox & Wilkes, 1996.

Mounier, Emmanuel. *Personalism.* Notre Dame, IN: University of Notre Dame Press, 1952.

Muravchik, Joshua. *Heaven on Earth: The Rise and Fall of Socialism.* San Francisco: Encounter Books, 2002.

Neuhaus, Richard John. *Death on a Friday Afternoon: Meditations on the Last Words of Jesus from the Cross.* New York: Basic Books, 2000.

Noll, Mark A. *A History of Christianity in the United States and Canada.* 1992; repr., Grand Rapids: Eerdmans, 2003.

Novak, Michael. *Will it Liberate? Questions About Liberation Theology* (New York: Paulist Press, 1986),

Patterson, Orlando. *Freedom in the Making of Western Culture.* New York: Basic Books, 1991.

Pius XI, Pope. Encyclical Letter *Quadragesimo Anno* (1931).

Rahner, Karl. *Foundations of Christian Faith: An Introduction to the Idea of Christianity.* New York: Seabury Press, 1978.

Rawls, John. *A Theory of Justice.* Cambridge, MA: Harvard University Press, 1971.

Raz, Joseph. *The Morality of Freedom.* Oxford, UK: Clarendon Press, 1986.

Santelli, Anthony J., et al. *The Free Person and the Free Economy: A Personalist View of Market Economics.* Lanham, MD: Lexington Books, 2002.

Segundo, Juan Luis. *The Liberation of Theology.* Trans. John Drury. New York: Orbis, 1975.

Spencer, Nick. *Doing God: A Future for Faith in the Public Square.* London: Theos, 2006.

Tocqueville, Alexis de. *Democracy in America.* 1835; repr., New York: Bantam, 2000.

Vatican Council II, *Gaudium et Spes* (Pastoral Constitution on the Church in the Modern World, 1965).

Veatch, Henry B. *Rational Man: A Modern Interpretation of Aristotelian Ethics.* 1962; repr., Indianapolis: Amagi Books, 2003.

Von Hildebrand, Dietrich. *Transformation in Christ: On The Christian Attitude.* San Francisco: Ignatius Press, 1990.

William G. Most, *Our Father's Plan: God's Arrangements and Our Response.* Front Royal, VA: Christendom Press, 1988.

Wojtyła, Karol. *The Acting Person.* Trans. Andrzej Potocki. *Analecta Husserliana: The Yearbook of Phenomenological Research,* vol. 10. Dordrecht, Netherlands: D. Reidel, 1979.

RACE AND RACISM

Ayittey, George B.N. *Africa in Chaos.* New York: St. Martin's, 1998.

Bell, Derrick. *Faces at the Bottom of the Well.* New York: Basic Books, 1992.

Cashin, Sheryl. *The Failures of Integration: How Race and Class are Undermining the American Dream.* New York: Public Affairs, 2004.

Cone, James H. *Martin & Malcolm & America: A Dream or a Nightmare.* New York: Orbis, 1991.

Cone, James H. *The Black Church and Marxism: What Do They Have to Say to Each Other?* New York: Institute for Democratic Socialism, 1980.

D' Souza, Dinesh. *Illiberal Education: The Politics of Race and Sex on Campus.* New York: Vintage Books, 1992.

Delgado, Richard, and Jean Stefancic, eds., *Critical Race Theory: The Cutting Edge.* Philadelphia: Temple University Press, 2000.

Du Bois, W.E.B. *Souls of Black Folk.* 1903; repr., Chicago: Bartlebys, 1999.

Dyson, Michael Eric. *Open Mike: Reflections on Philosophy, Race, Sex, Culture and Religion.* New York: Basic Civitas Books, 2003.

Dyson, Michael Eric. *The Michael Eric Dyson Reader.* New York: Basic Civitas Books, 2004.

Elkins, Stanley M. *Slavery: A Problem in American Institutional and Intellectual Life.* Chicago: University of Chicago Press, 1976.

Feagin, Joe R. *Systemic Racism: A Theory of Oppression.* New York: CRC Press, 2006.

Fischer, David Hacket. *Albion's Seed: Four British Folkways in America.* New York: Oxford University Press, 1989.

Genovese, Eugene D. *Roll, Jordan, Roll: The World the Slaves Made.* New York: Vintage Books, 1975.

Gitlin, Todd. "The Rise of Identity Politics," in *Race & Ethnicity in the United States: Issues and Debates.* Ed. Stephen Steinberg. Boston: Blackwell, 2000.

Goldfield, David R. *Black, White, and Southern: 1940 to the Present.* Baton Rouge: Louisiana State University Press, 2015.

Goldwin, Robert A. *Why Blacks, Women, and Jews Are Not Mentioned in the Constitution, and Other Unorthodox Views.* Washington, DC: AEI Press, 1990.

Hacker, Andrew. *Two Nations: Black and White, Separate, Hostile, Unequal.* New York: Charles Scribner's Sons, 1992.

Howe, Stephen. *Afrocentrism: Mythical Pasts and Imagined Homes.* London: Verso, 1998.

Keyes, Alan. *Masters of the Dream: The Strength and Betrayal of Black America.* New York: Harper Perennial, 1996.

Lasch-Quinn, Elisabeth. *Race Experts: How Racial Etiquette, Sensitivity Training, and New Age Therapy Hijacked the Civil Rights Revolution.* New York: W. W. Norton, 2001.

Lefkowitz, Mary. *Not Out of Africa: How Afrocentrism Became an Excuse to Teach Myth as History.* New York: Basic Books, 1996.

Levy, Jacob T. *The Multiculturalism of Fear.* Oxford, U.K.: Oxford University Press, 2000.

Loury, Glenn. *The Anatomy of Racial Inequality.* Cambridge: Harvard University Press, 2002.

Lovejoy, Paul E. *Transformations in Slavery: A History of Slavery in Africa*, 3rd ed. Cambridge, UK: Cambridge University Press, 2012.

Marable, Manning. *Race, Reform, and Rebellion: The Second Reconstruction in Black America, 1945–1990.* Oxford, MS: University Press of Mississippi, 1991.

McWhiney, Grady. *Cracker Culture: Celtic Ways in the Old South.* Tuscaloosa: University of Alabama Press, 1988.

McWhorter, John. *Authentically Black: Essays for the Black Silent Majority.* New York: Gotham, 2004.

McWhorter, John. *Losing the Race: Self-Sabotage in Black America.* New York: Harper Prennial, 2001.

McWhorter, John. *Winning the Race: Beyond the Crisis in Black America.* New York: Gotham Books, 2006.

Miers, Suzanne, and Igor Kopytoff. *Slavery in Africa: Historical and Anthropological Perspectives.* Madison: University of Wisconsin Press, 1979.

Ogbu, John U. *Black American Students in an Affluent Suburb: A Study of Academic Disengagement.* Mahwah, NJ: Lawrence Erlbaum Associates, 2003.

Omi, Michael, and Howard Winant *Racial Formation in the United States: From the 1960s to the 1980s.* New York: Routledge, 1986.

Patterson, Orlando. *Rituals of Blood: Consequences of Slavery in Two American Centuries.* New York: Basic Civitas Books, 1999.

Patterson, Orlando. *The Ordeal of Integration: Progress and Resentment in America's Racial Crisis.* New York: Basic Civitas, 1997.

Perazzo, John. *The Myths that Divide Us: How Lies Have Poisoned American Race Relations.* New York: World Studies Books, 1999.

Peterson, Jesse Lee. *From Rage to Responsibility.* St. Paul: Paragon House, 2000.

Phillips, Joseph C. *He Talk Like a White Boy: Reflections on Faith, Family, Politics, and Authenticity.* Philadelphia: Running Press, 2006.

Richburg, Keith B. *Out of America: A Black Man Confronts Africa.* San Diego: Harcourt, 1998.

Roberts, J. Deotis *A Black Political Theory.* Louisville: Westminster John Knox Press, 1974.

Roberts, J. Deotis. *Liberation and Reconciliation: A Black Theology.* Louisville: Westminster John Knox Press, 2005.

Schlesinger, Arthur M. Jr. *The Disuniting of America.* New York: Norton, 1992.

Sitkoff, Harvard. *A New Deal for Blacks: The Emergence of Civil Rights as a National Issue,* vol. 1, *The Depression Decade.* New York: Oxford University Press, 1978.

Smith, Robert C. *Racism in the Post-Civil Rights Era: Now You See It, Now You Don't.* New York: State University of New York Press, 1995.

Smith, Robert Charles. *We Have No Leaders: African-Americans in the Post-Civil Rights Era.* New York: SUNY Press, 1996.

Sowell, Thomas. *Affirmative Action Around the World: An Empirical Study.* New Haven: Yale University Press, 2004.

Sowell, Thomas. *Black Rednecks and White Liberals.* Jackson, TN: Encounter Books, 2006.

Sowell, Thomas. *Civil Rights: Rhetoric or Reality.* New York: Quill, 1984.

Sowell, Thomas. *Preferential Policies.* New York: William Morrow & Company, 1990.

Sowell, Thomas. *Race and Culture: A World View.* New York: Basic Books, 1994.

Sowell, Thomas. *The Economics and Politics of Race: An International Perspective.* New York: Quill, 1983.

Sowell, Thomas. *The Economics and Politics of Race.* New York: William Morrow & Co., 1985.

Stamp, Kenneth M. *The Peculiar Institution: Slavery in the Antebellum South.* New York: Vintage, 1964.

Steele, Shelby. *A Dream Deferred: The Second Betrayal of Black Freedom in America.* New York: Harper Collins, 1998.

Steele, Shelby. *The Content of Our Character: A New Vision of Race in America.* New York: HarperCollins, 1990.

Taylor, Charles. *Multiculturalism: Examining the Politics of Recognition.* Princeton: Princeton University Press, 1994.

Thernstrom, Abigail, and Stephan Thernstrom. "Black Progress: How Far We've Come—and How Far We Have to Go." *Brookings Review* 16 (Spring 1998).

Thernstrom, Abigail, and Stephan Thernstrom. *No Excuses: Closing the Racial Gap in Learning.* New York: Simon & Schuster, 2004.

Thernstrom, Stephan, and Abigail Thernstrom. *America in Black and White: One Nation, Indivisible.* New York: Simon & Schuster, 1997.

Thernstrom, Stephan. "One-Drop Still: A Racialist's Census." *National Review* (April 17, 2000).

Wade, Peter. *Race and Ethnicity in Latin America.* London: Pluto Press, 1997.

Walters, Ronald. *White Nationalism, Black Interests: Conservative Public Policy and the Black Community.* Detroit: Wayne State University Press, 2003.

West, Cornel. *Race Matters.* 1993; repr., Boston: Beacon Press, 2001.

West, Cornel. "Black Theology in Marxist Thought," in *Black Theology: A Documentary History*, vol. 1. Ed. James H. Cone and Gayraud S. Wilmore. New York: Orbis, 1993.

Williams, Juan. *My Soul Looks Back in Wonder: Voices of the Civil Rights Experience.* New York: Sterling, 2004.

Williams, Walter E. *The State Against Blacks.* New York: McGraw-Hill, 1982.

Wood, Peter. *Diversity: The Invention of a Concept.* San Francisco: Encounter Books, 2003.

SOCIAL WORK, PUBLIC POLICY, POVERTY, AND FAMILY

Beier, A. L. *The Problem of the Poor in Tudor and Stuart England.* Lancaster, UK: Lancaster Papers, 1983.

Beito, David T. *From Mutual Aid to the Welfare State: Fraternal Societies and Social Services, 1890–1967.* Chapel Hill: University of North Carolina Press, 2000.

Billingsley, Andrew. *Climbing Jacob's Ladder: The Enduring Legacies of African-American Families.* New York: Simon & Schuster, 1992.

Blankenhorn, David. *Fatherless America: Confronting Our Most Urgent Problem.* New York: HarperPerennial, 1995.

Bork, Robert H. *Slouching Towards Gomorrah: Modern Liberalism and American Decline.* New York: Regan/HarperCollins, 1996.

Brueggemann, William G. *The Practice of Macro Social Work.* Belmont, CA: Brooks/Cole, 2002.

Charen, Mona. *Do-Gooders: How Liberals Hurt Those They Claim to Help (And the Rest of Us).* New York: Sentinel, 2004.

Cherlin, Andrew J. *Marriage, Divorce, Remarriage.* Cambridge, MA: Harvard University Press, 1992.

Dalrymple, Theodore. *Life at the Bottom, The Worldview That Makes the Underclass.* Chicago: Ivan R. Dee, 2001.

Du Bois, W.E.B. *The Negro American Family.* Atlanta: Atlanta University Press, 1908.

Eastland, Terry. *Ending Affirmative Action: The Case for Color Blind Justice.* New York: Basic Books, 1996.

Frazier, E. Franklin *The Negro Family in the United States.* Chicago: University of Chicago Press, 1939.

Gilbert, Neil, and Paul Terrell. *Dimensions of Social Welfare Policy.* Old Tappan, NJ: Pearson Higher Ed, 2013.

Gilder, George. *Wealth and Poverty.* San Francisco: ICS Press, 1993.

Gilens, Martin. *Why Americans Hate Welfare.* Chicago: University of Chicago Press, 2000.

Gross, Robert A. "Giving in America: From Charity to Philanthropy." In *Charity, Philanthropy and Civility in American History*, ed. Lawrence Jacob Friedman and Mark Douglas McGarvie. New York: Cambridge University Press, 2003.

Guttmann, Herbert G. *The Black Family in Slavery and Freedom, 1750–1925.* New York: Pantheon Books, 1976.

Hendershott, Anne. *The Politics of Deviance.* San Francisco: Encounter Books, 2002.

Himmelfarb, Gertrude. *The Demoralization of Society.* New York: Alfred A. Knopf, 1995.

Hindle, Steve. *The State and Social Change in Early Modern England.* London: Macmillan, 2000.

Husock, Howard. *America's Trillion Dollar Housing Mistake.* Chicago: Ivan R. Dee, 2003.

Hymowitz, Kay S. "The Black Family: Forty Years of Lies." *City Journal* (Summer 2005).

Jordan, Cathleen, and Cynthia Franklin. *Clinical Assessment for Social Workers: Quantitative and Qualitative Methods*, 2nd ed. Chicago: Lyceum Books, 2003.

Kagan, Richard, and Shirley Schlosberg. *Families in Perpetual Crisis.* New York: Norton, 1989.

Lieberman, Myron. *Public Education: An Autopsy.* Cambridge: Harvard University Press, 1995.

Meinert, Roland G., John T. Pardeck, Larry Kreuger. *Social Work: Seeking Relevancy in the Twenty-first Century.* New York: Haworth Press, 2000.

Morse, Jennifer Roback. *Love and Economics: It Takes a Family to Raise a Village.* San Marcos, CA: Ruth Insitute Books, 2008.

Moynihan, Daniel P. *The Negro Family: The Case for National Action.* Washington, DC: U.S. Department of Labor, 1965.

Neukrug, Ed. *Theory, Practice and Trends in Human Services.* Pacific Cove, CA: Brooks/Cole, 1994.

Olasky, Marvin. *Renewing American Compassion: How Compassion for the Needy Can Turn Ordinary Citizens into Heroes.* Washington, DC: Regnery, 1997.

Olasky, Marvin. *The Tragedy of American Compassion.* Washington, DC: Regnery, 1992.

Popenoe, David. *Life without Father: Compelling New Evidence That Fatherhood and Marriage Are Indispensable for the Good of Children and Society.* New York: Free Press, 1996.

Ravitch, Diane, and Maris Vinovskis. *Learning from the Past: What History Teaches Us about School Reform.* Baltimore: Johns Hopkins University Press, 1995.

Reed, Lawrence W. *Great Myths of the Great Depression.* Midland, MI: Mackinac Center, 2008 (1981).

Reisch, Michael, and Janice Andrews. *The Road Not Taken: A History of Radical Social Work in the United States.* Philadelphia: Brunner-Routledge, 2001.

Rubin, Herbert J., and Irene S. Rubin. *Community Organizing and Development*, 3rd ed. Boston: Allyn & Bacon, 2001.

Ryan, William. *Blaming the Victim.* New York: Vintage Books, 1976.

Schansberg, D. Eric. *Poor Policy: How Government Harms the Poor.* Boulder: Westview Press, 1996.

Schiele, Jerome H. *Human Services and the Afrocentric Paradigm.* New York: Haworth Press, 2000.

Skocpol, Theda. "Bringing the State Back In: Strategies of Analysis in Current Research." In *Bringing the State Back In*, ed. Peter G. Evans. Cambridge: Cambridge University Press, 1985.

Skocpol, Theda. "Sustainable Social Policy: Fighting Poverty Without Poverty Programs." *American Prospect* 2 (Summer 1990).

Sowell, Thomas. *The Quest for Cosmic Justice.* New York: Free Press, 1999.

Sowell, Thomas. *The Vision of the Anointed: Self-Congratulation as a Basis for Social Policy.* New York: Basic Books, 1995.

Stone, Deborah A. *Policy Paradox and Political Reason.* Glenview, IL: Scott, Foresman, 1988.

Tanner, Michael D. *The End of Welfare: Fighting Poverty in the Civil Society.* Washington, DC: Cato Institute, 1996.

Tanner, Michael D. *The Poverty of Welfare: Helping Others in Civil Society.* Washington, DC: Cato Institute, 2003.

Trotter, Joe William. "African American Fraternal Organizations in American History: An Introduction." *Social Science History* 28 (Fall 2004): 355–66.

Watzlawick, Paul, John H. Weakland, and Richard Fisch. *Change: Principles of Problem Formation and Problem Resolution.* New York: Norton: 1974.

Weiss, Nancy J. *Farewell to the Party of Lincoln.* Princeton: Princeton University Press, 1983.

Wilson, William Julius. "From The Truly Disadvantaged: The Inner City, the Underclass, and Public Policy." In *The Blackwell City Reader*, ed. Gary Bridge and Sophie Watson. Malden, MA: Blackwell Publishers, 2000.

Wilson, William Julius. *When Work Disappears: The World of the New Urban Poor.* New York: Vintage, 1997.

Wormer, Katherine S. van, Fred H. Besthorn, and Thomas Keefe. *Human Behavior and the Social Environment: Macro Level; Groups, Communities, and Organizations.* Oxford, U.K.: Oxford University Press, 2007.

About the Author

Ismael Hernandez lives in Fort Myers, Florida, with his wife, Crystal. A native of Puerto Rico, he studied theology at the Jesuit Seminary in Rio Piedras, Puerto Rico, and holds a master's degree in Political Science from the University of Southern Mississippi. He has served in various positions in black Catholic ministry and social services, and, since 2005, has been a lecturer for the Acton Institute. In 2009, he founded the Freedom and Virtue Institute, which is committed to individual liberty, human dignity, and self-reliance. He can be reached at ismael@fvinstitute.org.

INDEX

Made in the USA
Monee, IL
27 December 2021

87390800R00167